D0801777

The United States
and
Inter-American Relations

The United States
and
Inter-American Relations

A CONTEMPORARY APPRAISAL

by

GEORGE WYTHE

UNIVERSITY OF FLORIDA PRESS

GAINESVILLE — 1964

FOR

Z . W .

A UNIVERSITY OF FLORIDA PRESS BOOK

PUBLISHED WITH ASSISTANCE
FROM
THE FORD FOUNDATION

PRINTED BY THE H. & W. B. DREW COMPANY
JACKSONVILLE, FLORIDA

Introduction

This sober and disquieting volume addresses itself to the major dilemma of United States policy toward Latin America. How does a great power get along with a number of weak nations? How does it get on with them in an age of strident nationalism, communism, anti-imperialism, anti-foreignism, anti-Yankeeism? While the question is not posed in this bald fashion, it is clear that this is Dr. Wythe's major preoccupation. The United States, a newcomer among the great powers after a long and fortunate history when it could pretend that other nations either did not exist or did not matter (for this is what isolationism meant), now finds itself suddenly playing a great role in an insecure world, and worrying about its "image." It wants to be well thought of. It has not yet learned the lesson that a great power can be feared, respected, disliked, but not "loved"—any more than a tiger can be, even a tame one. This complicates our relations with Latin America.

The Latin Americans are sensitive, proud, suspicious of our intent, dubious about our motives; and they dislike our ways. We ought to recognize that no matter what we do we will not really find a permanent place in their affections. The more we attempt, the more recalcitrant they become. Our proselytizing activities—our desire to improve, better, civilize, help, educate—our gifts by the bushel and the truckload only help "prove" America's "new imperialism." Our belief seems to be that we can wean these people away from nationalism, communism, anti-imperialism, anti-Yankeeism by increasing "good works," by stressing the importance of economic reform, and by undertaking larger and larger projects.

Long experience as a public official in inter-American relations leads the author to suggest that the greater the effort, the smaller the reward; that the more we undertake, the more we irritate; that eventually the Alliance for Progress may make our relations worse, rather than better. He suggests humbly enough that "love" cannot be bought because it is not for sale—that the relations between a great power and many weak powers belong on another plane. He would, I think, say that these relations may be better or worse but that they can never be good; that as the image of a nation is the by-product of all its activities, no amount of advertising and deliberate distortion will in the end do any good. Although the behavior of the American people in the days following President Kennedy's assassination made a profound impression on the world beyond our borders, it could not erase the deep imprint on Latin America made by the widely advertised riots in Little Rock.

I think the author is saying that the United States, with its enormous powers and responsibilities, should go on about its affairs without worrying about its image. It must do what it considers right and necessary without excessive concern about the impression being made, for this is the one thing it cannot really control. The author suggests that we are too sensitive and that we identify criticism with enmity, anti-Yankeeism with communism. We want too much to ingratiate ourselves. We overemphasize economic motives and pay too little attention to the demand by the Latin Americans for courteous and dignified treatment. We forget that every nation has a style of its own and its special sense of place in the world.

Dr. Wythe is concerned about our assumption that we can influence, change, modify, remake—when the world is replete with experiences proving this is one thing that one nation cannot do to another, and that the harder it tries, the more likely it is to fail. The end result of European colonialism is but one more item in a long story; our intervention in Haiti, Santo Domingo, Nicaragua, and Cuba is another. It is a difficult lesson to learn but a useful one.

I think the author concludes, without saying so, that we cannot remake Latin America and ought to stop trying. This is a painful theme for American policy, but one deserving careful examination. I recommend the book to all present and future policy makers.

Columbia University   FRANK TANNENBAUM

vi

Preface

In offering this book to the public, the author has attempted to present a general point of view and a long-range perspective, rather than a blueprint for specific policies or actions. It is not intended as a general treatise on Latin America, but as a frank and free-wheeling discussion of some of the more significant aspects of inter-American relations. Likewise, no profiles of individual countries have been included, although national experiences or points of view are cited frequently to illustrate the principles under discussion. Technical terminology has been avoided as far as practicable, although some acquaintance by the reader with the history of the area is assumed.

The points of view expressed herein are the outgrowth of long personal acquaintance with the countries and peoples of Middle and South America, as well as some knowledge of Spain, Portugal, and France—the three countries from which the languages and institutions of Latin America have been in large part derived. The author has found encouragement in the fact that other students of inter-American relations have expressed similar views on some, if not all, of the problems discussed. At the same time, the continuing widespread public confusion regarding some of the basic issues appears ample justification for a new approach and a new synthesis.

GEORGE WYTHE

Washington, D.C.

Contents

–I–

Americans, North and South

The United States and Latin America have much in common. There are also important differences. Failure to recognize that differences exist but need not act as a bar to fruitful cooperation and friendship is at the root of most of our difficulties.

From the earliest days of our history as an independent nation the lands to the south and southeast came to occupy a special place in our foreign policy. The Monroe Doctrine embodied the deep-seated conviction that the peoples of the New World, separated from the other continents by two oceans, share a common destiny. And some, but not all, would have added that they share common aspirations.

The thought of a special relationship was eloquently stated by José Joaquim da Maia, a Brazilian conspirator for independence, as early as 1787, when he wrote Thomas Jefferson, then United States Minister to France, that "nature in making us inhabitants of the same continent has in some sort united us in the bonds of a common patriotism."[1]*

Experience has shown the need for some revision of our early preconceptions about the southern lands and of our relations with them, but the essential elements in our views have changed surprisingly little since the early days of our independence. Both Hispanic America and Anglo-America were parts of the Western Hemisphere, with distinct sets of interests as compared to the countries of Europe. There was long a real danger of our encirclement by hostile dynasties. Our zeal for what was then called republican (i.e., nonmonarchical) institutions was sharpened by the tendency of continental European governments to look upon republicanism very much as we today look upon communism. The language of a projected Congressional resolution in 1811 on the Spanish American colonies, expressing "friendly

*Notes to chapter I begin on page 23.

1

interest" and "solicitude for their welfare," has a familiar ring today. Then, as now, our political leaders looked upon economic relations as instruments of enlightenment and good works.

THE UNITED STATES LOOKS AT LATIN AMERICA

At no time, to be sure, has there been complete agreement as to the outlook for the Hispanic nations nor as to our policy toward them. It is likely that the majority of Americans have entertained toward Latin America the sentiments felicitously expressed by Secretary of State Elihu Root at Rio de Janeiro in 1906, when he said that the United States made no claims for territory or privilege but desired "to help all friends to a common prosperity and a common growth, that we may all become greater and stronger together." But there has usually also been an active group of expansionists who believed that all of North America, at least, including Canada and southward to the Isthmus of Panama, would eventually gravitate into the orbit of the United States. Abraham Lincoln's Secretary of State, William Henry Seward, believed that all of Latin America would become "free, equal and self-governing members of the United States of America." But from the end of the Civil War until 1898, there was a reaction against territorial expansion; President Ulysses S. Grant's desire to annex the Dominican Republic was rebuffed by the Senate; our chief interests to the south were in the expansion of trade and investment. The Spanish-American War and the ousting of Spain from the Caribbean unleashed a new wave of imperialism, and acceptance, by many, of the philosophy of the "Big Brother," involving tutelage over the weaker nations which were on our doorstep and protected by the Monroe Doctrine from European intervention. The failure of most of the countries of this area to establish stable and responsible governments provided the immediate occasions for our assumption of police powers in the Caribbean. Such was the logic of events that even critics of this policy, like President Woodrow Wilson, ended by assuming increasing responsibilities in the area. But this policy soon brought about a strong reaction on the part of the American public, as well as criticism in Latin America and Europe, and in the 1920's the tide began to recede. In the 1930's we committed ourselves not to intervene unilaterally anywhere in the Americas.

In recent decades United States public opinion regarding Latin America has tended to polarize around one of two extremes: hemispheric solidarity, with an anti-Europe and isolationist animus; or, on the other hand, partly in reaction against exclusive concern with inter-Americanism, a tendency of other regional specialists and interests to exalt their own area of action (Europe, British Commonwealth, Near East, Africa, Far East) as the region where the future of mankind will be determined—and to unite in slapping down any spokesman for hemispheric points of view! Unfortunately, in the midst of this pushing and hauling there has been very little opportunity to examine objectively the realities of the situation.

Our inter-American relations are still suffering from the chill they received in passing from the hothouse of the early New Deal to the frigid atmosphere that surrounded the gestation and parturition of postwar universal organizations. Franklin Roosevelt, like Wilson, started with an inter-American policy (Wilson in 1915 proposed a Pan American Pact but later dropped it for the League of Nations Charter), but after Pearl Harbor became engrossed by other concerns. As the end of the war approached, planning for peace had to be global. Since at that time Roosevelt was very much concerned to find a basis for continuing cooperation with Soviet Russia, whose scorn for our Middle and South American "satellites" was well known, the Good Neighbors were in effect left out in the cold. The shock was all the greater because, in spite of the discontinuance of multilateral consultation from 1942 to 1945, several official agencies had continued to put out a heavy barrage of propaganda on the importance of the Latin American area, thus creating expectations that could not possibly have been fulfilled even under the most favorable circumstances. This fatal tendency of our public opinion specialists to see things larger than life succeeded in arousing antagonisms and jealousies that explain the glee with which the pro-European partisans went about cutting the inter-American concept down to size once the opportunity presented itself.

Latin America is, of course, an area of great importance to us, and

3

it should receive the attention and consideration it deserves. Our policies cannot be soundly based, however, unless they are founded on an understanding of realities, and it is therefore indispensable to clear up some of the misconceptions that exist.

Perhaps one of the most harmful of these preconceptions has been the tendency to assume that the United States and Latin America have essentially the same set of interests, the same ideology and scale of values, and will therefore naturally and harmoniously cooperate on all important matters. We have taken it for granted that all other countries, and particularly those in this hemisphere, would eventually come to enjoy the blessings of republican (or, as we now say, democratic) government and of private enterprise along Yankee lines. The other American republics have, indeed, as we shall see hereafter, been strongly influenced in various respects by United States customs and institutions. This "demonstration effect," as economists call it, shows up particularly in consumption patterns and in the externals of form, speech, and styles. We have perhaps been overimpressed by this froth and by the eddies on the stream but have ignored the depth and strength of the main currents of life. At international or inter-American conferences we have tended to side-step the real problems and to assume, because we succeeded in working out diplomatically worded compromises, that we had convinced them of the soundness of our views.

At the bottom of the trouble is what Professor Frederick B. Pike calls "sentimental one-worldism," which assumes "that once we become acquainted with people throughout the world, we will discover that they are basically the same as we: reasonable people, that is, who, when we have explained our basic concepts and value systems to them will warmly embrace our way of life." Professor Pike "feels that Latin Americans do not want to be treated as people who are the same as we; juridic equality they demand, but the notion of total equality, which sameness implies, they eschew."[2]

Another acute observer has pointed out that the crux of the Latin American problem is that the twenty republics want their own kind of statehood, which conflicts with "the kindly and condescending disposition of the United States to remold 'neighbor' selfhoods to its own image."[3] He concludes: "The twenty-one selfhoods, indeed,

4

might even become adjusted better if we and the 'neighbors' stopped making such strenuously self-conscious efforts to make ourselves like each other better."[4]

A distinguished American anthropologist has warned that "we make a fundamental error when we assume that Latin America is on the road toward developing into merely a Spanish-speaking version of the United States."[5] Dean Gillin feels that Latin American culture differs in significant respects from Anglo-American culture as regards "content, organization, values, and orientation."[6]

Another source of misunderstanding is what may be called the geographical illusion, which has been perpetuated and sanctified by a distortion of the original meaning of the term "Good Neighbors." The practice of referring to the Hispanic countries as "our friends and neighbors" goes back to the early period of our history. It appears frequently in our state papers, and was used by Clay, Adams, Madison, Lincoln, Blaine, Root, and Hoover, among others. The phrase, *buena vecindad*, which may be translated in this context as "good neighborliness," was current in Spanish and was used, for example, to apply to relations between Spain and the United States. It was, indeed, in this sense that President Roosevelt used the term in his first inaugural address: "In the field of world policy, I would dedicate this nation to the policy of the good neighbor." Shortly thereafter, however, the designation Good Neighbors came to be reserved for the Americas, as Roosevelt avoided politically unpopular European entanglements and began to emphasize hemispheric relations.

Geographically speaking, the countries of Middle America—i.e., Mexico, Central America, and the Caribbean area—are really neighbors in the spatial sense of the term, but Buenos Aires is farther from Washington by the Great Circle route than Washington is from Moscow. Furthermore, by sea, the large cities of eastern South America are farther from New York and New Orleans than from southern Europe.

It may also be noted that until the completion of the railway to Mexico City, trade and travel between the United States and the other American republics were almost entirely by water, the chief exception being considerable border smuggling. In the early days of commercial aviation, the Isthmus of Central America and the stepping stones of the Caribbean gave the United States some advantages over Europe in developing regular Latin American services, but modern jets have wiped out the differential.

That part of the hemisphere now occupied by the Latin American republics was colonized by Europeans a century earlier than the part now occupied by the United States. In spite of this longer history of settlement and development, Latin America is frequently referred to as a new land or new frontier, and its political upsets are blamed on inexperience. It is important to disentangle the various strands of reasoning involved in this judgment. There is, of course, a sense in which there is always a new frontier in every society—technologically, socially, morally. The illusion of newness in the case of South America probably arises from the low average population density (although most of Middle America is more densely populated than the United States) and the relatively underdeveloped state of their economies. But South America is not sparsely populated if one compares inhabitants per acre of arable land. The combination of unfavorable climate and poor soil has made a large part of South America unsuited to settlement by Europeans, and the local governments have not been disposed to open it up to Africans or Asiatics. There are no doubt important unused resources (in any case, resource is not a static concept, but is constantly changing with new technology and fashion), but there are also vast areas of eroded lands and burnt-out forests, as well as abandoned towns and mine sites.

Although the Latin American republics did not achieve their independence until half a century after our Declaration of Independence (and some not until much later), these countries are mature societies, with settled economic and social patterns.[7] A leading South American statesman, Dr. Alberto Lleras Camargo, ex-President of Colombia and former Secretary General of the Pan American Union, has stated: "Some people in the United States are under the delusion that there is still a frontier in the southern hemisphere, where free enterprise and adventure, individualism and economic liberalism should come to full flower just as they did in the United States a century ago."[8] A leading political scientist and historian has written that Latin Americans are "an old people, a people enmeshed in the

6

traditions of the past. Society is stratified, socially and economically, and this is also the heritage of the past."[9]

The argument that Latin American political conditions are due to inexperience during the colonial era tends to beg the question and is not accepted without qualification by experts in this field. In any case, most of the countries have been independent for well over a century. The truth is that very few Latin Americans have ever really wanted democratic government in our sense of the term; and those Latin Americans, like Domingo Faustino Sarmiento, who were genuine admirers of American institutions, did not hesitate to resort to autocratic measures when they were in power. It is not a lack of experience, but experience of a different kind, a different ideology and distinct set of values.

Some of our early statesmen did not share the general belief that the achievement of independence and the proclamation of a republic in South America would automatically ensure democracy and good government. Both Jefferson and John Quincy Adams were pessimistic about the outlook for democracy in the new republics. Some South Americans as well as most Americans of the North continued to put an unjustified faith in forms and names to solve substantive problems. Just as we took it for granted in 1917 that as soon as Russia got rid of the wicked Czar all would be well, so we insist today that all Latin America will consist of nice little democracies as soon as we can get rid of a few more dictators. There is no lack of democracy, even in some of the dictatorships, but it isn't necessarily our brand. It has a different ancestry.

LATIN AMERICA LOOKS AT THE UNITED STATES—AND THE WORLD

It is even more difficult to arrive at an accurate cross section of Latin American views historically than to sort out the different strands of opinion in the United States. There are great differences, of geography, of ethnic background, of historical experience, among the various countries, as well as important common elements. Strictly speaking, Latin America as a unit or bloc is a rather recent creation. Portuguese-speaking Brazil, both under the Empire and after 1889 as a republic, stood apart from the Spanish American nations, and

French-speaking Haiti also went its troubled way. As regards the Spanish Americans, the differences among the various provinces were sufficient to defeat attempts at unity, even on a very loose confederative basis. Prior to World War II an Argentine or a Mexican or a Brazilian would have been puzzled or insulted if called a Latin American.

In spite of the difficulties, it is possible to discern some broad trends of opinion in the area. During the early nineteenth century there was considerable sympathy for the United States, which, as the first of the important modern republics, served in some respects as an exemplar to the budding Latin American states. By that time the United States was making giant strides in population and economic growth, which excited the emulation of constitution makers and legislators. There was also sympathy for United States religious tolerance and educational progress. But there were also dissenting voices. Many of the leaders favored a monarchy or other authoritarian form of government; education was confined to the elite; and some disliked the Protestant religion and even more what they took to be the Protestant way of life. Many of the lower clergy had taken an active part in the revolutionary movements and were generally tolerant in religious matters, but among the hierarchy were many of European birth and conservative views.

In a proclamation to the Mexican nation upon the promulgation of the Constitution of 1824, the provisional executive stated: "If you wish to place yourselves on a level with the happy republic of our neighbors to the North, it is necessary that you should elevate yourself to the lofty heights of civic and moral virtue which characterize this singular people." But, alas, this liberal charter, modeled on the United States federal system, lasted only twelve years and was replaced by widely different points of view in 1836.

Simón Bolívar, the Liberator, in his famous letter written in 1815 while a refugee on the island of Jamaica, refers to the "talents and political virtues of our brothers of the North," but at the same time he apparently did not consider the United States as being in a position to make a positive contribution to the new South American states. He favored a close tie with Great Britain. Although he did not consider monarchy as suited to conditions in the Americas, he believed that the new federation he was trying to create should have a president and a senate chosen for life.

From around 1830 to the 1870's, United States influence was at a low ebb in Latin America, as we turned our energies to winning and developing the West, and became preoccupied by Manifest Destiny and Civil War. The Mexican War, filibustering in Central America, and other episodes aroused suspicion and hostility. But the abolition of slavery by Lincoln, the aid given the Mexican people in overthrowing the French-supported empire of Maximilian, and the revival of Spanish pretension in the Americas, again turned many sympathies toward their northern neighbor. An outstanding figure of this period was the Argentine educator and writer, Sarmiento, who met Horace Mann on a trip to the United States in 1847. Twenty years later Sarmiento was Argentine Minister to the United States, and was elected President of Argentina during his stay in this country. He remained throughout his life an ardent admirer of our political and educational systems, and was responsible for introducing American teachers into his country.

The last quarter of the nineteenth century was marked by rapid economic and population growth involving large foreign investment and European immigration as well as a huge expansion of production and trade. Most of the impetus for this development came from outside the area, but the change was facilitated by the triumph of the philosophy of positivism in most Latin American countries. During this period Latin America came to deprecate all indigenous elements, whether race, art, architecture, or literature, and to put a high value on external contributions, such as colonists, capital, or entrepreneurs. Mexico may be cited as an example in this connection.

Porfirio Díaz came to power under Benito Juárez, the leader of Reform, which resulted in *desamortización* (disentailing of Church communities), thereby reducing the enormous real estate holdings of the Church but enabling private landowners to extend their estates at the expense of the ancient landowning villages. In consolidating his power, Díaz followed the tradition of the great *caudillos,* but in his economic and social policies there is every reason to believe that he attempted to put into practice the principles of liberalism generally accepted at that time, summarized by the dictum of evolution from status to contract. Although himself a mestizo of perhaps predominantly Indian blood, Díaz apparently believed that his country's progress, if not indeed its continued existence as an independent nation, depended upon rapid modernization and Europeanization (in the sense of Western culture and race) of the country, and that this involved the effacement or amalgamation of the indigenous population, together with the removal of the Indian landmarks that were a symbol and citadel of an inferior civilization. The efforts of most other Latin American governments to accelerate immigration and investment reflected similar points of view: failure to progress would lead to capitulations and Balkanization.

During the heyday of positivism, United States investors and enterprisers, missionaries and educators, were generally welcome south of our border, but southern South America retained a predominantly European orientation. The growing economic and political power and prestige of the United States, especially after World War I, long continued to attract Latin American leaders and the burgeoning commercial and industrial classes, but the Spanish-American War and the subsequent interventions in the Caribbean set up a countercurrent that became increasingly vocal, first in literary circles and among the intelligentsia, and widening out to include middle- and upper-class conservatives who were never completely reconciled to American manners and ideology.

While to many Latin Americans the United States represented the dual ideals of science and democracy, to others this combination constituted an insidious danger—joining "the cult of Mammon to that of Hercules" but lacking God, in the language of Rubén Darío, Latin America's greatest poet. The classic protest against the encroachments of material power and utilitarian philosophy was made by the Uruguayan José Enrique Rodó in his essay, *Ariel,* named for the Shakespearean character from *The Tempest,* symbol of the nobleness and spirituality of disinterested culture, in contrast with the baser utilitarian elements symbolized by Caliban. Rodó favored a cultural and moral aristocracy; he criticized democracy as leading to mediocrity and "enthroning Caliban." He realized that the forces of democracy and science, as represented by the United States, were too powerful to be resisted entirely. He recognized some useful "northern traits," and hoped that these forces could be turned to "serve the cause of Ariel." But he objected to anything (such as excessively rapid immigration) that would denature the essential character of the Latin Americans or result in "delatinization."

Seen in the historical perspective, Rodó may be said to have expressed the point of view of the cultured minority in a small agrarian society not unlike that which prevailed in Virginia at the end of the eighteenth century. Jefferson likewise believed in an aristocracy of virtue and talent, and disliked the pushing new bankers and industrialists, but Jefferson's agrarian ideal was swamped by the influx of millions of immigrants and the growth of industrial centers, which gave rise to mass society and culture. As Uruguay and its large neighbors, Argentina and Brazil, become industrialized, skyscrapers and smokestacks have appeared to mar the serenity of Rodó's pastoral landscape. Latin America has now accepted the philosophy of the machine with almost religious fervor, but it clings to Rodó's aversion to anything that results in "delatinization."

In Mexico, Díaz's realization that the transformation he envisaged was impossible came too late to prevent the outbreak of revolution in 1910, a revolution which soon overflowed the narrow bounds of "effective suffrage, no re-election" (Madero's slogan and aspiration), and challenged the privileged position of the foreigner in Mexican life. One of the chief objectives of the Revolution has been the reduction of foreign economic, political, and cultural influences. Mexico has stuck to its determination to work out its own destiny along its own lines and has refused most offers of foreign aid and technical assistance. President Plutarco Elías Calles, although a personal friend of Ambassador Dwight Morrow and a great admirer of American technology and institutions, in 1929 refused an offer from one of the large American foundations to provide liberal financial aid for education on the grounds that every country should undertake its own education. Moisés Sáenz, Undersecretary of Education under Calles, himself a graduate of Teachers College of Columbia University, wrote in 1927: "Our trite phrase, 'incorporate the Indian into civilization,' should be changed to read, 'bring civilization to the Indian.' If there are thirteen million Indians and mestizos in Mexico and only a million and a half whites, there is no

11

other way but to take our white civilization (which is already a little dusky) to the Indian in order that it may become transformed, in the process of assimilation, into the Mexican civilization. To measure our people forever by the Nordic yardstick is to subject them to the disillusion of apparent failure and to relegate Mexico to play second fiddle in the white orchestra, when we might be able to produce in this land of ours the miracle of an Indio-Latin standard of civilization to which all the Indians and all the mestizos of this continent could aspire."[10]

In the United States the bumptious self-reliance of the nineteenth century has given place to an orgy of doubt and self-laceration that in some respects resembles the questionings of the Latin American *pensadores* before Spain's collapse in the Spanish-American War stirred their racial faith and feelings and caused them to close ranks against the heretic of the North. Our subsequent economic and military aggressions further aroused Latin American nationalistic reactions, which, combined with envy of the prowess and achievements of the northern neighbor, stimulated their sense of nationality, of national identity and pride. The great depression and the war also brought about a greater sentiment of national identity. Despite the importance of the aboriginal elements in most Latin American countries, and perhaps in large measure because of it, educated Latin Americans had tended to cling to European manners and ideas, and to look to Europe as their real home, to a greater extent than was the case in the United States. The recent renaissance of the arts, literature, and architecture in Latin America reflects the desire to find forms and expressions to fit their own context of life.

It would be desirable at this point to introduce some evidence as to Latin America's attitude toward Europe. Few of the Hispanic countries have ever been deliberately isolationist in the sense that that much abused word has been used in the United States. Until 1907, when all of the Latin American republics were invited to the Second Hague Conference at the instance of the United States, they were not considered of sufficient importance to be taken into international councils, although there was keen commercial rivalry from the earliest days of independence. They supported the "two spheres" doctrine of the separation between the Old and the New World whenever it appeared useful as a measure of defense against European encroachments, but they were not disposed to accept the American interpretation of that doctrine as excluding all European political and commercial influence. President Wilson in 1916 correctly interpreted the feelings of most Latin Americans when he pointed out their suspicions that we were trying to keep Europe out of "this side of the Atlantic" in order to set up protectorates of our own. Furthermore, Bolívar was not alone in thinking that Great Britain had more to offer than the United States, as protection against the pretensions of European powers, as a trading partner, and as a source of badly needed capital and enterprise. In fact, during the nineteenth century Britain was paramount in diplomacy, trade, and transportation, and also had important social and cultural influence.

Bolívar's famous Jamaican letter was full of venom against Spain. This heritage of bitterness persisted in Spanish America until the very end of the nineteenth century, and, indeed, has even now by no means disappeared. Spain only slowly and grudgingly acknowledged the independence of its former colonies and made efforts as late as the 1860's to retrieve them. Furthermore, Spain had neither money nor technology, nor fruitful social or political ideas, to assist her daughters in setting up housekeeping for themselves. Nevertheless, Spain's children could not forget the lessons they had learned at their mother's knee: they retained in large part the legal, administrative, fiscal, religious, and social forms and characteristics inherited from the mother country. Despite the dilution of the Spanish heritage through several centuries of exposure to other geographical and ideological influences and ethnic admixture with Indians, Africans, and all the races of Europe and the Near East, Spain still provides the key to an understanding of Spanish American politics and psychology.

If Latin American relations with Spain were a family affair and relations with the United States and Great Britain primarily a business affair, relations with France were a love affair. The term "Latin America" first came to be used in the days when Louis Napoleon, after unsuccessful attempts to establish French political hegemony over the Romance-speaking peoples of Europe, did succeed beyond all expectations in making Paris the center of the "Latin" world.

During the last quarter of the nineteenth century Paris became the mecca for every Latin American who could afford the price of a steamer ticket, and it has continued to exert a magnetic attraction, although its dominance has been weakened by two world wars, the great depression with its exchange controls, the increasing weight of the United States and the English language in diplomatic and industrial circles, the rise of nationalism, and the coming into fashion of native arts and customs. In Spain Latin Americans are apt to be considered as parvenus or Indians; in the United States they are Dagos or greasers; in England they feel cold and neglected; but in Paris they feel at home and their egos expand. Dictators and millionaires married their daughters to dukes and marquises. Until recently, at least, there was one president of a South American country who was as much identified with Paris as with his own country. Nor should the visitor be surprised to encounter a foreign minister who speaks Spanish with a French accent. At home, the sons and daughters of the middle and upper classes learned French as their second language; in the salons French poetry, novels, and art were the staples of conversation. The French language was the doorway through which Latin Americans entered European and world thought. Brazil, although strongly influenced by the United States in commercial and political matters, was perhaps more completely under the sway of French cultural and ideological influences than any Spanish American country. At the turn of the century it was said to be usual for the son of a well-to-do family to have a French mistress. It is possibly a sign of the times that whereas fifty years ago a budding poet would compose a lyric in the French style, now prize-winning *sambas* are written in honor of the native *mulatas*.

Brazil's relations with Portugal have deviated in several respects from those of Spain and Spanish America. For some years, during Napoleon's occupation of Lisbon, Rio de Janeiro was the capital of the Portuguese Empire. When the break came with the old country, Brazil retained the monarchical form of government under the Braganza dynasty. There was no bloodshed and no bitterness. Portugal has sent many hard-working migrants to Brazil, and Portuguese have been active in industry, trade, and banking. But in the early days, capital and technology came chiefly from Great Britain, with important later contributions from France, Germany, and the United States. In modern times Italian immigration has been numerically larger and has had more economic impact than that from Portugal. Despite the ostensible importance of other contributions, Portuguese influence is all-pervading and crops out at unexpected times and places.

In Brazil, as in Spanish America, there has been a revalidation of the native heritage. There is a new interest in the country's history, especially as interpreted by novelists and sociologists. President Juscelino Kubitschek, although himself half-Slav, apparently correctly interpreted his country's mood in his decision to move the capital to the interior and to spend huge sums in realizing the plans worked out by Brazilian architects, even though much of the materials had to be transported by air, and regardless of the inflationary spiral which the financing involved. Now a nation of nearly 80 millions, with several dynamic industrial centers and a large crop of multimillionaires who live like Renaissance princes (Hollywood version), Brazil is convinced of its destiny as a great power. Interviewed by *Visão* magazine, June 24, 1960, Érico Veríssimo, Brazil's leading novelist, expressed his "firm conviction" that within fifty years Brazil would be one of the Big Four.

Brazil was for many years the staunchest friend of the United States in Latin America. Brazil supported our position in inter-American and international conferences, and stood by our side in two world wars. It has been one of the tragedies of our postwar policies that Brazil, traditionally one of the friendliest and most internationally minded countries in the world, should have been alienated because our postwar schemes were too narrow to adjust to our new position as a world power. Brazil's reaction was partly inspired by the fear that our policies would force her back into a colonial status. But perhaps even more her response was feminine, that of a woman scorned, who, on the rebound, is in danger of falling into the arms of the first suitor. *Le coeur a ses raisons que la raison ne connait pas.*[11]

Argentina has traditionally been the chief holdout from official Pan Americanism, and, until recently, from international organizations in general. As far back as the first Lima Congress of 1864-65, Argentine spokesmen ridiculed the idea of American "sister-states"

15

setting themselves up apart from Europe. The Argentine delegate to the first of the present series of Pan American conferences, in 1889-90, objected to an all-American customs union because it would exclude Europe. At the Inter-American Conference for the Maintenance of Peace, held at Buenos Aires in 1936, the President of Argentina stated: "It is impossible to suppose that the work today beginning would fail to recognize the world interdependence which governs the economic and political life of these nations or to think that the action to be taken could alter age-old connections with the Old World."

Historically Latin America has in general followed a sort of balance of power concept in its attitude toward its foreign suitors. It does not want the United States too strong, lest it crush the weaker states, but it likewise does not wish the United States to be so weak that it cannot provide protection against aggressors from outside (and inside) the hemisphere. Great Britain and Germany have become more popular since their political and economic power declined. Spain's stock went up enormously as soon as it lost the last of its possessions in the Americas. Japan's popularity has risen since she lost the war, and several South American countries have shown a disposition to accept substantial numbers of Japanese immigrants. The fact that Russia has no investments in Latin America, has very little trade, and maintains very few resident representatives in comparison with the huge staffs of United States agencies, makes it difficult for Latin Americans to view them as rivals or a menace. Many wealthy and conservative Latin Americans are genuinely convinced that our constant harping on the communist menace is a smoke screen to conceal our own designs.

The Genesis of Anti-Americanism

It is, of course, to be expected that a great power like the United States will be envied, feared, and unloved, but the current wave of anti-Americanism is much more serious than the normal irritation against superior wealth and power. The situation has reached the point where to be successful a politician must be anti-American. All persons who have studied or spent much time in the United States are suspected. By way of compensation not a few of our former trainees have become vociferous critics of the United States. Just as in the United States anyone visiting Moscow is suspect, so in Latin America anyone who has received a grant or honor from the United States, or defends the American position, is apt to be called an *entreguista* (in the sense of collaborator as used in France during the German occupation) in Brazil or some more or less equivalent epithet elsewhere (e.g., *agringada* or *malinchista* in Mexico).[12]

As a rule, the resentment is not directed against individual Americans, who are usually popular. Visiting governors, professors, writers, and movie stars continue to get the red-carpet treatment. There has been virtually none of the surly attitude that Americans encountered in France in the late 1920's. Generally speaking, Latin Americans like to work for American firms or individuals, because they are better treated and better paid than by locals. But in this connection the careful observer can detect an important change of atmosphere: patriotic nationals are not content to work for foreigners, they want to be employers. This feeling has recently been given expression in novels as well as on the more prosaic business level. During the course of a debate on a resolution asking the Mexican government to establish a mixed commission to control foreign investment, at the meeting of the Confederation of National Chambers of Commerce in September, 1959, one member stated that he would never wish to see the day that the highest ambition of his sons should be to be employed by a foreign company.

This feeling began to appear in the difficult years of postwar readjustment, when the shifts in our policy were disconcerting. The Latin American bloc in the United Nations was formed and also the Economic Commission for Latin America (in imitation of the commissions for Europe and the Far East), thus isolating the United States in the Organization of American States. In the beginning, the criticisms were more in sorrow than in anger, but they took on some acerbity as the attention of our high officials was more and more engrossed in nonhemispheric issues. Differences of opinion developed over approaches to the problem of economic development, and particularly the financing thereof. At the end of the war there was a real need to rehabilitate the antiquated and inadequate port facilities, transportation, communications, and utilities, most of which had originally been European investments, or had been paid for out of proceeds of government bond issues in sterling, francs, or dollars. In 1946 the Brazilian Minister of Communications came to Washington to request a $50 million loan for such purposes, but our officials dragged their feet—there were pressing needs in Europe and Asia, perhaps these were jobs for private capital; so the Minister returned to Rio and lost his job.

In those innocent pre-Marshall Plan days the Latin Americans asked for loans or credits, and were prepared to accept substantial amounts of advice, technical assistance, and foreign private participation, but preferred not to take so much of the latter that the national character of their development would be unduly diluted. Prior to our massive grants to Europe and Asia it had not occurred to the Latin Americans to ask for gifts, but once grant aid became a continuing and prominent feature of our foreign policy, it became a matter of political necessity (as well as of pride and of personal interest) for every country to obtain its share. Curiously, Washington has never been able to understand either the psychology or the economics of this situation, that failure to treat one country or region *pari passu* with other countries or regions creates a psychology of discrimination no less than trade discriminations, and that economically it isn't possible to build up one area without affecting at least relatively the position of other areas.[13]

Other elements in the spread of the anti-American virus are summarized below:

1. Of prime importance is the overexpansion of United States interests and activities. In the eyes of many Latin Americans the tentacles of United States interests have penetrated into every phase of their society. Up to a point this might have been welcomed, but it has long since passed the point where the society could accommodate it. This is not the place to attempt an analysis of our wide-ranging activities, but it has long been clear that they were causing increasing misgivings and vexation. During the war years the late Arthur Bliss Lane, our Ambassador to Colombia, attended the customary New Year's diplomatic reception accompanied by such members of his staff as had diplomatic status. As the representative of a Latin Ameri-

can country fell back in dismay before this advancing horde, he muttered, "No es una misión, es una invasión" (it's not a mission, it's an invasion). During the war it was still possible to joke about such matters, but it has long since passed the joking stage. A 1959 public opinion poll of the university students of Chile showed that two-thirds felt that the United States had too much influence in Chile.

Once the saturation point is reached, even our activities that are definitely to the advantage of Latin America become objectionable. For example, the United States takes 45 per cent of Latin America's aggregate exports and supplies nearly 50 per cent of the imports. During the war and the Korean emergency Latin American requirements were given priority over our own nonmilitary needs. Not a few Latin American fortunes are due to this favorable treatment. Mexico's economic progress of the last two decades has been based on the large United States market for its products, her ability to obtain scarce materials during the years when submarine activities reduced the flow to nations overseas, and the growing outlays of tourists and investors. For years the United States supplied 80 per cent or more of Mexico's imports. Nevertheless, Mexico and other countries are not happy at finding themselves so dependent upon American suppliers and buyers, and have taken steps to broaden their markets and import sources.

Practically all of our activities in Latin America have been over-expanded and have become counterproductive, including our public relations. In psychology there is a law of reversed effort according to which our sensory apparatus sets up resistance when we try too hard to force our brain or organs to perform. This law illustrates our propaganda problem. We have been morbidly conscious about our "image" and standing, but the harder we try the less we succeed. This frantic effort to make ourselves liked is taken by Latin Americans (and others) to be a sign of weakness. As a consequence, we have lost respect as well as goodwill.

2. We have created anti-American sentiments among persons who are disposed to be our friends by our tendency to assume that anyone who differs from our official position in any particular is therefore anti-American. Many Latin Americans who have every respect for

19

our ideas and ideals do not feel that all of them are suitable for export. This comes out in the statement of Dr. Victor Urquidi, a Mexican economist, at the 29th Couchiching (Ontario) Conference in August, 1960: "We do not accept the American way of life. We are trying to evolve something of our own and we are frequently prevented from doing so because the slightest deviation towards social progress is immediately branded as Marxism or communism."[14]

3. We have made too much of economic motivations and have lectured others endlessly about their peccadillos. Now of course Latin Americans are not above material considerations; in fact, they have been bitten very hard by the gold bug, but no economic program, however vast or however favorable, will satisfy them or arouse any real enthusiasm. In fact, most such programs to date have caused more jealousy and backbiting than good will. As mentioned above, Latin Americans did not originate the demand for gifts. It was only after we started paying court to the other girls that their honor demanded some gesture on our part. The inspiration for large programs in Latin America has come as a rule from Americans who are doing a public relations job or have an interest in large expenditures in the area.

Admittedly, Latin Americans are a bit schizophrenic on this point, as are most people. But a student of human nature need not be surprised to find that those Latin Americans who have benefited most by our generosity may well be the first to criticize us for our materialism and vulgarity. Unfortunately, it is true that in countries like Venezuela and Cuba, which we once held up as examples of the achievements of private enterprise and American capital, we have become associated in public opinion with the vice and corruption that preceded revolution. A group of American journalists visiting in Venezuela in June, 1960, were told by spokesmen for the dominant political parties that most of the development brought about by petroleum wealth has been harmful; that Venezuela was better off in 1900, when it had no skyscrapers but was one of the most cultured countries in South America.

A Swiss journalist has recently made some acute comments following a trip to Mexico and South America. He points out that "scientific know-how and progressive optimism no longer possess the slightest mystery."[15] Latin American students come to the United States to study medicine and science but "the United States has not become the center of an ideology which would arouse the enthusiasm of other races."

4. It is frequently stated in the United States that the cause of our unpopularity is that we have "played footsie" with the upper crust and have not won the sympathy of the lower classes. Any broad generalization in this field is apt to be mistaken or misleading, but the evidence of a public opinion poll in Greater Santiago (Chile) in 1957 is striking: it showed that the upper class was less favorably disposed to the United States than the members of other classes. This is probably true in most of the other countries as well. The real opposition is not against our conservatism but against our particular brand of liberalism, which most Latin Americans feel is not suited to their traditions and way of life. Conservatives in Latin America constantly avow their devotion to democracy and free enterprise, but these words have a different content than in northern climes. Hence we find the apparent paradox that conservatives have some sympathy for Marxism, which justifies state direction and authoritarianism, while they are repelled by our concept of free enterprise and undirected democracy. Likewise the military has discovered in Marxism a modern and fashionable justification for dictatorship as an instrument for social and economic reform.

In recent years we have also alienated some of the less fortunate classes, since free enterprise does not always have agreeable connotations in Latin America. Furthermore, they are accustomed to the idea of benevolent dictatorship and doubt if reforms can be achieved any other way. Despite our attempts to court the intelligentsia, comparatively few have been won over to our position.

How can it have happened that so much effort, so much money, so much goodwill—and there has been a generous measure of all of these—went so far awry?

An answer to this question involves an examination of the various strands of inter-American relations and will be undertaken in the chapters that follow. Suffice it here to point out that the Latin American disaffection with our policies has been, and remains, serious. We have lost some ground that it will be very difficult to regain, since Latin American confidence in our basic goodwill and respect for our competence as a leader have been weakened.

There has always been an important group in Latin America representing what might be called hard-core anti-Americanism, and the size of this group has been increased by postwar events. Furthermore, an important recent development has been the emergence of a substantial nucleus of nationalist sentiment among sectors of the population that previously were without serious ideological commitment in these matters. Under favorable conditions, a large proportion of this group would prefer a policy of friendly cooperation with the United States in an inter-American system, but postwar developments have created widespread sympathy for at least an independent, if not a neutral, stance in relation to some of our objectives.

There is also, to be sure, a large reservoir of goodwill toward the United States, and many Latin Americans, although irked by our aberrations, have never lost faith in our basic fairness and generosity. Some of the anti-Yankeeism is of the deeply rooted variety that will hardly be affected by anything we do or refrain from doing, but much of it is based on passing irritations and only becomes vocal in times of stress. Even those least disposed to share our values and aspirations are seldom unaware of the importance to them of the United States, both in terms of economic well-being and of security against external pressures. Perhaps part of the pique against the United States grows out of this very feeling of dependence, in many respects comparable to European touchiness.

It is also illuminating to recall that the curve of anti-Americanism in Canada has followed much the same trajectory as in Latin America, and for much the same reasons: first, the feeling that the influx of United States capital and the subordination of public opinion media to American influences were undermining the national sovereignty and national identity; and, secondly, irritation at various aspects of United States foreign policy that seemed to reflect immaturity.

In recent years a large sector of the United States public has judged events in Latin America exclusively in the context of potential communist subversion. It is not within the purview of this volume to evaluate the world-wide communist problem in its various

22

ramifications, but rather to probe the basic issues in inter-American relations and to raise the question whether some of our policies have given aid and comfort to the communists by creating a favorable climate in which to operate. Obviously the communists have made the most of nationalistic and anti-American sentiments, but communism has merely capitalized on such attitudes and has been a minor element in creating them. It is not likely, therefore, that we shall be able to rebuild confidence and friendly cooperation on the assumption that, once the communist threat is surgically removed, the entire problem will be solved. In fact, one of the reasons why anti-Americanism became so widespread in recent years has been the resentment among all classes at our insistence that no one objected to our policies except the communists.

If we have to choose, it would, of course, be better to be right than to be liked. We must assure the security of the United States and of the nontotalitarian world even if we step on some toes in the process. But in practice we can achieve our major objectives without antagonism to men and women of good sense and goodwill, provided we act in good faith and do not use the communist scare as an excuse to promote private interests nor to upset genuine reform movements.

The Latin Americans demonstrated in October, 1962, as they have on various earlier occasions, that they are on the side of the United States whenever any real threat to Western values is involved. Fortunately, the United States government by its restraint as well by its readiness to meet any real challenge, helped to lay the groundwork for a better understanding. There are strong forces making for harmony, as well as for dissonance, and the opportunity to strengthen the former lies before us.

NOTES TO CHAPTER I

1. Joseph Byrne Lockey, *Pan-Americanism; Its Beginnings* (New York: The Macmillan Co., 1926), p. 264. Some time before this occurrence Jefferson had a conversation with a native of Mexico about the possibility of revolution in that colony. In his correspondence Jefferson recorded his view that "nature has placed it too near us to make its movements altogether indifferent to our interests." *Ibid.*

2. *Freedom and Reform in Latin America* (Notre Dame: University of Notre Dame Press, 1959), p. 14.

3. Duncan Aikman, *The All-American Front* (New York: Doubleday, Doran & Co., 1940), p. 11.　　　　　　　　　　　　4. *Ibid.*, p. 12.

5. John Gillin, "Modern Latin American Culture," in Leonard and Loomis, *Readings in Latin American Social Organization,* p. 10. (Originally published in *Social Forces,* XXV, 243-48.)   6. *Ibid.,* p. 15.

7. See article, "Latin America: Economic Factors," in *Encyclopedia Americana,* XVII (1956), 14-19.

8. "The Two Americas," *The Lamp,* XXXVI (September, 1954), 4.

9. N. Andrew N. Cleven, "The Political Heritage of Spanish America," in *Argentina, Brazil and Chile Since Independence,* A. Curtis Wilgus (ed.) (Washington, D.C.: George Washington University Press, 1935), p. 34.

10. *Boletín de la Secretaría de Educación Pública,* translated from the Spanish by George Wythe (México, D.F., julio 1927), p. 510.

11. This impression of a feminine reaction, which the author obtained during residence in Brazil in 1947-48, has been developed by Gilberto Freyre in *New World in the Tropics* (New York: Alfred A. Knopf, 1959), chapter X.

12. La Malinche was the Indian mistress of Cortés, who delivered her country to the invaders.

13. For further discussion of this point, see chapter VI.

14. *The Latin Americans,* Canadian Institute of Public Affairs (Toronto: University of Toronto Press, 1960), pp. 23-24.

15. Peter Schmid, *Beggars on Golden Stools,* translated from the German (New York: Frederick A. Praeger, 1956), p. 66.

–II–

Inter-American Cooperation Within a Regional System

The idea of cooperation among the American states, or nations, for the purposes of defense, maintenance of peace, and promotion of trade and common interests, goes back to the Era of Emancipation, when the Spanish provinces were still struggling for independence. There was early widespread sympathy in the United States for close ties with the emerging American nations, but this was submerged for a half century by Jacksonian isolationism and domestic preoccupations. The Monroe Doctrine was issued and interpreted unilaterally; various Spanish American overtures for bilateral alliances, as well as Brazil's suggestion of a "concert of American powers," were declined. It was not until the 1880's that the United States became interested in a multilateral approach to the common problems of the hemisphere.

Meanwhile, there had been various attempts on the part of the Spanish American countries to create a federation, league, or family of nations. Although these efforts came to naught, the various congresses and consultations served to keep alive the feeling of "continentalism" and gave expression to most of the basic principles now embodied in what is known as American international law.

THE PAN AMERICAN ERA, 1890-1945

A combination of internal and external forces induced the United States to take the initiative in bringing together, in 1889, what proved to be the first of a long series of inter-American conferences, and in laying the foundation for a continuing Union of American Republics that gradually extended its sphere of action and responsibility in hemispheric affairs.

25

The first fifty-five years of this movement, from the creation of a permanent office in 1890 until the Conference on Problems of War and Peace held at Mexico City in 1945, might be termed the Pan American phase of its history, since that was the name by which it was generally known. It is useful to recall the salient characteristics of this period.

1. The Pan American system was not confined to any one organization, but involved a complex of agencies, principles, and practices. There was no basic treaty or charter freezing the structure and workings of the system. The principal decision-making medium was the periodic International Conference of American States, in which all of the republics were entitled to representation and equal vote. Out of the modest commercial information office established in 1890 there gradually evolved a secretariat and technical staff, headed by a Director General and supervised by a Governing Board that served as a permanent committee of the International Conference. The practice soon developed of calling inter-American conferences at which the governments were represented by specialists or technicians, and out of these developed some permanent organs, such as the Pan American Sanitary Bureau, operating in a completely autonomous manner.

2. The Pan American Union and its Governing Board were enjoined from exercising functions of a political character. There were a number of reasons for this rule. A few countries, especially Argentina, did not want a strong Pan American system and were almost morbidly afraid of anything resembling a superstate. Some felt that the Pan American Union was under the thumb of the United States government and hence could not safely be entrusted with large powers. Of course, the no-politics rule did not apply to the International Conference of American States (although an effort was made to keep controversial items off the agenda), and indeed at these congresses were hammered out the main questions at issue between the United States and Latin America, such as intervention and rights of aliens. The machinery developed for the peaceful settlement of disputes was operated parallel to, but separate from, the Pan American Union. Nevertheless, from 1936 onward, with the development of the procedure of consultation and the expansion of activities in

26

response to the changing international scene, the need for a body with broader executive responsibility became evident. Hence it came about that the Governing Board was provisionally given broader powers pending the reorganization of the inter-American system, which occurred at Bogotá in 1948.

3. Throughout the period under review the chairman of the Governing Board was an American (the Secretary of State), and the Director General of the Pan American Union was an American citizen. In the early stages of the movement this circumstance was not considered unusual, for it was customary diplomatic practice to choose a chairman from the host country, but as permanent organs were established, a more democratic and elective type of organizational hierarchy appeared desirable. In 1923 the offices of chairman and vice-chairman were made elective, although in practice the Governing Board continued, until after the Mexico City meeting in 1945, to elect as chairman the American Secretary of State, who had before 1923 held the position ex-officio. In 1947, following the tragic death the preceding December of Dr. Leo S. Rowe, who had been Director General for twenty-six years, a Latin American was elected Director General of the Pan American Union (the title was changed the following year to Secretary General of the Organization of American States). Since that time the occupant of that office has always been a Latin American.

During the first decades of Pan Americanism, the composition of the Governing Board and the fact that it met only in Washington[1]* were also factors that made Latin Americans reluctant to confer extensive political powers upon its permanent organ. At the time of its establishment, the Governing Board consisted of the diplomatic representatives of the member states accredited to the United States government. This was a useful practical device, since any attempt to set up a permanent board of representatives to handle inter-American matters would have been self-defeating at that time. But the arrangement had the disadvantage that governments not recognized by Washington were without representation on the Board. Changes were made in the rule in 1910 and 1923, and in 1928 governments were permitted to send a special representative to sit on the

*Notes to chapter II begin on page 61.

Governing Board, even though they simultaneously had another diplomat accredited to the American government. There was some feeling that a special representative would have more freedom of action than an Ambassador to the United States, since the latter would be under the necessity of avoiding giving offense to the government to which he was accredited. Furthermore, in the case of the larger countries, it became impracticable for one man to do justice to both jobs. The Council of the Organization of American States, with enlarged functions, has its seat in Washington, but the Inter-American Conference and the Meetings of Consultation of Ministers of Foreign Affairs, are held in rotation in the various capitals.

It is, alas, very difficult in this world for one to have his cake and eat it, too. Once the Secretary of State had been ousted as chairman of the Governing Board, it was necessary to appoint an American diplomatic representative to the Board (and later to the Council of the OAS). This was, of course, appropriate, since the Latin American countries are not represented by their foreign ministers except at special conferences, but it inevitably downgraded inter-American affairs in relation to the times when men of the stature of Elihu Root, Charles Evans Hughes, and Cordell Hull sat at the head of the table.[2]

4. Despite the safeguards developed to prevent undue influence by any one power, it would be a mistake to put excessive emphasis on the negative factors. Actually, during the period under review there was a huge expansion in inter-American relations in all fields: trade, investment, travel, transportation and communications, press coverage, exchange of publications, improvement of health, sanitation, and also in a wide range of intellectual, cultural, and technical fields. Of course, most of this expanding activity was the result of dynamic private and official forces within the individual countries, but the Pan American organization can be said to have contributed significantly by helping to create a favorable atmosphere, by taking the initiative in some matters, and by providing counsel in others.

Likewise, the limitations on political activities by the Pan American Union should not be considered as purely negative; they were based on a positive concept of international relations. Dr. Rowe, a profound student of political science, believed that the functions of his office could best be performed by quiet, tactful diplomacy, rather than by building up a big staff or by throwing his weight around. In a lecture in 1938, Dr. Rowe addressed himself directly to the criticism which he said had been directed against the Pan American Union because it did not possess compulsory powers and therefore could not use force or impose sanctions. "This criticism is based," Dr. Rowe said, "upon a misconception of the purpose for which the Union was established, as well as upon a misinterpretation of the philosophy upon which its activities rest. For the promotion of peace, nations must develop the habit of cooperation. . . . Whenever a controversy arises between two or more of the American republics, the entire continent assumes, as a matter of course, that this controversy will be settled peaceably. Not only is it the fact that the machinery is at hand for the settlement of controversies, but there is also the far more important and significant circumstance that continental opinion demands that such machinery be used to arrive at a peaceful settlement."[3]

It is well to recall that during this period the association of the American republics was officially designated as a "moral union," resting "on the juridical equality of the republics of the continent and on the mutual respect of the rights inherent in their complete independence" (preamble to the draft convention on the Pan American Union, Sixth International Conference of American States). It was this sense of moral union and solidarity that rallied majority opinion of the continent behind the United States in two world wars. Brazil, in repealing its decree of neutrality in 1917, referred to its desire to give its foreign policy "a practical form of continental solidarity," and Uruguay, some two weeks later, in repealing its neutrality laws in favor of the American states that were at war, proclaimed the "principle of American solidarity as the criterion of its international policy." Similarly, the other countries taking action favorable to the United States and the Allies justified their course by such principles.

The New Organization of American States

At the end of World War II, some changes in the structure of the inter-American system appeared opportune in view of the situation

29

created by the formation of the United Nations, the vast expansion of inter-American activities during the war, and the need for greater coordination of the somewhat diffuse operations that had grown up over the years. Some interim measures were taken at the special conference in Mexico City in 1945, but the major step occurred at the Ninth Conference at Bogotá in 1948, with the signing of the Charter of the Organization of American States, which gave the system a new name and a new structure. The Charter was given provisional effect at once, and has since been ratified by all of the twenty-one republics of the hemisphere.

The new name replaced the little used and almost forgotten title of Union of American Republics. The word "organization" in the new title was chosen in preference to such words as "union," "society" or "association" that might be construed to have some implications of a superstate; and the word "states" replaced "republics" in order not to exclude Canada in case that great Dominion should eventually accept the standing invitation to associate itself with the system. (Brazil, the only New World monarchy with more than an ephemeral existence, was still an Empire when the invitations went out for the First International Conference of American States, but a republic was established on November 15, 1889, following the opening of the Conference on October 2.)

The Charter is an inclusive document that not only specifies the organizational structure with considerable detail, but also reaffirms the principles and practices evolved out of the experience of the previous decades. Aside from changes in terminology, the principal result achieved by the Charter was to give formal and permanent status to the association and to provide for a larger measure of coordination over the far-flung activities embraced in the inter-American system without restricting their technical autonomy.

The supreme organ of the system remains the periodic conference with its name shortened to the Inter-American Conference (used in the singular to indicate the continuity of the body). It convenes normally every five years. The Meeting of Consultation of Ministers of Foreign Affairs, for which provision was first made in 1938, has been retained. The old Governing Board of the Pan American Union is replaced by the Council of the OAS, which is composed of one representative of each member state. This has become pretty much of a full-time job, although some of the smaller countries designate their Ambassador to the United States as their Council representative as well in order to save money or to avoid personality conflicts. The Council has supervisory and coordinating functions and also carefully delineated political functions. It supervises the operations of the Pan American Union, which has been retained as the "central and permanent organ of the Organization of American States and the General Secretariat of the Organization." Although this name has now become somewhat misleading, it has both sentimental and practical value, and it provides a link with the past, when that name and the Union's headquarters, the imposing marble palace on Constitution Avenue in Washington, were popular symbols of inter-American cooperation and friendship. The Council's coordinating functions relate to the work of the specialized organizations, which have been brought into closer relationship with the central authorities. It is in the assignment of some political functions that the Council differs most sharply from the former Governing Board. At Bogotá this change (which had already been foreshadowed by the Mexico City Conference in 1945) was resisted by several delegates who disliked the trend toward a superstate and feared that it would open the door to intervention in the internal affairs of the members. Consequently, the limits of the political functions were carefully set forth in the Charter, but the Council was authorized to serve provisionally as the Organ of Consultation under the 1947 Treaty of Reciprocal Assistance, and furthermore it may take cognizance of any matter referred to it by the Inter-American Conference or the Meetings of Consultation of Ministers of Foreign Affairs.

In the light of the foregoing brief sketch of the evolution of the inter-American system, it is in order to undertake some general considerations on the achievements, weaknesses, and prospects of inter-American cooperation. The fact that the modern inter-American movement has survived for over seventy years and has indeed constantly enlarged its field of action and responsibility, provides some evidence of its vitality and apparent utility. At the same time it has come in for strong criticism in both North and South America. In both regions the chief complaint has been basically the same, that the marriage of the Anglo-Saxon North and the Latin South has been a *mésalliance,* and that each party might be better off with another partner. But despite some spats and charges of neglect and even unfaithfulness, it has not yet come to a divorce action.

If the association has survived, it has not been because it was perfect, but because it provided the best available solution to the problem of coexistence among the new nations of the Western world. Viewed in the historical perspective, then, the main contribution of Pan Americanism has been to provide an American solution, on a cooperative international basis, to the age-old problem of relations between a powerful nation and a group of weaker states in some manner associated with it through geography, history, and economic ties. Dr. Alberto Lleras, ex-President of the Republic of Colombia and former Secretary General of the OAS, has on various occasions given a moving tribute to the wisdom and restraint of the United States in refusing to follow the beckoning path of empire, as has been the almost invariable pattern in the past.[4]

There were times of genuine alarm that the United States might succumb to the imperatives of imperial power and gradually extend farther south its political and military sway, as it already had to a considerable degree financially and culturally. This was the time of dollar diplomacy, which, whatever its shortcomings in practice, had overall objectives essentially the same as the present-day dollar aid programs. In both cases the main objective was security; and in both private gain has been blended with idealistic motives. The rationale given by Secretary of State Hughes in 1923 was in almost identical language to that used later by Presidents Harry S. Truman and Dwight D. Eisenhower: that the troubles of the impoverished republics were due chiefly to the lack of development of their resources, for which capital is needed; and that private capital was obtainable only if the investment was reasonably secure. "We are not seeking . . . ," Secretary Hughes stated, "to exploit, but to aid; not to subvert, but to help in laying the foundations for sound, stable, and independent government."

There were Latin American misgivings, but there were also great advantages to be derived from association with the big northern neighbor. Despite the criticisms of jealous Europeans and embittered

Spanish Americans that the United States was using Pan Americanism as a device for establishing its hegemony, in practice Pan Americanism was from the beginning organized on the basis of equality of nations. The United States sponsored the international debut of the Latin American countries, and it has been through United States influence that Latin America has continued to receive much more international recognition than would otherwise have been the case. The Latin Americans were eager to profit from the large and growing United States market; their governments floated large bond issues in the United States, and also obtained capital through bank loans and private investments. American competition in the import trade was also welcomed, as affording them a wider choice of goods and in moderating prices. With the exception of the preferential arrangement with Cuba, which assured Cuba a large share of the American market for sugar, the United States did not ask for a preferred economic position.[5]

While the Monroe Doctrine and United States trade and financial competition provided a safeguard against undue European pressures (it is useful to recall that in the 1880's, when the first International Conference of American States was held, Asia, Africa, and the Near East were being carved up into colonies and protectorates), there was nothing about Pan Americanism that restricted relations with non-American countries. If the inter-American organization did not always protect Latin America in all respects against its protector, it provided a useful and effective mechanism for applying continuous moral and political pressures on the United States, and usually with gratifying results. The inter-American conferences offered a forum at which the member countries could and did air their grievances. By its very existence the inter-American system did, in some measure, "inter-Americanize" the Monroe Doctrine, and stimulated an international approach to problems of common interest. It helped to keep the peace in the Americas and moderated the ambitions of Latin American *caudillos* who might otherwise have been tempted—possibly with extracontinental help—to extend their boundaries. Hence United States policy during this period, whatever its theoretical shortcomings when judged in the context of a different era, had the great historical justification that any other policy might well have

33

precipitated Latin America into the scramble of the great powers—including the United States—for protectorates, extraterritorial rights in ports, and zones of influence, and postponed indefinitely the time when an international approach to world problems might be attempted.

BASIC PRINCIPLES OF INTER-AMERICANISM

Some critics have argued that the unequal power of the United States in comparison with that of the other members of the system vitiated the bases of genuine international association. For example, the Venezuelan Mariano Picón-Salas spoke of "the unbalanced alliance of the elephant and the ants," and the Argentine Manuel Ugarte called the Buenos Aires conference of 1910 "a congress of mice, presided over by a cat." Other critics inevitably have used the simile of the wolf and the lambs.

Actually it has been the power and resources of the United States that have made it possible for the inter-American system to perform a valuable historical function in an imperfect world. All Spanish American attempts at association and cooperation ended in failure, and it was primarily American moral and financial support that ensured continuity and the achievement of concrete results of mutual benefit to the members as well as to the world in general.

The United States has not insisted on a privileged position, and in the OAS, unlike the United Nations, there is no council of great powers nor a veto. Furthermore, the OAS Charter specifically recognizes the principle of universality in admission, all American states that ratify the Charter becoming members of the OAS with equal vote with all other members. In procedural and administrative matters, decision is by majority vote; in major policy or political matters, a two-thirds vote is normally required.

As relatively weak countries, the Latin American states have traditionally been interested in obtaining acceptance, from all of the great powers if possible, but particularly from the United States, of those principles of international law that would guarantee the rights of small states and afford protection against foreign pressures, either of a political nature or on behalf of foreign nationals and interests.

The United States has, from the beginning of the modern Pan American movement, shown sympathy with most of these doctrines, such as the juridical equality of states, peaceful settlement of international disputes, inviolability of national territory, and condemnation of wars of aggression. Until the 1930's the United States defended the accepted rule of international law regarding the right of intervention, or temporary interposition, in case of anarchy, or under circumstances where the breakdown of law and order put the lives and interests of its nationals in jeopardy, but by 1936 it had abandoned not only the practice of intervention but also the juridical right to do so.

In keeping with the views of some delegates to Bogotá that the Charter should be an all-embracing document, there are included those precepts of "American international law" which had been approved, in the same or modified form, in previous inter-American agreements, declarations or resolutions. In some cases the restatement is in extreme form. The provisions relating to equality of states in the Charter are essentially the same as the provisions in the Convention on Rights and Duties of States approved at the Seventh Conference at Montevideo in 1933: "States are juridically equal, enjoy equal rights and equal capacity to exercise these rights, and have equal duties. The rights of each state depend not upon its power to ensure the exercise thereof, but upon the mere fact of its existence as a person under international law." Also: "The political existence of the state is independent of recognition by other states."

These statements assert not only the equality of recognized states, but also oppose any attempt to use recognition as a weapon to extort conditions before granting recognition. Back of this lies a good deal of history. Early in the present century the United States became concerned with the frequent revolutionary upheavals, especially in Central America, and meditated methods that might be used to discourage revolution and encourage democracy. One means to this end, it was decided, would be to withhold recognition from governments coming into power by unconstitutional means. In 1907 the Central American countries and the United States signed a series of treaties by which the signatories agreed not to achnowledge any government coming into power as the result of a coup d'état until it had received the approval of the electorate. Despite the failure of the treaties to bring peace to the area, this principle of nonrecognition of a revolutionary government was reaffirmed in 1923 in the General Treaty of Peace and Amity, effective for ten years. President Wilson also applied the principle in Mexico. At the end of the 1920's, however, President Herbert Hoover abandoned the policy (except in Central America, where the relevant treaties did not expire or were not denounced until 1933 and 1934), which had not been successful in avoiding revolutions and was looked upon by the Latin Americans as an unwarranted interference in purely internal affairs.

In some of the Latin American countries, a revolution or coup d'état is actually the only way by which a government can be changed, since otherwise the governments in power either ignore the constitutional provisions regarding elections, or else go through the motions but rig them in a manner necessary to assure their continuance in power. In other words, a revolution is a sort of Democratic primary.

The general principles applying to recognition were set forth at Bogotá in Resolution 35, on the Exercise of the Right of Legation, which declared:

1. That continuity of diplomatic relations among the American states is desirable;
2. That the right of maintaining, suspending or renewing diplomatic relations with another government shall not be exercised as a means of individually obtaining unjustified advantages under international law; and
3. That the establishment or maintenance of diplomatic relations with a government does not imply any judgment upon the domestic policy of that government.

In other words, *de facto* recognition depends upon the traditional criteria, that the government actually controls its territory, and that it shows its intention to live up to its international commitments. Of course, the application of these criteria leaves a lot of room for judgment.

One other matter that has given rise to divergent interpretations relates to rights of aliens. During the nineteenth century the Latin American countries had frequently been subject to pecuniary claims on the part of foreigners, some of which were unfair or downright scandalous. But there were also cases in which it was impossible to obtain justice either through normal administrative processes or through the courts. Hence foreign governments frequently resorted to diplomatic pressures and at times to naval demonstrations, naval bombardments, or military intervention. As early as 1868 Carlos Calvo of Argentina had pronounced the doctrine, which came to bear his name, providing for final jurisdiction of local courts and the denial of the privilege of diplomatic recourse. The Latin American countries embodied the Calvo doctrine in their constitutions, laws, and contracts and attempted to have it written into treaties and multilateral agreements.

While the United States has given up the right of intervention, it has never admitted the right of an individual to contract away the right or duty of his government to protect him. The Montevideo Convention on Rights and Duties of States had provided that "nationals and foreigners are under the same protection of the law," but the United States made a reservation that it did not waive any rights it may have under international law. When the Charter came to be written, a similar clause was proposed for article 12, but as the result of the objection of the United States delegation, it was modified to read, "The jurisdiction of states within the limits of their national territory is exercised equally over all the inhabitants, whether nationals or aliens," to accommodate the American position that while both nationals and aliens are subject to the jurisdiction of the state in which they reside, they are not necessarily under the same protection.[6]

The question of intervention was long the hottest issue in inter-American relations. The principle of absolute nonintervention is stated very broadly in the Charter. Article 15 reads: "No state or group of states has the right to intervene, directly or indirectly, for any reason whatever, in the internal or external affairs of any other state. The foregoing principle prohibits not only armed force but also any other form of interference or attempted threat against the personality of the state or against its political, economic and cultural elements." Also article 17: "The territory of a state is inviolable; it may not be the object, even temporarily, of military occupation or of any other measures of force taken by another state, directly or indirectly, on any grounds whatever. No territorial acquisition or special advantage obtained by force or other measures of coercion shall be recognized." Despite the ring of finality about these declarations, one cannot but wonder if the chapter on intervention has yet been closed. The question at once arises, what is intervention? At the Fifth Meeting of Consultation of Ministers of Foreign Affairs, the Council of the OAS was requested to prepare an instrument listing the greatest possible number of cases that constitute violations of the principle of nonintervention. The Council turned the job over to the Inter-American Juridical Committee, which prepared a report and draft resolution on the subject. The examples of violation of the principle of nonintervention were culled from various inter-American documents and treatises on public international law. The American member of the Committee entered a dissenting statement, pointing out that attempts to define a primary notion like nonintervention tends to limit and distort rather than clarify the concept. He added that both the League of Nations and the United Nations had refused to define a comparable term, aggression.

In the 1930's, when the principle of nonintervention was approved at the Seventh and Eighth International Conferences of American States, it was still a distinctly American doctrine, but a somewhat similar proscription has now been made a part of the United Nations Charter. Article 2(4) states: "All members shall refrain in their international relations from the threat or use of force against the territorial integrity or political independence of any state, or in any other manner inconsistent with the Purposes of the United Nations." Article 2(7) reads: "Nothing contained in the present Charter shall authorize the United Nations to intervene in matters which are essentially within the domestic jurisdiction of any state or shall require the Members to submit such matters to settlement under the present Charter; but this principle shall not prejudice the application of enforcement measures under Chapter VII."

The Inter-American Security System

The inter-American system of peace and security, as embodied in the Charter and other documents, has two distinct but interrelated strands, one the traditional American regional system and the other the collective security system of the United Nations.

Traditionally, the American states have always made, and still make, a distinction between external aggression, on the one hand, and disputes between American states, on the other hand. The late Dr. Rowe summarized the situation in a statement on the Fiftieth Anniversary of the Pan American movement: "The unity of the Americas means the safety of the Americas from aggression from without and it also means the maintenance of peace within the confines of the twenty-one republics of the American continent."[7]

In practice, during the period under review, the Monroe Doctrine has been the main defense against encroachments from outside the hemisphere but—to paraphrase NATO terminology—the Doctrine was long both a shield and a two-edged sword, a shield against noncontinental attacks or threats, but a weapon to chastise unruly American republics. The Latin American policy, therefore, was to retain the shield but to blunt one edge of the sword. With the triumph of the doctrine of complete nonintervention, the first steps were taken, at Buenos Aires in 1936, toward what has been called the continentalization of the Monroe Doctrine through the declaration that "every act susceptible of disturbing the peace of America affects each and every one of them," and the agreement to "consult together" in "the event that the peace of the American republics is menaced." But this agreement, as well as subsequent ones, made a distinction between international war and conflicts between American states. For example, in 1940, at the Second Meeting of Consultation of Ministers of Foreign Affairs, one declaration was made "that any attempt on the part of a non-American state against the integrity or inviolability of the territory, the sovereignty or the political independence of an American state shall be considered an act of aggression against the states which sign this declaration," while another declaration related to the "maintenance of peace and union among the American Republics." At Mexico City in 1945, having in mind the Dumbarton Oaks proposals for the organization of the United Nations, specific provision was made, for the first time, for the application of sanctions, in cases of aggression whether "against any of the American states by a non-American state" or by "an American state against one or more American states." This agreement was applicable only during the war emergency, and was replaced by the Treaty of Reciprocal Assistance (Rio Treaty) in 1947.

During the course of negotiation of the Rio Treaty, some countries wanted to confine the application of the treaty to extracontinental aggression, and avoid the possible application of coercive measures against American states. As approved, the treaty represents a compromise, since it establishes general principles applicable to all types of aggression, but provides that "in the case of a conflict between two or more American states," the first objective of collective action shall be to bring about a suspension of hostilities and the restoration of the *status quo ante bellum*. Article 20 of the treaty provides that sanctions agreed upon by the Organ of Consultation (i.e., Meeting of Ministers of Foreign Affairs) are binding upon all signatory states which have ratified the treaty but that no state shall be required to use armed force without its consent.

The Charter of the OAS reaffirms, among its Principles, that (a) "an act of aggression against one American state is an act of aggression against all the other American states" and (b) "controversies of an international character arising between two or more American states shall be settled by peaceful procedures." The Charter has a chapter, "Pacific Settlement of Disputes," which provides that disputes between American states shall be submitted to the procedures made available by existing inter-American treaties before being referred to the Security Council of the United Nations, and also a chapter entitled "Collective Security," which incorporates by summary and reference the provisions of the Rio Treaty. Since article 51 of the United Nations Charter provides for "collective self-defense" by nations having regional arrangements, the provisions of the OAS Charter and the Rio Treaty come within the framework of the world organization. NATO and other regional organizations were set up under this same article, and modeled after the Rio Treaty.

Up to the end of 1962 the Rio Treaty had been invoked ten times.[8] In all but one instance threats to peace originating within the hemisphere were involved. The first seven cases involved disputes among the smaller countries of the Caribbean area (the five Central American countries, Panama, Haiti, and the Dominican Republic), and eight of the cases were settled by the Council of the OAS acting provisionally as the Organ of Consultation. Most of the difficulties in these seven cases arose out of the existence of large numbers of refugees from dictatorial governments in the Caribbean, swollen at times by mercenaries and adventurers, and the attempts of these expatriates—aided in some cases by the government of the country in which they had taken refuge—to overthrow their political adversary. In one case, Guatemala in 1954, the government was overthrown by an invasion from Honduras having the moral and perhaps material backing of the United States. In most cases a peaceful adjustment has been worked out by the Council through committees of investigation aided by military advisers, which personally visited the countries involved in the dispute. In at least one case, the threatened invasion of Costa Rica from Nicaragua in 1955, the decision of the United States to sell planes to Costa Rica proved adequate to readjust the balance on that troubled frontier.

The eighth case in which the Rio Treaty was applied is of special interest, since it involved the complaint of a major country, Venezuela, against the Dominican Republic, and also resulted in the first instance of the application of sanctions (but not involving the use of force, which nominally—although the precedents on this point are a bit fuzzy—would have required prior approval by the United Nations Security Council. The Sixth Meeting of Consultation of Ministers of Foreign Affairs, in session at San José, Costa Rica, in mid-August, 1960, concluded that the government of the Dominican Republic had participated "in the acts of aggression and intervention against the state of Venezuela that culminated in the attempt on the life of the President of that country," and agreed upon (a) the breaking of diplomatic relations of all the member states with the Dominican Republic and (b) partial interruption of economic relations with the Dominican Republic, beginning with the immediate suspension of trade in arms, and to be followed by such other measures as might be recommended by the Council of the OAS. Although all of the American republics broke diplomatic relations (but left consular representatives), there was less unanimity in January, 1961, when the Council of the OAS took up the matter of economic sanctions. After impassioned debate, it was decided, by a vote of 14 in favor, 1 against (Dominican Republic), and 6 abstentions (Argentina, Brazil, Guatemala, Haiti, Paraguay, and Uruguay), to recommend that members cut off exports of oil, oil products, trucks, and spare parts. The United States took action along these lines, and in addition moved to reduce the Dominican sugar quota and to deprive the Dominican Republic of the bonus normally received on sales in the United States at a price about 2 cents above the world market prices (this was done by charging a 2-cent-per-pound entry fee).

Intervention vs. Democracy and Human Rights

There are various aspects of the case of Venezuela vs. the Dominican Republic that illustrate vividly some of the vital current issues in inter-American relations. One of these is the question as to whether the Organization of American States should take an active role in promoting the cause of representative government and human rights within the various countries, some of which have long had notoriously harsh dictatorial regimes (of course, no country is 100 per cent perfect in the matter of human rights, especially since the orthodoxy of one generation is the heterodoxy of another). Theoretically, this approach has offered the prospect of joint pressures against the more objectionable types of dictators, while at the same time providing for common action in cases of communist infiltration. Already as early as the time of the Mexico City conference in February-March, 1945, there was some concern over the possibility of "subversive influences" of a Nazi-Fascist character (e.g., Argentina), and soon thereafter at the San Francisco meeting to set up the United Nations (April-June), as rifts began to appear in the Washington-Moscow honeymoon, the fear that the Soviet Union might use its veto in the Security Council to block collective action against a communist takeover was an important factor leading to the decision to include article 51 (providing for collective self-defense) in the United Nations Charter.

In October 1945, Foreign Minister Alberto Rodríguez Larreta of Uruguay, a small country under heavy Peronista pressure from across the Río de la Plata, made a proposal espousing collective intervention in any American state to guarantee human rights and democracy. The Minister referred to the "parallelism between peace and democracy," and insisted that the principle of nonintervention should not shield without limitation "the notorious and repeated violation by any republic of the elementary rights of man and the citizen." United States Secretary of State James Byrnes promptly supported the Uruguayan initiative, but only Venezuela, Cuba, and four Central American countries were in agreement; the other countries were unwilling to open this Pandora's box.

These various currents of opinion were to play an important role at the Ninth Inter-American Conference at Bogotá. In keeping with the well-established tradition in Pan American documents, the Charter, as approved, makes a bow, in its preamble, to democratic institutions and also affirms, as one of its basic Principles, that, "the solidarity of the American states and the high aims which are sought through it require the political organization of these states on the basis of the effective exercise of representative democracy" (article 5a). An effort by the Brazilian and Uruguayan delegations to include a statement of the basic elements of representative democracy (and, in the Brazilian proposal, to make them a condition of membership) was, however, abandoned.[9]

The Ninth Conference also adopted a resolution, "The Preservation and Defense of Democracy in America," which called attention to the "anti-democratic nature" and "interventionist tendency" of international communism and urged the countries to adopt measures to eradicate activities "instigated by foreign governments." At the same time the Latin American sensitivities on the subject of intervention led to the broadening of article 15 of the OAS Charter in two respects beyond any previous statement of the principle of nonintervention: prohibiting intervention by any group of states as well as by a state, and also proscribing threats as well as direct intervention. The first of these additions reflected the nervousness of the majority of delegations over attempts, such as the Larreta proposal, to justify intervention in the name of democracy.

GROWING HEMISPHERIC DIVERGENCES DURING THE 1950's

It was at Bogotá that there began to appear the cleavage, destined to widen with the passing years, in United States and Latin American

43

points of view regarding the nature and solution of postwar problems. As the United States became engrossed by the cold war, Latin Americans, preoccupied with social, economic, and political problems at home, became increasingly critical of the United States' use of its anticommunist slogan as an excuse to shelter dictators and to oppose as socialistic Latin American attempts at social reform and economic development. President Roosevelt's cozy deals with the Trujillos and Somozas had been accepted during the late '30's and war years, especially since the other leaders were also flattered and pampered, but by the decade of the '50's Latin Americans were less inclined to accept uncritically our leadership in either regional or world affairs.

Bemused by frequent optimistic official utterances regarding the progress of democracy and free enterprise in Latin America, Washington did not awake to the gathering storm until the cataclysmic year 1958, which opened with the overthrow of President Marcos Pérez Jiménez in Venezuela, flickered on to the mobbing of Vice-President Richard Nixon, and ended with the advent of Fidel Castro in Cuba. Tension mounted in the Caribbean as new and old governments screamed at each other through radio broadcasts, attempted to stir up revolt through subversive leaflets dropped from airplanes, and sent bands of armed exiles and adventurers to carry on a war of nerves by land, sea, or air, according to the available means.

The Inter-American Peace Committee, composed of five representatives chosen from the OAS Council, operating with flexible permissive procedures, had had some minor successes in settling disputes between 1948, when it was activated, and the summer of 1959, when the Fifth Meeting of Consultation gave it a general mandate to study the problem of international tensions in the Caribbean and to take the initiative, subject to the express consent of the parties concerned, to prevent aggression or intervention designed to overthrow established governments. It was the Peace Committee that paved the way for the Sixth Meeting of Consultation by establishing the responsibility of the Dominican Government in connection with a flight from Ciudad Trujillo for the purpose of dropping leaflets over a Venezuelan city, and also finding that international tensions in the Caribbean had been aggravated by "flagrant and widespread violation of human rights." It also received extensive documentation from the United States and Cuban governments prior to the Seventh Meeting of Consultation, which was held in 1960 in the same city as the Sixth Meeting (San José, Costa Rica) and immediately following that session.

BEGINNING THE 1960's

The Seventh Meeting was convoked at the request of Peru, but the United States and Cuba were recognized as the chief protagonists. It had been the original hope of the United States that both the Dominican Republic and Cuba might be called before the bar of inter-American public opinion for violations of human rights and democratic principles. In the case against the Dominican Republic, Venezuela had asked for and obtained the convocation of the Organ of Consultation, pursuant to article 6 of the Rio Treaty, to consider acts of "intervention and aggression." But when the Council of the OAS came to consider the other aspects of Caribbean tensions, it found no grounds for calling a Meeting of Consultation under the Rio Treaty, in the absence of specific evidence of aggression; hence the Seventh Meeting was convoked under the provisions of the Charter authorizing meetings, if approved by majority vote of the Council, to consider matters of an urgent nature and of common interest. Neither the agenda for the meeting nor the decisions proceeding from the conference made specific mention of Cuba.

In an address before the Seventh Meeting, United States Secretary of State Christian Herter emphasized his concern with "threats of extracontinental intervention," and put the bee directly on Cuba by citing evidence of communist control, and pointing out that Cuba was violating the seven principles and attributes of the democratic system set forth in the Declaration of Santiago the previous August. He called attention to the welcome Cuban officials had given to statements by the Russians that they were ready to support Cuba with rocket fire against the United States. In concluding, he asked the American states to "indicate grave concern over Cuba's toleration and encouragement" of communist intervention in the hemisphere. "Last week the Sixth Consultative Meeting of Foreign

Ministers acted courageously to meet one threat to peace in this hemisphere," Secretary Herter said. "Now we must act with equal courage to meet another threat to peace in the hemisphere, this time greatly magnified by an extracontinental menace."

The principal result of the meeting was the approval of the Declaration of San José, which condemned the intervention or threat of intervention of an extracontinental power as jeopardizing American solidarity and security, and stated that "the inter-American system is incompatible with any form of totalitarianism." At the same time the Declaration reaffirmed the principle of nonintervention and reiterated "that each state has the right to develop its cultural, political, and economic life freely . . . and as a consequence, no American state may intervene for the purpose of imposing upon another American state its ideologies of political, economic, or social principles." Secretary Herter issued a statement on August 29, the day of adjournment, that the Declaration of San José "constitutes a clear indictment of the Castro government of Cuba," but the Mexican delegation took the opposite view, in a statement insisting that the Declaration was in general terms and did not "constitute a condemnation or a threat against Cuba, whose aspirations for economic improvement and social justice have the strongest sympathy of the Government and people of Mexico." During the discussions the representatives of eight countries came to the defense of Cuba. The foreign ministers of Peru and Venezuela refused to sign the declaration but were replaced by their governments. The Dominican Republic was not represented at the conference, and the Cuban delegation walked out as the Declaration of San José was voted.

In the light of this sequence of events, it will be desirable to examine the significance of the outcome of the Sixth and Seventh Ministerial Meetings. The importance of the Sixth Meeting clearly lies in the decision to impose sanctions for the first time in inter-American history. At the same time the governments were not disposed to approve any action that would involve actual intervention within the country. Secretary Herter had proposed to the conference that it ask the Dominican Republic to accept the appointment of a committee empowered to supervise free elections, with the understanding that if the Dominican government did not accept the proposal, then sanctions would be applied. But to the Latin Americans this was intervention, the great bugbear. It was easy for the Latin Americans to vote sanctions, since their trade with the Dominican Republic was negligible, thus putting practically the entire onus and loss on the United States.[10]

Since the actions taken by the Sixth Meeting were designed to force a change of government in the Dominican Republic, it has been difficult for some people to see how the breaking of diplomatic relations and the imposition of sanctions were less a matter of intervention than the proposal of Secretary Herter for the supervision of elections. As a matter of fact, there was considerable difference of opinion among the Latin American countries, as is shown by the split vote on sanctions. At that time the Brazilian delegation put on record an explanation of its dissenting vote that received little attention at the time but, to anticipate events somewhat, is of significance for an understanding of the crosscurrents operating at the Eighth Meeting of Consultation, held at Punta del Este in January, 1962, when the foreign ministers unanimously (except for Cuba) declared communism to be incompatible with the principles of the inter-American system, but split (with six of the principal countries abstaining) on a resolution stating that such incompatibility "excludes the present Government of Cuba from participation in the inter-American system." The Brazilian reservations will be discussed hereafter in connection with the Eighth Meeting of Consultation.

There were, however, a number of reasons why all of the American republics were prepared to condemn Generalissimo Rafael Trujillo. His harsh rule had resulted in the existence of clusters of plotting Dominican exiles in various countries, and had made him the number one target of liberal or leftist governments in the Caribbean, even though some of the latter were also of the authoritarian type. This necessarily resulted in the organization of a large Dominican counter-espionage force, but prior to his entanglement with Rómulo Betancourt, the embattled President of Venezuela, Trujillo had managed to remain within recognized bounds. Indeed, the investigations of the Inter-American Peace Committee in 1949 and of the Council of the OAS in 1950 indicated that the Dominican Republic was as much sinned against as sinning in this matter of "subversive and

47

seditious movements." But by 1960 Trujillo had become a definite political liability not only in the United States but also throughout most of Latin America, where it was felt that he was bringing discredit to the region as a whole. His ruthlessness was greatly feared. He did not play the game of political asylum according to the rules. The moral stench that arose from the island, as it did from Cuba in the last years of the Batista regime, offended many nostrils that normally are not oversensitive. Seven Latin American countries had broken off diplomatic relations with Trujillo before the San José meeting. But it was his bitter feud with Betancourt that proved his undoing, that led him to go too far, and to get caught in specific acts of aggression.

By this time Trujillo was also out of favor in Washington, owing, in part, to the wave of indignation that followed the publication of charges of Trujillo's complicity in the disappearance of Professor Jesús Galíndez of Columbia University, and, in part, to the need to conciliate President Betancourt, since the United States could not risk the possibility of his ire against the large United States investment in Venezuela, and furthermore needed Venezuela's powerful support of the indictment against Cuba. Hence the United States not only voted to condemn Trujillo and to impose sanctions, but it also took actions beyond the strict requirements of the Council's recommendations. In fact, the most serious sanction applied against Trujillo was the action of the United States in connection with the Dominican sugar quota. When the United States proposed additional sanctions, the other countries refused to go along.

To complete the story of Dominican sanctions, it may be noted that the OAS Council withdrew its economic measures against the Dominican Republic on January 4, 1962, exactly one year after the sanctions had been voted. During this period of a year, there were some dramatic developments: on May 30, 1961, General Trujillo was assassinated, and a tense period followed during which it was feared that a coup either by the Trujillo dynasty or by Castroites might be attempted. A subcommittee of the OAS visited the Dominican Republic in June, October, and November to ascertain whether the "Government of the Dominican Republic had or had not ceased to be a danger to the peace and security of the Continent," but the lifting of sanctions was withheld until the remaining members of the Trujillo clan had been expelled in mid-November and a seven-man council of state, including representatives of the opposition parties, was installed. Even after the withdrawal of the sanctions, a new attempt at a military coup d'état was narrowly averted.

The United States restored diplomatic relations with Santo Domingo (the historic name of the capital was restored after the death of Trujillo) on January 6, and shortly thereafter took steps to extend a $25 million credit to the Dominican Republic and also to allot a regular sugar quota of 43,204 short tons for the first six months of 1962, and a nonquota entry amount of 315,987 short tons for the same period.

It is difficult to assess the influence of OAS economic measures and the diplomatic rupture on the course of events. It appears likely that the condemnation of the Trujillo regime, and particularly the change in the previous United States policy of benevolent neutrality, encouraged the bitter enemies of the self-styled Benefactor of the Dominicans to bolder action. At the time of the crisis in mid-November, the avoidance of either a rightist or a leftist coup was in large measure due to the presence of American warships on the high seas near the three-mile limit within plain view of the capital. Well-informed observers have declared that "unquestionably it was the sight of the Yankee warships that saved the day for President Balaguer."[11]

THE CUBAN CASE

It is now in order to examine more closely the reasons for the failure of the United States to enlist full hemisphere support against Castro at the Seventh Meeting of Consultation in 1960 similar to the action taken a few days earlier, at the Sixth Meeting, against Trujillo. The difficulty of verifying any specific acts of aggression by Castro eliminated the possibility at that time, as has been noted, of bringing the case under article 6 of the Rio Treaty, although by the end of 1961 two-thirds of the countries were prepared to consider *"threats* to the peace and to the political independence of the American states" as justification for the convocation of a meeting under article 6. In 1960 the majority of the countries were inclined to stand on a strict construction of the nonintervention doctrine, since the feeling prevailed that the United States was using the communist scare as an excuse to snuff out the social revolution in Cuba and to restore the status quo before Castro. Rightly or wrongly, Cuba had at that time become a symbol throughout the hemisphere of the efforts of a small country to throw off the economic imperialism and political tutelage of a large neighbor, efforts which were considered to have much in common with the Mexican revolution beginning in 1910. The fact that the United States applied sanctions unilaterally against Cuba by cutting its sugar quota after the Cuban government seized the refineries of the Texaco and Esso Standard Oil companies reminded Mexico of a chapter in its own history. Even those Latin Americans who were somewhat nervous about Castro's leftist predilections found it hard to avoid sharing in the sympathy for the underdog and in taking pride in the fact that a Latin American could stand up to Uncle Sam.

It was difficult in those days for most Latin Americans to take seriously our charges against Cuba as a security menace, in view of the disproportionate size and strength of the two countries, to say nothing of the existence of a United States naval base at Guantánamo. We were also stymied in any attempt to base a case on violation of human rights and responsible democracy, since we had cooperated closely with several notorious violators of such rights, especially Trujillo and Pérez Jiménez, as well as the Batista regime in Cuba. As a matter of fact, most Latin Americans blamed the United States for the unhappy developments in Cuba, just as many Americans blamed Belgium for events in the Congo. Furthermore, just as the United States insisted, through the United Nations, on getting the Belgians out of Katanga, so Latin Americans felt that Cuba could not really be considered as a free nation until the large United States economic interests were cut down to a reasonable size. According to this point of view, political colonialism as represented by Europe is rapidly disappearing, but economic colonialism, as represented by the United States, has been overcome only in Mexico. One writer has noted that the reactions in the United States to the economic decolonization process are essentially the same as the reaction of European countries to the loss of colonies.[12]

With the passing of time, however, some of the countries, especially those in the Caribbean, began to have second thoughts and to show increasing concern over the trend of events in Cuba culminating in Castro's open avowal of his Marxist-Leninist affiliations. One government after another severed diplomatic relations with Castro, and others refrained from doing so only for special reasons, such as the reluctance to sacrifice the Cubans who had found asylum in their Havana embassies, or because the embassy had become a depository for Church art works and treasure turned over when Catholic priests and nuns were expelled. As Cuban refugees, many of them persons who had risked their lives in the struggle against Batista, poured into the neighboring countries, there was rising indignation against Castro's treachery and butchery. In various countries there was clear evidence of the use of the Cuban embassies as centers for communist propaganda and also for espionage and intrigue against the governments in power. Finally, on December 4, 1961, on the initiative of Colombia, the OAS Council convoked a Meeting of Consultation of Ministers of Foreign Affairs to consider the threats to the peace and to determine the measures necessary to be taken. Cuba was not specifically mentioned in the convocation. This decision was taken on the affirmative vote of 14 countries, with 2 negative votes (Cuba and Mexico) and 5 abstentions (Argentina, Brazil, Bolivia, Chile, and Ecuador), calling the Eighth Meeting of Consultation into session at Punta del Este, Uruguay, from January 22 to 31, 1962. (This was the ninth application of the Rio Treaty, but only the second case to be taken up by a Meeting of Foreign Ministers acting as the Organ of Consultation under the Rio Treaty.)[13]

At this meeting there was general agreement, Cuba excepted, "that the subversive offensive of communist governments" is a danger, and in recommending that those governments "whose structure or acts are incompatible with the effective exercise of representative democracy, hold free elections in their respective countries," but some of the countries demurred when a majority of the representatives wanted to pass from the pronouncement of general principles to specific action. The principal resolution adopted at the meeting, providing for the exclusion of the Cuban government from participation in the inter-American system, had four executive clauses:

51

1. That adherence by any member of the Organization of American States to Marxism-Leninism is incompatible with the inter-American system and the alignment of such a government with the communist bloc breaks the unity and solidarity of the hemisphere.

2. That the present Government of Cuba, which has officially identified itself as a Marxist-Leninist government, is incompatible with the principles and objectives of the inter-American system.

3. That this incompatibility excludes the present Government of Cuba from participation in the inter-American system.

4. That the Council of the Organization of American States and the other organs and organizations of the inter-American system adopt without delay the measures necessary to carry out this resolution.

The preliminary voting showed that all of the republics except Cuba were prepared to accept the first two points, but six of the countries (Argentina, Bolivia, Brazil, Chile, Ecuador, and Mexico) abstained on the last two clauses and hence in voting on the adoption of the resolution as a whole.

This outcome has led to a divergence in interpretation as to the significance of the vote. The declaration of incompatibility in the first clause did not go beyond the Declaration of San José, approved by the Seventh Meeting of Consultation in 1960, which reaffirmed that the inter-American system "is incompatible with any form of totalitarianism" but did not mention Cuba. In specifically declaring the incompatibility of the "present Government of Cuba," the second clause of the Punta del Este resolution did carry the argument a step further. But it was the abstention of six countries on the exclusion of Cuba that caused the chief concern, especially since this important group of dissidents account for two-thirds of the population and three-fourths of the area of Latin America.[14]

There was a vote of 20 to 1 (Cuba) to exclude Cuba from the Inter-American Defense Board, but this vote merely recorded a *fait accompli*. There were four abstentions (Brazil, Chile, Ecuador, Mexico) on the resolution to suspend immediately trade with Cuba in arms and implements of war, and to instruct the OAS Council to study the feasibility and desirability of extending the suspension of trade to other items. Since the trade in arms had already been discontinued, and commercial exchanges were minimal, the chief significance of this resolution was the leverage it might afford the United States in preventing transhipment of strategic goods from other American republics, and in bringing influence to bear against trading with Cuba on the part of Canada and the European countries. As regards the United States, its trade of over a billion dollars with Cuba in 1958 (exports plus imports) had dwindled to less than $50 million in 1961. In that year imports from Cuba consisted chiefly of tobacco filler, while exports were confined to such food and medicinal items as were approved by the export control authorities. On February 3, 1962, President John Kennedy prohibited all Cuban imports into the United States.

The United States also attached some importance to the adoption of a resolution directing the OAS Council to establish a Special Consultative Committee of experts on security matters, modeled on the lines of the Emergency Committee for Political Defense which functioned at Montevideo from 1942 to 1948. Cuba voted against this resolution, and Bolivia abstained. There was likewise one abstention (Uruguay) on a resolution recommending that the Council revise the Statute of the Inter-American Commission on Human Rights so as to strengthen the Commission's faculties, and "permit it effectively to further respect for these rights in the countries of the hemisphere."

Growing Sentiment for Collective Intervention

This last-mentioned resolution again brought into the open the smouldering conflict between those insisting that the inter-American system should take a more active role in the protection of human rights and the promotion of democracy, and those fearful of opening loopholes in the doctrine of nonintervention. It may be noted that Uruguay, the only country abstaining on this resolution, had in earlier years been the staunchest supporter of multilateral action in this field. Venezuela has become a leading spokesman for concerted action against governments denying fundamental human rights or violating international obligations. Its representatives have followed the line of their statement at the Fifth Meeting of Consultation at Santiago that "there is a danger that too much emphasis may be

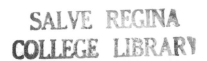

given to the question of nonintervention while overlooking the importance of liberty and self-determination for the development of the hemisphere."[15] It was Venezuela that successfully forced the imposition of sanctions on the Dominican Republic. In a telegram to the Secretary General of the OAS congratulating the foreign ministers on taking this action, President Betancourt of Venezuela also proposed that the Eleventh Inter-American Conference, at that time scheduled to meet in Quito, should draw up a treaty "in which it is defined and made explicit that those governments not elected by the people may not form part of the regional judicial community."[16]

Some of the Central American states likewise have, at times, insisted that the doctrine of nonintervention should not serve as a shield for dictators.

In the United States there has also been a growing sentiment that the rule of nonintervention has become too absolute and inflexible, and does not take into account that the chief danger to the hemisphere today is not military aggression but the subversion of legitimate governments by agents of the international communist movement. Both at the Ninth and at the Tenth Inter-American Conferences the United States made the adoption of a resolution on this topic the main order of business. However, United States policy has not been entirely consistent in the matter of intervention. At the time of the Santiago meeting in 1959, the United States was much concerned about Caribbean tensions resulting from the war of nerves in which Cuba was playing a leading role, and, therefore, wished to discourage revolutionary sallies and interventions. Secretary Herter, in an address before the Ministers, stated, "To weaken the principle of nonintervention and the principle of collective security in an effort to promote democracy is, therefore, a self-defeating activity." He expressed his conviction "that the basis for the soundest and most durable growth of democratic institutions within a country stems from the people themselves. History has shown that attempts to impose democracy upon a country by force from within may easily result in the mere substitution of one form of tyranny for another."[17] A year later at San José some shift of emphasis was observable. At the Sixth Meeting of Consultation, the United States had gone along in condemning the Dominican government, but wanted to postpone the imposition of sanctions until an approach had been made to that government to obtain its consent to the holding of free elections under the supervision of an OAS committee. Had this proposal been accepted it would have been a return to the tutelary policy followed unilaterally by the United States during the early decades of the century but subsequently discarded. At the Seventh Meeting of Consultation, which was directed chiefly against Cuba, Secretary Herter argued that communist control in Cuba demonstrated extra-continental intervention in the hemisphere, and he therefore asked for a "positive decision" and "effective resistance" to the efforts of the Sino-Soviet bloc.[18] Likewise, at the Eighth Meeting of Consultation at Punta del Este, the United States called for the exclusion of Cuba from participation in the inter-American system.

The problem of human rights was on the agenda for the postponed Eleventh Inter-American Conference. In preparation for this conference, and pursuant to instructions from the Fifth Meeting of Consultation, the Inter-American Council of Jurists (or its permanent committee, the Inter-American Juridical Committee, with headquarters at Rio de Janeiro), prepared two studies in this field, one a Draft Convention on Human Rights, including a proposed Inter-American Commission for the Protection of Human Rights and a proposed Inter-American Court of Human Rights, and the second, a *Study on the Juridical Relationship between Respect for Human Rights and the Exercise of Democracy*.[19] The document on *Protection of Human Rights*[20] set forth a code on human rights, treated under the two headings, "civil and political rights" and "economic, social, and cultural rights." As regards the enforcement machinery, the proposed Inter-American Commission for the Protection of Human Rights may receive complaints of violations, "after all domestic remedies have been applied and exhausted," and attempt to bring about a friendly settlement. If a solution is not reached, the Commission shall draw up a report for submission to the states concerned. The proposed Inter-American Court of Human Rights may deal with a case only after the Commission has acknowledged that it has not been possible to reach a settlement.

Argentina, Mexico, and the United States made reservations to this draft convention. The United States called attention to its

55

reservation to Resolution VIII of the Fifth Meeting of Consultation, which reservation was as follows: "The United States, as is well known, has since its birth as a nation strongly defended human rights. The promotion of respect for human rights in the inter-American system is therefore supported by the United States. While the United States, because of the structure of its Federal Government, does not find it possible to enter into multilateral conventions with respect to human rights or with respect to an Inter-American Court of Human Rights, it, of course, raises no objection to other states' entering into conventions on these subjects should they find it possible to do so. Accordingly, while the United States has voted in favor of Resolution VIII, Human Rights, it reserves its position with respect to its participation in the instruments or organisms that may evolve."

In its study of the juridical relationship between respect for human rights and the exercise of democracy, the Inter-American Juridical Committee concluded that at present there is no legal authority to ensure the effective exercise of democracy. The inter-American system authorizes sanctions only in cases in which the peace and security of the hemisphere are involved. The Committee goes on to ask, "What agency . . . could set itself up as the judge of the democratic nature of this or that government? Who could say, with all the intermediate shades there are between one and another regime, where democracy ends and autocracy begins?" The Committee felt that the Inquisition "would be an example of continence beside this tribunal of grace, this tribunal that would fulminate excommunications and anathemas against a state that was not in a state of democratic grace. . . . Democracy," the study observed, "is a way of life."

The Committee argued that the protection of democracy is a matter exclusively of domestic jurisdiction. Although Resolution 93 of the Tenth Inter-American Conference provided that "the domination or control of the political institutions of any American state by the international communist movement, extending to this hemisphere the political system of an extracontinental power," would be cause for action under the Rio Treaty, "domestic corruption of democracy, so long as it does not stem from foreign aggression or result in an act of this sort, escapes completely from the control of the Organization."

The Colombian representative on the Committee submitted a dissenting opinion in which he urged a more active policy in bringing about the ideal expressed in article 5 of the OAS Charter, namely, "The solidarity of the American States and the high aims which are sought through it requires the political organization of those States on the basis of the effective exercise of representative democracy." The necessary measures, he stated, "could be taken gradually," first directing the attention of the nondemocratic state to the condition, then other suggestions or recommendations of a "moral nature," and finally, in extremely serious cases, "action might go as far as temporarily or definitively suspending such state from participation in one or more organs of the association or in the Organization itself." This reservation is significant, because it was Colombia that took the initiative in calling the Eighth Meeting of Consultation, and the action voted by a two-thirds majority called for the exclusion of Cuba from participation in the various organs of the OAS. The Colombian Minister of Foreign Affairs, José Joaquín Caicedo Castilla, who headed the Colombian delegation at Punta del Este, was the member of the Inter-American Juridical Committee who signed the dissenting opinion.

A reservation by the Brazilian representative on the Juridical Committee is also of interest. It recommended that Meetings of Consultation of Ministers of Foreign Affairs be given the authority, through a convention, to make recommendations designed to encourage respect for human rights and the rule of representative democracy. Such recommendations would have only moral force. It is of interest in this connection to hark back to the dissenting opinion of Brazil on the vote to impose sanctions on the Dominican Republic, which may be summarized as follows: The real solution to cases like this one does not lie in coercive action, but must come from moral force, which, while preserving inter-American solidarity, will move toward integration of the country into the democratic way of life. The condemnation voted by the Sixth Meeting of Consultation was not against the internal regime of the Dominican Republic as such, but against specific acts of aggression. The sanctions which have been proposed are injurious to the people of the Dominican Republic, and may not be efficacious in achieving the desired result.[21] These views anticipate the position taken by the Brazilian delegation at the Eighth Meeting in Punta del Este in January, 1962: That collective sanctions against Cuba would be not only illegal but unwise since such action would force Cuba to "become even more integrated with the Socialist world, toward which it would have to gravitate";[22] that Cuba would realize in time that it could not depend upon Russian support, and that the door should be left open so that Cuba could reintegrate itself into the geopolitical system to which it belongs.

Perhaps it would not be straining the imagination too much to fill in the assumptions which lay behind this reasoning, i.e., that Castro was seen essentially as a political adventurer with burning ambitions to become a new conquistador [after all, Cortés and his followers were *barbudos* ("bearded ones"), too, and likewise started their odyssey from Cuba], that had he achieved his hopes of setting up satellite governments elsewhere in Latin America he might well have preferred to maintain his independent position in the world, free of communist or other discipline, and that if ever he perceived Russia as a long way away with no missiles to expend on his behalf, he—or his successor—would seek ways of accommodation with Western concepts and policies. Meanwhile, Cuba could serve as a hostage for use in negotiations with the United States.

THE OCTOBER, 1962, MISSILE CRISIS

This Brazilian policy of neutrality and philosophical detachment did not find much sympathy, however, among the smaller Caribbean countries subject to constant harassment from Castroite agents. Since most of these countries had authoritarian governments, Cuba became the mecca for refugees desirous of learning the latest tricks in the revolutionary arts. Even in Mexico sympathy for Castro chilled rapidly after his communist affiliations became evident. Mexico continued its policy of firm opposition to intervention but Mexican communist leaders were hustled off to jail. Several of the Central American countries proposed an anti-Castro bloc. In South America, Peru early lined up with the United States "in the struggle against communism in the world and in our hemisphere."[23] By the second half of 1962, only Bolivia, Brazil, Chile, and Uruguay, in addition to Mexico, retained diplomatic relations with Havana. In the early days of October, when the Latin American foreign ministers assembled in Washington at the invitation of Secretary of State Dean Rusk, it was evident that most of the ministers were prepared to accept the "guidelines of U.S. policy." In fact, the *New York Times* correspondent reported his impression that the Latin American governments "would not take an exaggeratedly hostile view of any U.S. attempt to seek to annihilate the Castro regime through internal subversion aided from abroad" by turning the communists' own tactics against them in the form of a "democratic war of national liberation."[24]

By this time it was clear that most of Latin American officialdom was sick and tired of Castro and ashamed to have him appear in the world press as the number one Latin American. The leaders of some of the countries, specifically Venezuela, had come to hate and fear Castro much as they had hated and feared Trujillo—and for much the same reasons. The stage was therefore set for the next act of the unfolding drama: President Kennedy's dramatic confrontation of the Soviet missile installations in Cuba, and his call for a Meeting of Consultation, under the Organization of American States, to consider the threat to hemisphere security. On the following day, October 23, 1962, the Council of the OAS, meeting as the Provisional Organ of Consultation, adopted a resolution (1) calling for the immediate dismantling and withdrawal from Cuba of all missiles and other weapons with any offensive capability; (2) recommending that member states take all measures, individually and collectively, including the use of armed force, which they may deem necessary to ensure that the government of Cuba cannot continue to receive military material and supplies from the Sino-Soviet powers, and to prevent the offensive missiles in Cuba from ever becoming an active threat to the peace and security of the continent; and (3) providing for the informing of the Security Council of the United Nations of this resolution, and expressing the hope that the Security Council would dispatch United Nations observers to Cuba at the earliest moment.[25] Detachments from Argentina and the Dominican Republic participated with the United States forces in a Combined Quarantine Force. Various countries offered port facilities to vessels of the armada.

There was fairly general agreement throughout the hemisphere that Russia had gone too far in undertaking a military build-up in Cuba. Even some ultranationalists and extreme anti-Americans fulminated against Russia for converting Cuba into a pawn in the cold war. But the decision to establish a blockade around Cuba revealed a sharp difference of opinion between those who were willing to prevent Cuba from becoming a military base for an extracontinental power, but still opposed internal intervention in an American republic, on the one hand, and those whose chief objective was direct action to destroy any communist regime that might appear in the hemisphere, on the other. The former view is, of course, in accordance with the traditions of the inter-American system, which has always made a distinction between measures to repel external aggression and action involving intervention within an American country. At the Council session on the afternoon of October 23, 1962, there were three abstentions (Brazil, Mexico, and Bolivia) on the second part of article 2 of the resolution relating to Soviet build-up in Cuba. The Brazilian delegate, in explaining the views of his government, stated that actions under article 8 of the Rio Treaty could apply only to prevention of further arms build-up and not to a total blockade nor to invasion.[26]

There was a considerable group both in the United States and in Latin America that would have preferred actual invasion of Cuba, and members of this persuasion expressed concern that President Kennedy's understanding with Khrushchev might have the effect of protecting the Castro regime as a communist sanctuary. Thanks, however, to Castro's intransigence in the matter of inspection, President Kennedy avoided the necessity of completing the mutual agreement made through letters with Khrushchev on October 27, 1962.[27]

It appears likely that the difficult problem of how to deal with dictators, whether of the right or of the left, without violating the principles of nonintervention and self-determination, and without doing more harm than good to the long-run cause of democratic evolution (there are still people who remember that some of the worst dictators evolved out of our attempts to impose good government on Central America and the Caribbean), will remain on the agenda of inter-American conferences for some time to come.

Nor is this the only important issue likely to receive attention. Some of the new forces appearing in Hispanic America, such as Latin American regionalism, nationalistic political and economic aspirations, and the desire on the part of the larger republics for a more independent foreign policy, are bringing new questions to the fore. The implications of these developments will be considered in the next chapter.

NOTES TO CHAPTER II

1. Washington was the only capital in which all of the other republics were normally represented.

2. Despite Latin American sensitivities on the subject of undue United States influence in the inter-American organizations, it is not on record that any country has objected strenuously to the fact that the United States contributes two-thirds or more of the budgets of the various organs.

3. "The Promise of Pan Americanism," in *Pan Americanism: Its Justification and Its Future* (Washington, D.C.: George Washington University Press, 1938), p. 17.

4. *The Inter-American Way of Life* (Washington, D.C.: Pan American Union, 1957).

5. Some trade preferences were also involved in the Republican reciprocity agreements, but these were of short duration and relatively unimportant from a trade standpoint.

6. The Drago Doctrine, announced in 1902, was narrower than the Calvo Doctrine, since Drago's protest lay solely against the use of armed force in the collection of public debts. Drago made it clear that his doctrine was not intended as a defense "for bad faith, disorder, and deliberate and voluntary insolvency." See E. M. Borchard, "Calvo and Drago Doctrines," *Encyclopaedia of the Social Sciences*, III (1930), 155.

7. "The Pan American Union and the Pan American Conferences," *Bulletin of the Pan American Union*, LXXIV (April, 1940), 199.

8. This count does not include the extraordinary meetings of the Council in April and May of 1962 to hear the charge of Bolivia announcing "an imminent aggression by Chile against Bolivian territory by virtue of the diversion of the waters of the Río Lauca," since the conclusions of the Council did not call for application of the OAS collective security machinery. On September 3, Bolivia suspended its participation in the Council, basing its action on the failure of the Council to effect a satisfactory solution of the Lauca River problem. The Government of Bolivia was, however, again represented in the OAS deliberations at the time of the Cuban missile crisis, and continued to attend sessions until June 11, 1963, when it again suspended attendance in the Council (although continuing participation in the other organs of the OAS).

9. A list of "principles and attributes of the democratic system" is included in the Declaration of Santiago, adopted at the Fifth Meeting of Consultation of Ministers of Foreign Affairs, Santiago, Chile, August 12-18, 1959. This question was on the agenda for the Eleventh Inter-American Conference, originally scheduled to meet at Quito, Ecuador, in May, 1961, but subsequently postponed indefinitely.

10. Substantial amounts of Venezuelan petroleum are normally sold to the Dominican Republic but the problem of finding an alternative market falls primarily upon the international oil companies.

11. Tad Szulc, *New York Times,* November 26, 1961, p. E 3.

12. H. Hoetink, "Cuba and the New Experts," University of Puerto Rico, Institute of Caribbean Studies, *Caribbean Studies,* I (July, 1961).

13. To avoid confusion, it is necessary to keep clearly in mind the distinction between the two principal numbered series of high level inter-American conferences and meetings, which are under discussion in this chapter. The Inter-American Conference, which before 1948 was known as the International Conference of American States, is the supreme organ of the inter-American system, and considers the whole range of inter-American problems. The Tenth Conference was held at Caracas in 1954; the Eleventh was scheduled to be held at Quito, but was postponed. In practice, several unnumbered special conferences have been held, in most cases to deal with specific problems, such as the International Conference of American States on Conciliation and Arbitration, held at Washington in 1929, and the Inter-American Conference for the Maintenance of Continental Peace and Security, held at Rio de Janeiro in 1947.

Another numbered series of conferences are the Meetings of Consultation of Ministers of Foreign Affairs, the first being held at Panama City in 1939 to consider the problems arising from the outbreak of war in Europe. The Eighth of this series was held at Punta del Este, Uruguay, in January, 1962. Meetings of Consultation may be called, by a majority vote of the OAS Council, "in order to consider problems of an urgent nature and of common interest," or to serve as the Organ of Consultation under the Rio Treaty; that is, to consider cases of armed attack or threats to the peace. The OAS Council may act provisionally as the Organ of Consultation, and in fact most of the cases involving application of the Inter-American Treaty of Reciprocal Assistance were resolved satisfactorily by the Council without a meeting of Ministers of Foreign Affairs. There have been two cases in which applications of the Rio Treaty came before ministerial Meetings of Consultation, namely, the Sixth (at San José, Costa Rica, in 1960) and the Eighth (at Punta del Este in 1962). In addition to these numbered series of meetings at the level of Ministers of Foreign Affairs, dozens of other inter-American conferences are held annually, many of them falling within the category of "specialized conferences" and others being of a less official character. Some of these may also involve high-level representation, for example, Ministers of Education, but as a rule the delegations are composed chiefly of technicians or specialists. In 1961 provision was made for an annual meeting of the Inter-American Economic and Social Council at the ministerial level.

The only strictly "summit" conference in inter-American history met at Panama City in July, 1956. At the invitation of the President of Panama, nineteen presidents and presidents-elect met to commemorate the 130th Anniversary of the Congress of Panama convoked in 1826 by Simón Bolívar. At the suggestion of President Eisenhower, a committee of presidential representatives was set up in Washington "to prepare concrete recommendations for making the Organization of American States a more effective instrument of cooperative effort."

14. It would be seriously misleading to speak of the conference at Punta del Este as either a victory or a defeat. Perhaps the most valuable result was the sympathy gained for Secretary of State Dean Rusk by his calm, patient, and fair-minded approach to the issues and the influence this will have on Latin American attitudes in the future. Despite the tragic situation of the Cuban people, and our understandable impatience to get rid of Castro in a hurry, the conservatism of some of the Latin American countries in the matter of sanctions and intervention may well have, over the longer run, some useful consequences,

including the strengthening of anti-communist sentiment in the Americas. It may be noted that the six countries that abstained at Punta del Este on the resolution to exclude Cuba from the inter-American system, voted against Cuba's attempt in the United Nations in February, 1962, to bring charges of aggression against the United States.

15. Quoted by C. Neale Ronning, *Journal of Inter-American Studies*, III (April, 1961), 265.

16. *New York Times*, August 24, 1960.

17. Department of State *Bulletin*, XLI, No. 1053 (1959), 303.

18. *Ibid.*, XLIII, No. 1107 (1960), *passim.*

19. OAS, Eleventh Inter-American Conference, Document 16, November 24, 1959.

20. *Ibid.*, Document 8, November 5, 1959.

21. Pan American Union, *Aplicaciones del tratado interamericano de asistencia recíproca: Suplemento 1960-1961* (Washington, D.C., 1962), pp. 17, 18.

22. *New York Times*, January 19, 1962.

23. Address of President Manuel Prado before the United States Congress, reported in the *Congressional Record*, September 21, 1961, p. 19296, and the Department of State *Bulletin*, XLV, No. 1165 (1961), 676.

24. Szulc, October 7, 1962.

25. Council of the OAS, "Resolution on the Adoption of Necessary Measures to Prevent Cuba from Threatening the Peace and Security of the Continent," October 23, 1962; also Department of State *Bulletin*, XLVII, No. 1220 (1962), 722-23.

26. Consejo de la OEA, *Acta de la sesión del Consejo de la O.E.A. actuando provisionalmente como órgano de consulta celebrada en la tarde del 23 de octubre de 1962.* Serie del Consejo (OEA/ser. G/II, C-a-463 provisional) (Washington D.C., October 23, 1962). The Uruguayan representative also abstained pending the receipt of instructions from his government, but subsequently recorded an affirmative vote.

27. In his letter President Kennedy stated that in return for the undertaking of the Soviet Union to remove the weapon systems from Cuba, the United States agreed—upon the establishment of adequate enforcement arrangements through the United Nations—"(a) to remove promptly the quarantine measures now in effect, and (b) to give assurances against an invasion of Cuba. I am confident that other nations of the Western Hemisphere would be prepared to do likewise." (*New York Times*, October 29, 1962.) See chapter IX for further discussion of the Cuban problem.

–III–

Globalism, Regionalism, Nationalism

Hispanic America, like the United States, has not quite made up its mind regarding the relative place of global and regional organizations in international relations.

At San Francisco in 1945 the Latin Americans were more zealous in their defense of the inter-American system than the United States. It was also the Latins who pressed for, and eventually obtained, a commitment from the United States to conclude a regional defense pact, which eventuated in the Rio Treaty of 1947. It was not until after the reorganization and strengthening of the inter-American structure under the new name of the Organization of American States that some of the Latin Americans began to have second thoughts, arising, in part, from disillusionment over United States policy, and also, in part, from their satisfaction with the opportunity to play a role on the broader stage at New York.

LATIN AMERICA AND THE UNITED NATIONS

At the United Nations organization conference at San Francisco the Latin Americans were successful in obtaining several changes in the original proposals that were of vital importance to them. They were particularly concerned about the provisions relating to regional arrangements which made all action subject to Security Council veto and control. After protracted discussion and negotiations at the highest levels, there was approved a new section, which became article 51 of the Charter, recognizing the right of individual or collective self-defense. New provisions in article 52 provided for efforts "to achieve pacific settlement of local disputes through . . . regional arrangements . . . before referring them to the Security Council," and also directed the Security Council to "encourage the development of pacific settlement of local disputes through such regional arrangements or by such regional agencies either on the initiative of the states concerned or by reference from the Security Council."

Under the Charter, enforcement action involving the use of armed force is reserved to the Security Council by article 41. The one exception: individual or collective self-defense. When the Sixth Meeting of Consultation of Ministers of Foreign Affairs met at San José, Costa Rica, in August, 1960, the sanctions voted against the Dominican Republic did not involve the use of armed force.

Another amendment successfully backed by ten of the Latin American countries provided that the General Assembly may discuss any question or any matters within the scope of the Charter. Although they were not successful in attempts to enlarge the Council or to provide for regional representation by rotation, they supported a successful initiative by Canada providing that United Nations members not represented on the Council be entitled to participate in decisions concerning the employment of forces which they might be called upon to implement. The Latin Americans were also successful in obtaining the admission of Argentina as a charter member of the United Nations.

The Latin American countries have occupied a strategic position in the United Nations and have wielded considerable power. In the early days the twenty republics comprised two-fifths of the voting strength of the Assembly. With the admission of new members, the Latin American bloc is now less than one-fifth of the membership but is still a significant, and at times a decisive, group. Despite the nominal dilution of their strength, the Latin Americans have found sympathy among the new members for their points of view on such matters as anticolonialism, universality of membership, and special consideration in economic matters for the less developed countries. Although some of the countries have not been happy about the special position of the five great powers, in practice the Latin Americans have always had two members on the Security Council. Furthermore, the adoption of the "Uniting for Peace" resolution in 1950 converted the Assembly into the key organ of the United Nations.

United Nations membership provides many tangible and intangible advantages to the Latin Americans. It gives status and recognition to the countries, and also a place in the sun to their delegates. Five Latin Americans have served as President of the Assembly, and under the monthly rotation system of the Council a Latin American frequently presides over this body. Given the wide coverage of the Assembly meetings and United Nations activities by press, radio, and TV, they achieve some of the glamour of movie stars. Likewise, they obtain a much wider audience for their views than the OAS can provide. This is particularly important when their views diverge from those of the spokesman for the United States. United Nations membership also confers considerable bargaining power, so much so that the United States is constantly under the necessity of granting financial or other favors to the various countries in order to keep as many as possible lined up with her position. International law is a field that has long attracted some of the best minds in Latin America, and is therefore one in which their talents show up to good advantage.

In the United Nations Latin Americans have seldom voted as a solid bloc on any issue, but the majority have spoken out against colonialism, aggression, intervention, and racial discrimination. In practice, they have not always found it easy to be consistent, since some of their attitudes conflict with others. On issues involving the status of dependent peoples, for example, Latin Americans have tended to be more lenient and sympathetic toward France, Italy, and Portugal than toward the remnants of non-Latin empires. Latin Americans, like North Americans, had some difficulty in finding the proper criteria by which to judge the Spanish post-Civil War government. In the early days of the United Nations only two Latin American countries stuck by the principle of domestic jurisdiction sufficiently to oppose excluding Spain from United Nations membership, and in 1946 eleven Latin American countries voted in favor of breaking diplomatic relations with the Franco government, while six opposed and three abstained. By 1950, however, only three Latin American nations opposed recision of this action while one abstained. One of the three in opposition was Mexico, the government of which has consistently refused to recognize the Franco government, although such action violates the spirit, at least, of one of Mexico's most cherished doctrines, that recognition should not imply any judgment upon the domestic situation and should not be used as a means of indirect intervention.[1]*

Latin American delegates are very active in debate and in corridor politicking and bring collective pressure to bear to assure the success of their candidates for elective office and for appointments to the staff. They are not bashful about expressing their views on the entire gamut of issues coming before the United Nations. The Latin Americans have, however, shown considerable reserve about participating in enforcement of decisions taken by either the Assembly or the Council. In the case of Korea, for example, the Latin Americans were nearly unanimous in approving the "Uniting for Peace" resolution, but the only Latin American country that placed forces at the United Nations' disposal was Colombia. At the Sixth Session, when the Collective Measures Committee presented the case for further action, the Latin American "preoccupation with regional and domestic matters were sharply highlighted."[2]

Brazil and Colombia participated in 1956 with contingents in the United Nations Emergency Force in the Middle East (UNEF). In order to meet the costs of this operation, the Secretary General recommended that a Special Account outside of the regular budget be set up for UNEF and that its costs be shared by member states on the basis of the scale of assessments adopted for the 1957 budget, and that an initial assessment of $10 million be made to meet the immediate cash needs. The Latin American countries, in a joint statement, disputed the Secretary General's position. They pointed to the primary responsibility of the Big Five for keeping the peace and proposed that only 10 per cent of the costs be assessed according to the regular scale. The question of financing arose in an even more acute form in connection with the United Nations' Force in the Congo (ONUC). The Latin American countries again suggested that the expenses be paid largely by the permanent members of the Security Council. In practice, this has meant that the United States has picked up the tab for a large proportion of the cost of both operations.[3] According to the financial records published by the United Nations as of November 30, 1961, all of the Latin American countries were in arrears on ONUC, all but Brazil and Ecuador in arrears on UNEF, and all but five countries in arrears on the annual budget assessment. Under article 19 of the Charter, countries two years in arrears lose their voting privileges.

Pursuant to a request from the United Nations for a ruling, the International Court of Justice decided on July 20, 1962, by a vote of nine to five, that the expenditures made in connection with UNEF and ONUC constitute "expenses of the organization" within the meaning of article 17 (paragraph 2) of the United Nations Charter. The Assembly on December 19 endorsed this opinion, but some of the larger countries, like France and Russia, have made it clear that they do not accept the opinion as binding, and some of the Latin American countries have proposed a new assessment plan that would throw most of the costs of the United Nations on the great powers.

Some of the Latin American countries are also in arrears on the "local cost" operations of the United Nations technical assistance projects, which were originally requested by the defaulting governments.

Some observers have been inclined to blame the Latin Americans for shortsightedness and selfishness in failing to give more substantial backing to the United Nations actions, just as they have been criticized for reluctance to take action against Castro through the Organization of American States. The fact is that Latin Americans not only have a built-in resistance to outside intervention in their own affairs, but their experience has taught them to be skeptical of the prospects of collective intervention as an instrument for achieving democracy and stability. Under the Rio Treaty no state is required to use armed force without its consent. Since the United Nations Charter reserves to the Security Council the decision as to the use of armed force, the Latin American countries have been inclined to feel that the application of such measures is primarily the responsibility of the great powers. In the case of Korea, for example, the feeling was widespread in Latin America that the trouble grew out of the mistakes of United States policy and that hence Latin American forces should not be used as a cat's-paw to retrieve our lost chestnuts.

At the same time, it should be noted that, on the whole, the Latin Americans have given the United States considerable moral support on most critical cases arising in the United Nations. The two Latin American members of the Security Council in June, 1950, when the Korean crisis developed, supported the resolution recommending that the United Nations members furnish assistance to South Korea. Likewise, Cuba did not find much support in its various attempts in 1960 and 1961 to obtain an airing of charges of intervention and aggression against the United States.

It is impossible at the present time to foresee with clarity what shape the political and economic structure of the world will take over the next few decades. Will the United Nations survive in its present form? If not, will a new world organization take its place? What shape will the various postwar regional organizations then take? What will be the effect of the European Economic Community on the other countries of Europe? And outside Europe? Will the United Kingdom join the Common Market, and if so, what will be the effect on the Commonwealth? What is the destiny of the new nations of Africa? and Asia? Will international economic relations expand or contract?

In this welter of uncertainties, the inter-American system may well prove to be one of the stabler elements, but it also has come in for attack both from the North and from the South. Not a few observers in the United States have long felt that Pan Americanism was merely an excuse for hemispheric isolationism, and that the sooner it is ended the better. This general line of thought has received support from the finding of Professor Arthur P. Whitaker that the "Western Hemisphere Idea"—that is, the "proposition that the peoples of this Hemisphere stand in a special relationship to one another which sets them apart from the rest of the world"—has entered a period of "euthanasia."[4]

LATIN AMERICA AND THE INTER-AMERICAN SYSTEM

Latin American doubts regarding the present inter-American structure appear to be based on a number of important changes since the war, which, it is feared, invalidate the previous bases of the system. Perhaps the most important of these is the changed position of the United States, which is now a world power, and from its metropolitan position feels a bit out of place in a neighborhood with its country cousins. At the same time some of the countries have attained sufficient population, wealth, and influence to feel that they have come of age and no longer need our guardianship. With the shifting of the main center of interest of American policy, Latin Americans feel that the United States is no longer in a position to represent their interests. In 1947 the Venezuelan critic and writer, Mariano Picón-Salas, expressed the view that unless the Latin American countries were united, they would remain acolytes of the United States. Furthermore, he stated, "the policy of the United States is no longer Pan-American, but rather ecumenical, and the ideological struggle which Yankee capitalism is now undertaking against Russia may possibly compromise us in the future."[5] A fuller and soberer statement of this position was given by a Mexican Foreign Office official in 1956. He felt that the Rio Treaty was being transformed "from a regional instrument of defense into an instrument of world policy." Since Pan Americanism has become one of the many facets of U.S. policy, "there is danger that the Latin American countries will be caught up in political and military risks unnecessarily."[6]

As the United States expanded its far-flung commitments, Latin Americans became increasingly nervous about the risks of involvement in view of their relationship with the United States in the inter-American system. "The Latin American republics . . . are more afraid of the commitments the United States has assumed all around the world than of Soviet interference in the affairs of their own continent," a leading Brazilian publisher has written. "They do not feel bound to support NATO, the Baghdad Pact, or SEATO, since they were not consulted when such power blocks were set up."[7]

Although the enthusiasm of many Latin Americans for the inter-American system has waned, none of the twenty republics, not even Cuba, has withdrawn (See chapter II, note 8). Castro criticized the OAS on various occasions, and in a speech beginning late on the night of March 29 and continuing into the early hours of March 30, 1960, he declared that his government did not feel obligated to the Rio Treaty because the revolutionary government did not sign it. Despite this midnight oratory, Castro did not take any formal steps to denounce the agreement, and furthermore Cuba was represented at the Sixth Meeting of Consultation, which was convened under article 6 of the Rio Treaty. Cuba was also represented at the Seventh and Eighth Meetings, and, far from withdrawing voluntarily, strenuously resisted efforts to exclude Cuba from inter-American organs. Cuba also applied for admission to the Latin American Free Trade Association but was rejected. However, Cuba did not join the Inter-American Development Bank and did not sign the Charter of Punta del Este.

In some quarters the idea of Hispanic American solidarity has been offered as a substitute for Pan Americanism, and this has found a nucleus in the creation of the Latin American Free Trade Association.[8] Of course, the idea of continental solidarity and unity goes back as far as Bolívar, as we have seen, but union has never achieved widespread backing. In its present-day form, Latin American regionalism is the resultant of several forces, not least of which has been the precedent established by United States financial and moral support of European unity. The formation of Latin American groups or blocs in the various international organizations likewise has had an important influence by revealing the strength that unity confers and by accustoming officials to the idea of regional cooperation. Following the establishment by the United Nations of the Economic Commission for Europe and the Economic Commission for the Far East, the Latin Americans insisted on the creation of the Economic Commission for Latin America (ECLA), with headquarters in a South American capital. It is perhaps significant, however, that when the Inter-American Development Bank was organized, it was the Latin Americans rather than the American representatives who wanted it located in Washington. The plans for the new Latin American Institute of Economic Development Planning, which is being financed for five years by the Inter-American Development Bank and the United Nations Special Fund, provide that thereafter it will be converted into a permanent organization maintained and directed by the Latin American governments.

It is likely that the concept of a Latin American region will continue to have considerable influence, especially in the psychological and cultural spheres, through the strengthening of the common elements in the Spanish heritage, such as language, customs, and ideology. The fact that the Commonwealth of Puerto Rico is associated with the United States is galling to many Hispanic superpatriots; contrary to the opinion apparently widely held on the mainland, the basic trouble does not come from the communists but from the conservatives.

Mexico has been making a strong bid for leadership, both culturally and as the exemplar of a maturing nationalist revolution, and these considerations appear to have played an important part in Mexico's decision to join the Latin American Free Trade Association. Mexico is now the largest Spanish-speaking country in the world.[9] Mexico City has become an important publishing center in the Spanish language, and substantial quantities of books are exported. Former President Miguel Alemán took the initiative in promoting the first Congress of the Academies of the Spanish Language, which undertakes to work against the fragmentation of the language and to standardize vocabulary and grammar. The Third Congress, held at Bogotá in 1960, established the Cervantes prize to honor outstanding works in the Spanish language. Mexico City is the headquarters of the Inter-American Cultural Council created by the 1948 Charter of the OAS, despite the expense and inconvenience of having the operations at such distance from the Secretariat of the Council. The scenic beauty of Mexico, the many tourist attractions, the barbaric splendor of Mexico's history as recorded on its blood-stained monuments, and the wide range of opportunities offered to the present-day *bon viveur,* have conspired to put Mexico on the tourist circuit in a big way.

But even upon the most optimistic assumptions regarding current integration plans, it is evident that the Latin American countries cannot go it alone either politically or economically, and this has been made even clearer by the formation of the European Economic Community. However much the Latin Americans may criticize the United States for the inadequacy of its financial aid, they know that they couldn't do one-tenth as well elsewhere, and furthermore they have discovered the secret of extracting additional aid from us by threatening to go neutral or to put our investments over a barrel.

It is also possible that the regional concept will be strengthened through the admission of new members to the OAS. A handsomely carved chair with the seal of Canada awaits an occupant at the

Council table in the marble palace near the banks of the Potomac. Canada is already a member of the Inter-American Statistical Institute and of the U.N. Economic Commission for Latin America. When Cheddi Jagan was in Washington in October, 1961, he told reporters that British Guiana would join the inter-American system when Guiana became independent. This precedent might well set in motion the application for membership by various former dependencies, such as Jamaica, Trinidad, and Surinam. The admission of these states, especially Canada, would bring Latin America closer to such North Atlantic organizations as the Organization for Economic Cooperation and Development and reduce its dependence upon the United States as an intermediary. Developments along these lines might also prepare the way for the merging of ECLA with the OAS.

The staff and budget of the Pan American Union at Washington and of its various organs and specialized agencies have been increased enormously since the war. Some observers feel that this mushroom growth has been at the cost of the organization's prestige and effectiveness. A veteran international civil servant has called attention to the fact that the inter-American system made its greatest contributions during a period when its budgets were small. "Obviously," he says, "progress and achievement cannot be measured in dollars and cents."[10] The present OAS structure does in many respects reflect the war-born tendency to emphasize organization and machinery in international affairs, ending in top-heavy mechanisms that create personal and national rivalries but tend to crush any real spirit of cooperation or internationalism. Unfortunately it has been felt necessary to compete with the United Nations in visibility and in bureaucratic empire building. The budgetary quota of the various Latin American countries for the various organizations, to say nothing of the costs of representation (that is, salaries and expenses of national representatives accredited to these organizations), have tended to become real burdens on many treasuries.

Despite the tendency to overexpansion, part of which reflects national or individual log-rolling, the OAS performs many valuable functions and includes many able and devoted officials among its ranks. Its various specialists perform cheerfully and competently the staff functions involved in the endless round of conferences. It serves the public with information on travel, educational exchanges, literature, art, and trade. The monthly magazine, *Américas,* published in English, Spanish, and Portuguese, with handsome illustrations, deserves a wide circulation.

NATIONALISM AND INTERNATIONAL ORGANIZATION

Apparently our policy makers have not quite caught up with some of the more significant trends of the postwar world, such as the tendency of international organizations and rapid economic development to stimulate national consciousness and sharpen resentment against inferior status. Most of the elaborate international machinery developed since the war, however desirable otherwise, has had the practical effect of heightening nationalism. To cite one illustration, some observers feel that the creation of UNESCO has exacerbated rather than diluted nationalistic feelings. For decades scientific and professional associations had held international meetings where they exchanged ideas and formed personal friendships. The superimposition of UNESCO has added governmental, political, and nationalistic elements to the situation. "Is culture a fit object of international relations such as diplomatic matters or commercial treaties might be?" a leading Mexican historian has asked. When culture is made a governmental and intergovernmental activity, doesn't its spontaneity suffer? "Is is possible to adapt it to foreign information organs without running the risk of its being influenced by the aims of propaganda?"[11] The official character of postwar internationalism also has stimulated linguistic nationalism. Spanish Americans have been very zealous in insisting on Spanish as one of the working languages of international conferences. In fact, the Spanish Americans have made more of a point of this than Spain. The Brazilians have been somewhat less chauvinistic in linguistic matters, but at times they insist on having all documents put into Portuguese. Haitian representatives are required by law to speak French at international conferences.

The organization of the United Nations and its methods of operation, especially since the adoption of the "Uniting for Peace" resolution in 1950, has given the smaller countries a political weight out of proportion to their economic and military power. This circumstance naturally bolsters the nationalistic ego of the countries, since the vote of a country with a population of less than a million counts as much as that of the United States or the Soviet Union. It is this circumstance, combined with the rapid economic and population growth of some of the countries, that has led to insistent demands for a greater voice in decisions relating to world affairs and for an "independent" policy, involving, if necessary, neutrality in matters which they feel they cannot control. In two public addresses published in the Havana daily, *Revolución,* on September 8 and 10, 1959, Cuban Under Secretary of State Marcelo Fernández stated that after fifty years of frustration, Cuba had inaugurated a new foreign policy of its own. Whatever the element of exaggeration in this pronouncement, the feeling elsewhere in the southern republics that in foreign affairs they have been tied to the chariots of the great powers has been a major factor in provoking sympathy for Castro.

In the introduction to an important volume published for the Council on Foreign Relations, the late Lyman Bryson pointed out that "there is one kind of hostility toward another power which is the natural outcome of continued dependence," and that in some of the larger republics, at least, the "resentment of the debtor" has been "replaced by the more vigorous and self-respecting hostility of the rival."[12] A distinguished historian has pointed out that the major conflicts of history have been between advanced nations, and then proceeded to the pertinent question, "Can there be any clear assurance of gain for peace in the multiplication of well-to-do, industrialized states, modelled primarily after those which have been the principal war-makers of modern times?"[13]

NATIONAL RIVALRIES IN THE AMERICAS

Nationalism is not, of course, an entirely new phenomenon in Latin America. The histories of the individual countries reveal strongly aggressive and imperialistic tendencies at times. The unsettled state of the national boundaries at independence has been a fruitful cause of conflict from the early days down to the present time, despite the frequent resort to arbitration rather than to arms for settlement of their differences. During the nineteenth century the

Latin American countries were partners to eighty-four arbitrations, many of which involved boundary disputes.[14]

In the Río de la Plata region, Argentina and Brazil inherited the Spanish-Portuguese rivalry of colonial days. Of the five or six real wars among South American states during the nineteenth century (some authorities do not classify the clashes of 1828-29 between Colombia and Peru as a real war), three grew out of the struggle to dominate the left bank (Banda Oriental) of the Río de la Plata and to obtain control over the shipping on the Plata River system and its tributaries. The first of these wars, from 1825 to 1828, was settled by the mediation of the British Government and resulted in the creation of the Eastern Republic of Uruguay in 1830 as a buffer state. The precarious equilibrium established by this settlement was disturbed in the 1830's when the Argentine dictator, Juan Manuel Rosas, intervened in the bitter struggle between Uruguay's political parties. Argentine army and naval forces participated in the nine-year siege of the port of Montevideo. The unsatisfied territorial ambitions of Argentina and Brazil were also important elements in the chain of circumstances that brought about the war between the Triple Alliance (Argentina, Brazil, and Uruguay) and Paraguay, 1865-70, one of the bloodiest in South American annals.

Brazil, the largest of the South American countries, has been extraordinarily successful in expanding its domains both by the sword and by diplomacy. Since 1850 Brazil has expanded at the expense of all of the seven contiguous states except Peru. At the other end of the power scale, Bolivia has lost territory to all of its neighbors. The long-drawn-out Chaco War between Bolivia and Paraguay in the 1930's had psychological roots in the memory of Bolivians, who recalled their "continual despoilment by their neighbors. The West bank of the River Paraguay and the Acre Territory had gone to Brazil, the south had been taken by Argentina as long ago as 1840, and the west by Chile."[15] The Chaco War resulted in the loss of additional territory by Bolivia.

Both Argentina and Brazil have forced Bolivia to grant them important oil concessions in the regions adjacent to the territories of the two big powers. According to authoritative accounts, Bolivia's sudden action in 1937 in annulling the petroleum concession of the

Standard Oil Company and in confiscating its properties resulted from Argentine pressure in demanding control of Bolivian oil resources in return for support at the Chaco Peace Conference.[16] Chile also has used its investments in Bolivia and its control of Bolivia's outlets to the Pacific to influence Bolivian policy.

Argentina has on various occasions shown a yearning to restore the boundaries of the Viceroyalty of Buenos Aires (or La Plata), which included present-day Bolivia, Paraguay, and Uruguay as well as the territory of modern Argentina. As the largest of the Spanish American republics in area and long the commercial leader of the South American continent, Argentina has tended to regard itself as the natural political leader as well. As early as the 1860's Carlos Calvo wrote: "The Argentine Republic is called upon to be, within the next half century, if we have peace, as great a power as are the United States in the North."[17] Again, in the 1880's, the Argentine press began to advocate the reconstruction of the old viceroyalty, apparently as a counterpoise to growing Chilean power.[18] From 1909 on, various Argentine publicists promoted the idea of a Southern Union, or Southern Customs Union, to embrace the former viceregal territory plus Chile. The neighboring states were under heavy pressure during the Perón regime.

On the West Coast of South America, rivalry between Chile and Peru has paralleled in some respects the traditional Argentina-Brazil duel. The first serious clash came in 1835 when the Bolivian dictator, Andrés Santa Cruz, established a Peru-Bolivia Confederation with himself as Supreme Protector. Both Argentina and Chile were alarmed at this disturbance to the balance of power and declared war. Santa Cruz was defeated, and in 1838 the Confederation was dissolved. During the 1840's and 1850's the need for common action against outside threats, both from Europe and from the United States (in 1854 the United States signed a convention with Ecuador regarding the Galápagos Islands), brought the West Coast countries closer together, and in the 1860's they joined in war to resist Spanish aggression on the West Coast. With the re-establishment of peace, however, the Chilean-Peruvian rivalry took on a more acute form, as Chilean economic interests became active in the guano and nitrate fields of the previously neglected desert coastal regions of Bolivia and

Peru. From this conflict the Pacific War (1879-83) resulted. Chile triumphed, owing to stronger naval power, superior governmental organization, and able diplomacy. As the consequence of the war, Chile enlarged its territory at the expense of both Bolivia and Peru, and emerged as one of the two leading countries of South America (following Brazil) both as regards the value of its foreign trade and in international prestige.

As the leading viceregal capital in South America during the colonial era, Lima has had difficulty at times in accepting its limited territorial jurisdiction. Unsuccessful in the south (although it retrieved the province of Tacna in 1929 through direct negotiations aided by the good offices of President Herbert Hoover), Peru took a firm if not aggressive stand in handling border disputes with Ecuador and Colombia. A dispute in 1932 over the Leticia Trapezium, which gave Colombia access to the Amazon River at a point below the Peruvian port of Iquitos, was settled under the auspices of the League of Nations. The difficult nature of the terrain between the Andes and the upper Amazon River, and the lack of fixed boundaries and settlements during the colonial era (during most of which the Presidency of Quito was administratively under the Viceroyalty of Peru) long delayed the establishment of Peruvian-Ecuadorian boundaries, but through superior economic and military strength Peru succeeded in establishing its claims to most of the eastern territory. When military clashes occurred in 1941, the dispute was taken to the Third Meeting of Ministers of Foreign Affairs, in session at Rio de Janeiro. A protocol fixing the boundary line was signed at Rio on January 29, 1942, with the United States, Argentina, Brazil, and Chile as guarantors. In the process of marking the line, however, a previously unknown river, the Cenepa, was discovered, and Ecuador claimed that this discovery invalidated the survey. In his inaugural address on September 1, 1960, President José María Velasco of Ecuador declared that "Ecuador will never accept as legal and just that it be cornered between the Pacific and the Andes after having been the discoverer of the Amazon and having colonized and administered vast regions of eastern Amazonia." On December 7, 1960, the United States joined the other guaranteeing powers in a statement upholding the validity of the 1942 protocol.

It is noteworthy that Argentina and Chile have succeeded in avoiding serious clashes despite boundary disputes and power rivalries. The Andean boundary in the Puna de Atacama region was settled in 1898 by the arbitration of the United States Minister to Buenos Aires, while the dividing line in southwestern Patagonia and Tierra del Fuego was based on the award of King Edward VII in 1902. These peaceful settlements were commemorated by the erection of the giant statue of Christ the Redeemer amid the perpetual snows at the point where the main pass crosses the frontier. Meanwhile, in the Pactos de Mayo of 1902, Argentina and Chile had agreed upon the limitation of naval armaments and the division of spheres of influence.

In the Caribbean region, the ideological conflicts and personal ambitions that have kept it in a turmoil since World War II conform to a long-established pattern. There are numerous precedents both in South America and in Central America for intervention on ideological grounds. On various occasions the chief executives in Colombia and Peru gave their moral and/or material support to a liberal or conservative aspirant to power in Ecuador, depending upon the views of the presidents in office at Bogotá or Lima at the time. In Central America, following the breakdown of the Federal Union in 1838, the governments of the separate states faced the "constant threat of intervention by neighboring state governments which were in the hands of the opposite party" (i.e., liberal or conservative).[19] In fact, intervention has become "a way of life" in Central America.[20] Since 1948 all of the Central American countries have been involved in some way in disputes relating to disturbance of the peace, and all of the actions under the Rio Treaty or by the Inter-American Peace Committee have involved situations arising either among Central American countries or from the Antillean republics.

Conflicts between Haiti and the Dominican Republic also have a long history, and in this case the racial factor has usually been more important than the ideological. In 1822 President Jean Pierre Boyer of the black Republic of Haiti conquered the eastern part of the island, which was administered as a part of Haiti until 1844. In recent decades the Dominican Republic has been much stronger than Haiti, and most of the complaints of plots and aggression have come from Haiti. The vexatious boundary dispute between the two countries was not finally settled until 1935, and even this settlement did not terminate border clashes. Apparently with the intention of discouraging the infiltration of Haitians in search of work, a massacre of several thousand Haitian workers in the Dominican Republic was carried out in October, 1937. As the result of mediation under the Gondra Treaty (Treaty to Avoid or Prevent Conflicts) of 1923 and the General Convention of Inter-American Conciliation of 1929, the controversy resulting from the bloodletting was resolved. By the terms of settlement, the Dominican Republic agreed to pay the sum of $750,000 to be used by the Government of Haiti in benefit of the interests of Haitian nationals who suffered damages. This settlement is of particular interest since it is the only one that has been accomplished within the framework of the inter-American treaty structure for the pacific settlement of international disputes.

A study of the histories of the area suggests that the Middle and South American countries have been influenced in resort to arms or intrigue against their neighbors by the same motivations as have actuated other nations: popular patriotic fervor, personal ambition of rulers, maintenance of the balance of power, and crusading zeal for particular ideologies. In some of the capitals, memories of the spacious authority of colonial days have stimulated hopes for the revival of larger national or federal units. The political and social structures of the countries have been contributing factors, but it is not possible to make a clear correlation between the prevalence of the military in the government and the frequency of aggressive or imperialistic ventures. In the early period of independence, there was considerable confusion and uncertainty before the national states as we now know them became established, and during this period a number of ambitious *caudillos* arose. Bolívar himself was not without vaulting personal ambition, as well as vision and patriotism, but his Gran Colombia broke up into separate units (Colombia, Venezuela, Ecuador) during his lifetime. As regards the history of the republics during the last century, it could be argued that countries like Argentina and Chile, which are among the most democratic in South America, have shown a more aggressive foreign policy than some (like Venezuela) that have been mostly military dictatorships.

Only a few of the southern republics have put sufficient premium on peace and general welfare to forego the expense of military establishments or nationalistic gestures. Psychologically, it has been difficult for most of the Latin American nations to envisage the status of what might be called the intermediate nation. "Everyone now knows that a country has either the economy of a colony or that of a world power," an Argentine army officer remarked during the war.[21]

Beckoning Destiny

The course of international events during recent decades, combined with the greater weight of the Latin American countries in international affairs, has conspired to accentuate the nationalistic ambitions of the Hispanic countries. Among the changes that have influenced opinion are the decline in the relative international position of Western Europe, the swarming of the new nations of Asia and Africa, the Soviet challenge to what the Latin Americans like to call "nineteenth century orthodoxy," and the weakening of Latin American confidence in United States leadership both in their own area and in the rest of the world. However egotistic and unrealistic it may appear to many, not a few Latin Americans are convinced that their hour has struck and that they are called upon to play an important role on the world stage. A Frenchman with extensive experience in Latin America has written: "A great many brilliant minds in Latin America are convinced that a great destiny awaits their continent," he says, since they feel that Latin America can combine "the most modern and bold accomplishments" of the New World with "the art of living and the delightful traditions of its true elite" and thus make the contribution to civilization for which the century is searching.[22] The word "destiny" is a very popular one in the Hispanic countries and is now frequently used in much the same sense as was attached to Manifest Destiny in the United States around the middle of the last century.

Growing nationalism is reflected in the zeal of the Latin American states to press Antarctic claims, extend the breadth of their territorial seas, and take over any real estate still held by European countries in the Western Hemisphere (as well as enclaves under the jurisdiction of the United States). Brazil, a satisfied nation territorially, has been more conciliatory on these questions than the Spanish Americans, but a correspondent for the *New York Times* reports that Janio Quadros, during his brief tenure as President of Brazil, ordered his army to prepare for a possible incursion into British Guiana, and that he planned to use as his excuse that the Cheddi Jagan regime might prove to be a communist danger to Brazil.[23]

The territorial claims were stimulated by wartime developments. Chile's claim to a sector of Antarctic territory dates from 1940. Argentina's claim is older but was not pressed until the time of President Juan Domingo Perón. The Chilean and Argentine claims overlap, and both conflict with the British sector. Although Chile and Argentina attempt to maintain a common front in favor of an American Antarctic, the rivalry between the two South American countries has, at times, been very sharp. A visit by President Arturo Frondizi of Argentina to Deception Island early in 1961 resulted in rioting in Chile, and a note of protest from London. The United States has not made any claims in the Antarctic but does not recognize the claims of other states. The Antarctic Treaty signed at Washington on December 1, 1959, in effect holds in status quo all territorial claims during the life of the treaty, thirty years. Representatives of both Chile and Argentina signed the agreement, which became effective on June 23, 1961.

The Latin American countries, like the United States, have traditionally shown sympathy for colonial peoples, but in practice, as has been seen, they have been more tolerant of colonialism by Latin nations than by others. The anticolonial zeal of the last two decades, and particularly the pressure against the continuance of dependent territories in the Americas, take their point of departure from decisions of the first two meetings of Ministers of Foreign Affairs, at Panama in 1939 and at Havana in 1940, designed to prevent the Nazis from obtaining a foothold on the American continents or on the islands adjacent to the continents. The resolution adopted at Panama in October, 1939, merely provided for calling a consultative meeting "in case any geographic region of America subject to the jurisdiction of any non-American state should be obliged to change its sovereignty," but the Havana meeting, held shortly after

Norway, the Netherlands, Belgium, and France had been overrun by the German armies, went a step further and set up machinery for the provisional administration of European colonies and possessions in the Americas which might be "in danger of becoming the subject of barter of territory or change of sovereignty." These actions have been described as constituting the "panamericanization" of the historic No-Transfer policy of the United States.[24] In practice, there was never occasion to give specific application to the Act of Havana.

The Monroe Doctrine had opposed new European conquests in America but had stated that the United States " shall not interfere" with the then existing colonies or dependencies of any European power. The even older No-Transfer principle provided that the United States cannot see with indifference the transfer of European colonies in the Western Hemisphere to another non-American power.[25]

The agitation for termination of the colonial system in the Americas has been kept alive since the war chiefly by those countries which feel they have a chance to gain territory if European sovereignty is ended. Argentina, which has claims against the Falkland Islands (known as Las Malvinas in Spanish), and Guatemala, which disputes British control of Belize (British Honduras), have been particularly active. Under the doctrine of *uti possidetis* of 1810, Mexico also claims to have inherited the rights to northern Belize. Since the Anglo-Mexican treaty of 1893, Mexico has not made claims to the territory as against Britain, but has made it plain that in the event of a change in status of the territory of British Honduras, her interest in the northern half would revive.[26] In recent years the chief nationalist group in Belize has indicated its desire for independence, or self-government within the Commonwealth, rather than absorption by Guatemala. However, President Miguel Ydígoras Fuentes of Guatemala is reported to have told the Ambassador of the United States that "as soon as the first atom bomb drops anywhere, my troops will invade Belize."[27]

The complicated technical problems involved in the law of the sea affecting the breadth of the territorial sea and in the question of the continental shelf need not be discussed here, other than to note the boldness of the claims of some of the Latin American countries.

The West Coast countries of South America and some of the Central American states have, in effect, claimed exclusive fishing rights in the high seas in a zone of two hundred miles from their coasts.[28]

Can any valid conclusions be drawn from this brief historical sketch as regards the future trends of Latin American nationalism or internationalism? The Latin American countries have by no means been insensitive to the idealistic aspects of international cooperation and world organization, but, as with all peoples, their vision is colored by their own particular history, culture, and interests. The Hispanic countries are still striving to find themselves and their place in the world, but some of their aspirations can find satisfaction in a framework larger than the nation. It is likely that the southern republics will follow a more "independent" line and exact a higher *quid pro quo* for collaboration in the future than in the past. But there is little reason to doubt that they would respond to inter-American common interests if we consistently occupy the high ground of principle and avoid deceptive appeals designed to conceal expediency.

UNIVERSAL HUMANISM AND CONTINENTAL NATIONALISM

Latin American nationalism is not lacking in imperialistic longings, and in every country some frankly chauvinistic spokesmen are to be found. But some exponents of nationalism among the intelligentsia have attempted to find a broader justification either in universal humanism or in continental nationalism—continental being the traditional term for the Bolivarian concept of Spanish American unity or federation. A strong sense of nationality is necessary, they feel, not only as defense against external penetration and as a cohesive force required to maintain unity against the centrifugal internal pressures, but also as an indispensable element in the effort to mobilize the national will in the drive for modernization.[29]

But there is some reaction against the telluric or "blood-and-soil" school of thought, and also a desire to get away from the purely negative aspects of nationalism, which arose out of the struggle of the Latin American countries to free themselves from foreign cultural and economic predominance. But once a country has estab-

84

lished its national character, its nationals can lift their heads above the struggle and act as free citizens of the world. "For the first time in our history, we are contemporaries of all men," Octavio Paz, Mexican poet, scholar and diplomat, has written.[30]

Both nationalistic sentiment and the persistent feeling in Latin America that Europe and the United States have let them down have resulted in a strong urge for a more independent foreign policy. There was a brief period at the beginning of the '60's when several of the larger Latin American countries appeared to be moving in the direction of neutralism. Cuba was an official participant in the Belgrade Conference of nonaligned countries, which closed on September 6, 1961; and Bolivia, Brazil, and Ecuador were represented by observers. In his inaugural address of January 31, 1961, President Janio Quadros of Brazil denounced the "new imperialism" of communism but at the same time stated that Brazil would follow "a sovereign policy sovereign in the real and full sense," and would open its arms to all countries, "without any political or philosophical prejudices." A little later Quadros announced that he had invited President Tito of Yugoslavia to visit Brazil, an action that was interpreted by some as indicating his sympathy for some of Tito's views, such as the rights of small nations and the doctrine that there is a cultural and economic middle ground between orthodox communism and capitalism of the American type.[31]

This neutralist phase, strictly speaking, may be said to have passed with the dramatic departure of Quadros from his high office. Although his successor, João Goulart, followed the same general lines of foreign policy as Quadros and Juscelino Kubitschek, his ambassador in Washington explained that the Brazilian position is one of independence rather than neutralism. "We are not systematically 'non-aligned,' as the neutralists pretend to be, nor systematically aligned, as the satellite countries are. While faithful to the inter-American system, we may in specific circumstances follow independent policies, if that serves the cause of peace or the cause of economic development."[32]

Mexico has, of course, followed an independent foreign policy (independent, that is, of the United States) much longer than Brazil, but President Adolfo López Mateos has made it clear that

Mexico is independent but not neutralist. In his message to Congress on September 1, 1961, President López stated that neutrality is incompatible with the principles of collective security contained in the charters of the United Nations and the OAS, and in the Rio Treaty of reciprocal assistance. Although Mexico has shown its independence by having diplomatic relations with the Soviet Union and in eschewing relations with Franco Spain, recent administrations have avoided flamboyant gestures or aggressive tactics. As Mexico has consolidated its political stability and economic prosperity, and as its *revolucionarios* have become *millonarios,* an attitude of greater confidence has replaced the former touchiness and defensiveness. Openly expressed anti-Americanism has come to be considered as bad taste and as reflecting the outworn slogans of another era.

Both Mexico and Brazil have shown a desire to step out on the world stage and play a more important role than in the past. President López took occasion to visit Canada in 1959 at the time of his official visit to Washington, and he was the first President of Mexico to visit India and other leading countries of the Far East. These trips were designed not only to emphasize Mexico's independent position, but to promote trade, especially in manufactured products.

The search of educated and cosmopolitan Latin Americans for a broader loyalty has provided an opportunity for the revival of continentalism, a concept that not only offers spiritual consolation to those seeking *la patria grande,* but also coincides with postwar trends towards regionalism. As indicated earlier, Mexicans have been sensitive to this type of appeal, and President López was also the first President of Mexico to visit South America while in office.[33] President López's visit to Brazil was followed by a commercial mission, which agreed upon the establishment of a direct shipping line between the two countries. There was also some discussion of joint industrial arrangements, and for a time Brazil looked hopefully to Mexico as a possible market for automotive parts, as well as other manufactured items.

At the time of President Goulart's return visit to Mexico early in 1962 there were reports of a political understanding between the two governments that some commentators called a Brazil-Mexico axis. President Goulart also had been to the Far East and had included

Peking in his itinerary. But the distinctive feature of Brazil's new stance in foreign affairs has been the repudiation of European colonialism in Africa and the launching of claims of a special position for Brazil in Africa. One of the early acts of President Quadros was to set up a Brazilian Institute of Afro-Asian Studies and to send an Ambassador to Ghana. In an article published in *Foreign Affairs* (New York) for October, 1961, Quadros stated that Africa "represents a new dimension" in Brazilian policy, and that Brazil is suited by its geographic situation, its history, and its ethnic and cultural roots to serve as the link or bridge between Africa and the West. Although little understood in the United States, this new orientation in Brazilian foreign policy had been in the making since the early 1950's. The theoretical groundwork had been laid down by Brazilian historians and diplomats. In 1955 a Brazilian diplomat, Adolpho Justo Bezerra de Menezes, published a book on Brazil and the Asian-African world, which urged Brazilians to "think big" and realize that they had the possibility of achieving the leadership of the Asian-African world.[34] This thesis also received support from a distinguished Brazilian historian, José Honório Rodrigues, in 1961.[35]

Juscelino Kubitschek was the first person of the first or second generation of non-Portuguese descent to attain high office. Despite this racial background, or possibly on account of it, in the beginning Kubitschek supported the Luso-Brazilian community concept. He visited Portugal and received the President of Portugal in Brazil. Kubitschek agreed with the Portuguese thesis that the Portuguese territories are provinces and need not furnish information to the United Nations. Nevertheless, by 1960 Kubitschek's policy began to reflect the new currents stirring in Brazil, and in December Brazil supported in the United Nations the Declaration on the Concession of Independence to Colonial Peoples and Countries.[36]

President Goulart has continued the African policy by establishing direct air and shipping connections with that continent. Although some have criticized this policy,[37] others feel that Brazil cannot "adopt the same indiscriminate policy of 'anti-colonialism' in regard to Portuguese Africa as is now followed by British and U.S. politicians," and that Brazil is "the potential leader of a possible confederacy of Portuguese-speaking peoples."[38]

Leaving Cuba aside as a special case, one may say that Brazil and Mexico have been the chief spokesmen for the new nationalism and the new declaration of independence in international policy. Historically, Argentina has been one of the more assertive of the South American countries as regards its national aspirations, and also, in view of its close cultural, economic, and personal ties with Europe, the one American republic least enthusiastic about Pan Americanism. During the last decade, however, there has been a tendency in Argentina to favor stronger inter-American ties. In each of the countries there is awareness of the advantages of the inter-American system, but also a desire to preserve its distinct historical and regional characteristics according to which hemispheric relations are subject to a different set of rules from those applying to outside relations or to United Nations actions. This view conflicts with the opinion widely held in Washington that the OAS is a sort of bush league United Nations that has to be a busybody in order not to be overlooked.

In concluding this chapter, the opinion may be ventured that the inter-American system will undergo further changes but that most of its traditional values and principles will survive. Professor Whitaker is no doubt correct in his conclusion that the "Western Hemisphere Idea," in the sense of exclusive concern with the Americas, will not be revived importantly—if, indeed, it ever really existed in a pure and unalloyed form.[39] Nor would such a policy be to the advantage of either the United States or Latin America. There is no reason to believe that Latin America would desire to depend exclusively upon the United States either politically or economically, nor can the United States ignore the fact that it is a world power located geographically in the Northern Hemisphere. On one occasion Charles Evans Hughes complained that the Monroe Doctrine was misunderstood because "it has often been treated as though it were our sole policy in this Hemisphere."[40] Likewise, there has been considerable misunderstanding of inter-American cooperation because it has frequently been identified exclusively with some extreme version of some aspects of Pan Americanism, while ignoring the deeper and quieter currents of the movement. In inter-Americanism, as in internationalism in general, there is need for tolerance of differences and flexibility in structure and policies to meet changing conditions.

88

Notes to Chapter III

1. Mexico's policy was formulated by Foreign Minister Genaro Estrada in a statement on September 30, 1930, as follows: "The Mexican Government does not grant recognition which implies judgment; it confines itself to the maintenance or withdrawal, as it may seem advisable, of its diplomatic agents." This came to be known as the Estrada Doctrine. The doctrine is equivocal, since the decision to grant, or not to grant, recognition, obviously implies a judgment. But the doctrine is significant as reflecting the aversion of Mexico to become involved in the internal affairs of other countries.

2. John A. Houston, *Latin America in the United Nations* (New York: Carnegie Endowment for International Peace, 1956), p. 144.

3. John G. Stoessinger, "Financing the United Nations," *International Conciliation,* No. 535 (November, 1961), pp. 33-52.

4. *The Western Hemisphere Idea* (Ithaca: Cornell University Press, 1954), pp. 5, 131, 155. Also see three interesting articles under the heading "Abrazo vs. Coexistence," in Albert O. Hirschman, ed., *Latin American Issues* (New York: The Twentieth Century Fund, 1961).

5. "Imperialismo y buena vecindad," *Cuadernos Americanos,* XXXV (Mexico, D.F., septiembre-octubre de 1947), 68.

6. Jorge Castañeda, "Pan Americanism and Regionalism: A Mexican View," *International Organization,* X (August, 1956), 373-89.

7. Luis Alberto Bahia, "A Brazilian Defines Our Choice in Latin America," *The Reporter,* XXIV (February 2, 1961), 31.

8. ". . . economic integration cannot be conceived except as based on and at the same time ultimately aimed toward political integration," according to Felipe Herrera, President of the Inter-American Development Bank. See chapter IV, footnote 22.

9. That Mexico's cultural claims are not without an imperialistic tinge is illustrated by the statements of some of the intelligentsia. For example, a Mexican sociologist has written that Mexico has "unavoidable responsibilities" that "project themselves over the whole Ibero-American area." Luis Recaséns Siches, *Proyección de México en Latinoamérica* (México, D.F.: Universidad Nacional Autónoma de México, 1960).

10. William Manger, *Pan America in Crisis* (Washington, D.C.: Public Affairs Press, 1961), p. 81.

11. Silvio Zavala, in *Responsible Freedom in the Americas,* Angel del Río, (ed.), Columbia University Bicentennial Conference Series (Garden City: Doubleday & Co., 1955), p. 411.

12. *Social Change in Latin America* (New York: Harper and Brothers, 1960), p. 9.

13. Rupert Emerson, *From Empire to Nation* (Cambridge: Harvard University Press, 1960), p. 415.

14. Edwin M. Borchard, "Arbitration, International," *Encyclopaedia of the Social Sciences,* II (1930), 157-62.

15. Royal Institute of International Affairs. *The Republics of South America* (London: Oxford University Press, 1937), p. 151.

16. Bryce Wood, *The Making of the Good Neighbor Policy* (New York: Columbia University Press, 1961), chapter VII.

17. Royal Institute, *op. cit.,* p. 346.

18. Robert N. Burr, "The Balance of Power in Nineteenth-Century South America: Exploratory Essay," *Hispanic American Historical Review,* XXXV (February, 1955), 55.

19. Dana G. Munro, *The Five Republics of Central America* (New York: Oxford University Press, 1918), p. 32.

20. J. Lloyd Mecham, *The United States and Inter-American Security 1889-1960* (Austin: University of Texas Press, 1961), p. 391. The bibliographical note, pp. 481-89, contains references to materials on inter-American conferences and on the inter-American system in general.

21. Statement by Colonel Mariano Abarca, Director General of Industries, in a speech before the Unión Industrial, reported in *El Cronista Comercial,* June 1, 1944. Similar statements by others have appeared in recent years.

22. Georges Friedmann, "A Frenchman Looks at Latin America," *Américas* (January, 1962), p. 40.

23. C. L. Sulzberger, *New York Times,* December 27, 1961.

24. John A. Logan, Jr., *No Transfer: An American Security Principle* (New Haven: Yale University Press, 1961), pp. 333, 335.   25. *Ibid.,* p. 1.

26. D. A. G. Waddell, "Developments in the Belize Question 1946-1960," *The American Journal of International Law,* LV (April, 1961), 462.

27. C. L. Sulzberger, *New York Times,* December 27, 1961.

28. A convenient summary is given by Max Sorensen, "Law of the Sea," *International Conciliation,* No. 520 (November, 1958).

29. This view has been expressed on various occasions by Roberto de Oliveira Campos, Brazilian Ambassador to the United States.

30. *El laberinto de la soledad* (México, D.F.: Ediciones Cuadernos Americanos, 1950), p. 192. This valuable survey of Mexican thought is now available in English translation as *The Labyrinth of Solitude: Life and Thought in Mexico* (New York: Grove Press, 1962). Another distinguished Mexican scholar, Daniel Cosío Villegas, has warned that European and American concepts of nationalism do not really apply to Latin America, since there are no modern states in Latin America. "Nacionalismo y desarrollo," in Banco Interamericano de Desarrollo, *Conferencia sobre tensiones del desarrollo en el hemisferio occidental,* Organizada por el consejo sobre tensiones mundiales y la Universidad de Bahia. Salvador, Bahia, Brasil, 6-11 agôsto 1962.

31. Cf. Paul Willen, "Neutralism—the Tito Brand," *The New Republic,* CXLIV (March 27, 1961), 11-12.

32. Ambassador Roberto de Oliveira Campos, letter, *New York Times,* January 19, 1962.

33. Before taking off on his trip, President López quipped, "Y no voy de paseo!" (I'm not going merely for the ride).

34. *O Brasil e o mundo Ásio-Africano* (2d ed. rev. and enl., Rio de Janeiro: Ediçãoes GRD), pp. 7 and 9. The first edition appeared in 1955.

35. *Brasil e África: outro horizonte (relações e política brasileiro-africana)* (Rio de Janeiro: Editora Civilização Brasileira, S.A., 1961). Also see Sr. Rodrigues' article, "The Foundations of Brazil's Foreign Policy," *International Affairs,* XXXVIII (July, 1962), 324-38.

36. Maria Y. Leite Linhares, "Brazil's Foreign Policy and Africa," *The World Today,* XVIII (December, 1962), 534.

37. *Ibid.* The author points out that Brazil historically has had connections with only a small part of Africa, that Brazil's nondiscrimination in racial matters is not sufficient reason to make Brazil useful and beloved to Africans, and that Brazil's trade with Africa is very small and is chiefly with the South African Republic and with Morocco.

38. Gilberto Freyre, "Misconceptions of Brazil," *Foreign Affairs,* XL (April, 1962), 460.

39. It is not without interest and is possibly of significance that the United

States Congress in the preamble to the American Republics Cooperation Act, adopted by the Senate and the House on August 31, 1960, made the following statement "as the sense of the Congress": "the historic, economic, political, and geographic relationships among the American Republics are unique and of special significance and, as appropriate, should be so recognized in future legislation."

40. Quoted in Clarence H. Haring, *South America Looks at the United States* (New York: The Macmillan Co., 1928), p. 102. Also of interest is the comment of the late Thomas W. Palmer, Jr.: "The fact that some diehards have indeed continued to stress hemispheric interests exclusively should not lead anyone to suppose that a significant number of genuine Latin Americanists have at any time been hemisphere isolationists." *Search for a Latin American Policy* (Gainesville: University of Florida Press, 1957), pp. 8-9.

–IV–

The Changing Latin American Economic Structures

Since the war, economists have come to use per capita national income (or product) as the yardstick for measuring a nation's economic status. On this basis the Latin American countries as a group occupy a middle position between the upper bracket of Western industrial nations and the basement level of Asian and African states.

There are serious objections, as we shall soon see, to the use of income as the chief or sole measuring rod, but first it should be noted that there is a very wide spread between the per capita income of the more prosperous Latin American countries like Venezuela and Argentina and the least developed, to wit, Bolivia, Paraguay, and Haiti, being from six to twenty times as much in the richest as in the poorest. This gap is considerably larger than the gap between the richer Latin American countries and the nations in the top bracket. In fact, per capita income in Venezuela is on the level with the more prosperous European countries, approximately double that of Italy, and three times that of Japan.

Now it must be admitted that international comparisons of income, although useful, are subject to serious limitations. There are formidable statistical problems, such as finding reasonably exact purchasing power equivalents for different currency units, the lack of reliable data in some countries, differences in method of computation, and above all, the inherent lack of comparability arising from different social and economic structures. Even climate makes a difference: in New England, central heating is considered a necessity, but in Panama neither one's economic nor social status is affected by the lack of it. In the United States the value added by each additional motor vehicle produced is included in national income, and no deduction is made for the reduction in utility and pleasure caused other owners by traffic and parking problems, nor for other costs (including that of human life) chargeable to the motor car industry. In other words, per capita income cannot be automatically translated into units of welfare.

Another source of possible misunderstanding is that per capita income expresses an arithmetical average and reveals nothing regarding the distribution of the income. In Venezuela, for example, a small group of people have very high incomes but well over half of the population would be considered worse off, by most criteria, than the low-income groups in many countries having lower per capita incomes than Venezuela.

Traditional Characteristics of Latin American Economies

Countries in the lower half of the national income curve are today generally designated as "underdeveloped." Other words sometimes used to characterize their economies are "passive," "reflex," or "derivative." Dr. Raúl Prebisch, Director General of the United Nations Economic Commission for Latin America, calls them "peripheral." Before the war the Latin Americans frequently referred to their economies as "colonial," emphasizing certain traditional structural characteristics, such as the high degree of economic specialization, the predominance of primary production, high export coefficient, and dependence on foreign initiative and financing.

All of the Latin American republics still have two or more of these characteristics, and some show all five (including low per capita income), but developments of recent decades have brought about structural changes that reduce the applicability of some of these categories. Not that all of them are necessarily unfavorable. Economic specialization, to take one important characteristic, is apt to yield the maximum economic return in a country where population and capital are scarce in relation to natural resources. But as population increases and further investment in basic export industries tends to yield diminishing returns under prevailing world market conditions, some diversification and industrialization become indispensable if per capita income is to be maintained or increased.

Historically the Latin American countries have had "export"

economies in the sense that the return from exports was the chief determinant of income changes in the commercial sectors of the economies. Furthermore, it was characteristic that one or two products (coffee in Brazil, copper and nitrates in Chile, sugar in Cuba) accounted for most of the export return. This situation still prevails in a number of the countries, including some of the larger ones. In the case of Venezuela, for example, the export coefficient is around 38 per cent, while petroleum accounts for 92 per cent of the total value of exports. But expansion of the internal economies and diversification of the list of export products have produced some important changes in the traditional picture. In recent years the export coefficient for the twenty republics has been around 16 per cent, while in some of the larger countries like Brazil and Mexico it is less than 10 per cent. This is still considerably higher than in the United States, where exports comprise less than 3 per cent of the national product, but it is substantially less than in some of the so-called developed countries, for example, the Netherlands (34 per cent), Belgium (30 per cent), West Germany (22 per cent), and New Zealand (27 per cent). In the United Kingdom, the export coefficient has been around 16 to 18 per cent in recent years, but was 30 per cent or more in the days of Britain's greatest prosperity. In a very real sense, the highly industrialized countries might be said to be more dependent on foreign trade than the underdeveloped countries.

RECENT STRUCTURAL CHANGES

The structural shifts of recent decades have involved a decline in the relative importance of the primary industries (agriculture, mining, forestry) and an expansion of the secondary industries (manufacturing, power, construction). In two of the countries (Argentina, Chile) the industrial sector accounts for a larger proportion of the national product than the primary sector. Industrialization has reinforced the tendency toward urbanization, but this trend was in evidence even before significant industrialization as the result of strong sociopolitical forces. It is estimated, however, that about 55 per cent of the active population of Latin America is engaged in agriculture or grazing. In fifteen of the twenty republics the rural population still exceeds the urban dwellers (in countries like Haiti, the rural population is 80 per cent of the total), but the drift to the cities is proceeding at a startling rate.

As a general rule, the per capita income is lowest in those countries in which a large proportion of the population is of non-European extraction. A distinctive feature of many of the countries is the existence of large concentrations of peoples of Indian or African blood or mixture, retaining their characteristic dress, way of life, and, in some cases, language. Since these elements are at a low cultural and technical level, their per capita contribution to the national income is minimal. In fact, some economists have coined the phrase "dual economy" to emphasize the gap between the urban industrialized sectors and the traditional economy of the indigenous elements. Even in Mexico, about 10 per cent (that is, three and a half millions) are Indians in the sense that they belong to Indian communities with a distinct Indian way of life, including the use of native languages. Furthermore, another large segment of the Mexican population, which may be 50 per cent of the total, is close to the indigenous group as regards standards of living and methods of production, although ethnically the members of the group may be of mixed blood (mestizo). Most of both groups are illiterate and neither technically nor culturally able to take advantage of the changes taking place in the modern sectors of society.

Yet it is in some respects very misleading to refer to Mexico or to four or five of the leading South American countries as underdeveloped.[1]* In each there is much wealth, luxury, and culture. Buenos Aires, São Paulo, and Mexico City are among the ten leading metropolises of the world. Each country boasts its quota of multimillionaires—although some of these, including several ex-presidents, find it convenient to reside abroad from time to time. In each there is an important nucleus of enterprising and knowledgeable business leaders, bankers, industrialists, and traders. Four or five of the leading Mexican financial groups perpetuate prerevolutionary dynasties. These groups, as well as some of more recent origin, have organized hundreds of new enterprises in the fields of manufacturing, merchandising, insurance, banking, hotels, etc. Most of these leaders

*Notes to chapter IV begin on page 120.

have shown a high degree of civic and social responsibility. Practically all of the technology is derivative in the sense that it was originally developed abroad (to a large extent the same applies to Japan), and consequently the introduction of new technology involves the temporary employment of foreign experts or the sending of Mexicans abroad for training. But within the established fields there is no shortage of Mexican entrepreneurs, managers, or technicians; indeed, Mexico has begun to export them, particularly to adjacent regions like Central America or for employment by international agencies.

Outlook for 1960's

During the postwar decade the Latin American area taken as a whole enjoyed a spectacular rate of economic growth, higher than the growth rate of any other important geographical area in the world. Even after allowing for an equally spectacular rate of population growth—more than twice as fast as in the United States—the per capita growth rate was nearly 3 per cent as compared to the secular rate of around 2 per cent in the United States. As the result of this population explosion the aggregate population of Latin America has since the early 1950's surpassed that of the United States and by 1975 is expected to be 50 per cent larger than that of the United States.

Not all of the countries have shared in this prosperity. Per capita, Argentina, Uruguay, Paraguay, Bolivia, and Haiti are not better off, and possibly are worse off, than in 1939. The rate of growth in the other countries is also uneven. In some, growth is still at a high level, but in others there has been a slowing down as the terms of trade—the chief factor in the postwar boom—have become less favorable, and there is growing concern as the decade of the sixties unfolds.

In drawing up a balance sheet of Latin America's prospects during the coming years consideration must be given to a wide range of factors, including attitudes and institutions, as well as the more strictly economic elements. Latin America's expectations of rapid economic progress were fired by wartime pronouncements and by the postwar emphasis in the United States and by international agencies on accelerated economic development. In practice this has meant a continuation, with enlarged external resources, of the movement for "economic independence" that took shape during the 1930's.

One of the earliest instances in Latin America of a formal approach to this problem was Mexico's Six-Year Plan (1934-1939), which put considerable emphasis on social objectives, such as the distribution of land, assistance to small farmers, and participation of workers in the profits of industry, but devoted chief attention to national objectives, including the Mexicanization of economic activities, acceptance by the state of the responsibility of regulating the economy, and the expansion of irrigation and resettlement programs, especially in the North, with preference to Mexicans repatriated from the United States.

The Getulio Vargas revolution in Brazil also provides an outstanding example of an attempt to form a nation-state out of previously semiautonomous regions, and in the process promoting the domestication of operations long in foreign hands. A strong nationalistic movement likewise got under way in Argentina in the 1930's, a decade before Perón came to power. This included the establishment of regulatory boards for the basic export products, the creation of a central bank, the formation of mixed companies in the minerals field, the strengthening of the government petroleum enterprise, and nationalization of two railways.

ROLE OF THE STATE

The vital forces behind Latin American developments of recent decades have had two principal constituent elements: nationalism, and state programming and support of economic activities. Programming first attracted attention in the United States. The original inspiration for planning appears to have come from the *Planwirtschaft* of republican Germany, which in turn took some ideas from Soviet Russia. President Plutarco Elías Calles of Mexico was a great admirer of Germany and visited President Friedrich Ebert.

As the national development programs of the other republics moved into high gear, words and gestures were borrowed from the New Deal in the United States, from Keynesianism, from the Soviets, from fascism, from national socialism, from the Portuguese New State, but these influences were mostly superficial. More important has been the corporate concept of society that has deep roots in Hispanic legal, social, and ecclesiastical structures. Furthermore, the state as the agent of national resurgence has the sympathy of all classes. Rugged individualists of all countries know how to use the state to run interference for them. In a deeper sense, the stimulation of national pride and loyalty has been an essential part of the process of economic development everywhere.

It is not unusual for Latin American political leaders to talk of socialism as the ultimate goal, and in some countries there has been a considerable growth of state socialism. As a rule, however, state enterprise has been confined to large undertakings either too big or not sufficiently remunerative to attract local entrepreneurs; the alternative is usually foreign control. These developments have not prevented, and indeed have hastened, the emergence of a strong entrepreneurial class in most of the countries. Most of the additional income that has accrued to the Latin American countries since the 1940's has gone to this class, with little if any gain for most of the workers. Considerable statistical evidence on this point has recently been published. Professor Nicholas Kaldor of King's College, Cambridge, spent some time in Chile in 1956 and documented the increasing inequality in the distribution of income in that country. A recent Mexican study shows that from 1950 to 1957 the family income of the bottom fifth of the population declined, on the average, from $22 monthly to less than $20. In the mid-1950's President Adolfo Ruiz Cortines estimated that 65 per cent of the Mexicans were worse off than they were a quarter of a century earlier. A Brazilian Minister of Labor and Social Security has stated that it is not unusual in Brazil for the profits of an industrial enterprise to exceed the total wage payments, even in cases where the number of workers exceeds ten thousand.[2]

CONSUMPTION VS. INVESTMENT

Heretofore, the Latin American governments, even those nominally furthest to the left, have justified this unequal distribution of income on the grounds that if wages were increased, consumption would increase and savings would decline. This is essentially the same attitude as that taken, at a certain stage of development, by both high capitalism and by Marxists. The strongly nationalistic governments have successfully courted labor and have given it some recognition and status it did not enjoy before, but the financial rewards have been confined to the labor leaders and to certain special groups, while the rank and file have been induced to believe that they were contributing to the social peace essential to national advantage.

Serious inequalities in the distribution of income have occurred in all countries, particularly during a dynamic stage of development, but there are some differences in the current Latin American situation as compared to the historic processes in the industrialized countries of Western Europe, the United States, and Japan, that throw considerable light on the process of economic growth. At the critical period of their development the entrepreneurial classes of the industrial countries were mostly hardworking people who spent little on their personal satisfactions, putting most of the profits back into the business. One finds numerous examples of this class in Latin America, and it may well be that in some areas they will provide the leaven needed to raise the general level, but the statistical evidence clearly shows that, taken as a group, the employer and proprietary classes have invested only a small part of their income (from profits, dividends, interest, rents) and furthermore pay comparatively little in taxes, thus limiting the amounts available for government investment. As regards Mexico, the Economic Commission for Latin America reported: "While the share of profits, interest, and rentals in net income rose from 34.5 per cent to 51.0 per cent between 1939 and 1952, the proportion which the propertied sector invested rose only from 19 to 22.6 per cent of the total available goods and services during the same period." The Commission concludes that the higher income group in Mexico increased their consumption about ten times more than their investment.[3] A more recent study by a leading Mexican economist points out that the 5 per cent of Mexican families in the highest income category receive 37 per cent of the total personal income.[4] Given the historical and institutional situation in Mexico, the author points out, personal saving is low and is not increasing. Since this upper income group pays little in taxes, the remedy lies in a personal income tax that will provide the government with means to make the necessary social investments.

Professor Kaldor, in the study mentioned earlier in this chapter, asks why it is that Chile, with natural conditions more favorable than in Switzerland or Sweden, has only one-third of the per capita income of those countries. He finds the answer in the "social factors that curb the free development of productive forces."[5] He estimated that, taking into account the greater inequality in the distribution of income in Chile, the level of living of the masses in Chile is only one-sixth of that in Switzerland and Sweden, and hence they have not been able to benefit from the cumulative process that, in improving living standards, increases efficiency through education, better health, and longer working life.

In Chile personal consumption by the proprietary class absorbs 21.2 per cent of the national resources, as compared to only 7.4 per cent in the United Kingdom. Considered on an individual basis, it is estimated that the sumptuary consumption of the well-to-do in Chile is three or four times as great as in the United Kingdom. "Despite the frequent statement that Chile is not able to generate savings because of the poverty of the people, these figures demonstrate that through a reduction in sumptuary consumption by the rich a higher rate of savings could be generated without reducing the living levels of the poor."[6]

The World Bank has estimated that more than one-fourth of the national income of Nicaragua accrues to 1 per cent of the population. "If 10 per cent of the incomes of the upper 1 per cent of income recipients were to be invested productively, the current productive investment would increase by 50 per cent."[7]

A distinguished American economist arrived at a similar conclusion two decades ago: "In a number of industrially backward countries the principal obstacle to domestic investment is not the absence of local funds that might be invested but a scale of social values, combined with political instability, which causes the wealthy groups within the country to spend their incomes on foreign travel or on foreign and domestic luxuries. In more than one Latin American country that is reputedly 'short of capital,' the sums that have been spent in Paris in the last half century by wealthy natives would have endowed the country with a modern transportation system and a well-equipped industrial plant."[8]

Before World War I, Argentines had the reputation of being the freest spenders, and their wives the most fashionably dressed, among the foreigners who congregated in Paris and fashionable watering places, although they had stiff competition at times from Russian Grand Dukes, Indian princes, and henequen planters from Yucatán. More recently, the international playboys are more likely to hail from Brazil, Mexico, the Dominican Republic, or Venezuela.

Since there is a huge gap between the highest and the lowest real incomes in all countries, inequalities in income cannot alone be considered a major obstacle to economic development. More important perhaps has been the relative absence in Latin America in the past of a middle class, and especially the numerous gradations in income and status, as well as opportunities for advancement, that might encourage young men and women to attempt the next rungs up the ladder of economic improvement. The psychology and environment in Latin America have been such that this slow bourgeois pattern has not offered much attraction to the majority of the population. Hence it is that a chance at the *gordo* in the national lottery makes a greater appeal than saving or investment. Hence it is that the army and politics have been the chief instruments of democratic opportunity. Poor boys from the mountains or the plains, with little education, have risen by ruse, daring, and ruthlessness to the highest positions in the land. In politics, too, the rewards are great, since some of the largest fortunes are based on political preferment.

The Middle Income Groups

With the rise of industry and the expansion of the service activities, the middle-income group has expanded numerically throughout Latin America, and it is this group that has provided much of the drive for economic betterment. It is also this group that is most nationalistic and that supplies many of the anti-American recruits. Many of the people in this group, especially those with experience abroad, are very unhappy that their countries have been stigmatized as underdeveloped or that members of their nationality should constantly be typed, on the screen and in fiction, as vicious or improvident. When Castro banned from Cuba the use of the word "underdeveloped," which he considered humiliating, his action had an echo in the hearts of millions of Latin Americans.

Perhaps even more serious, from the standpoint of economic development, has been the lack of a vigorous and informed class of farmers, whether big, little, or medium. There are, to be sure, many enlightened landowners, but a disproportionate share of the land is in the hands of proprietors who are primarily interested in maintaining the status quo. At the other end of the land tenure scale, there are, in most of the countries, large numbers of extremely small farm units, where the yields are low because the soil is eroded and exhausted and the cultivation is carried on in a primitive manner.

Nor have the policies of the Latin American governments in connection with land reform been notably successful in creating highly productive new farm units. The type of policy that has been followed in countries like Brazil, with large unsettled areas, involves the opening up to colonization of lands situated at considerable distance from population centers and without adequate transportation facilities to move the produce to market at reasonable cost. The consequence has been that this type of pioneer settlement has created new nuclei of small subsistence farmers at a low economic and technical level using the "slash and burn" system of cultivation.

During the last decade conservative Brazilians have become alarmed by the organization of Peasant Leagues in the densely populated and impoverished Northeast. At one time a safety valve was found in the migration of the landless and hungry to other areas of Brazil: during the nineteenth and early twentieth centuries to the Amazon Valley, attracted by the rubber boom (and where thousands perished), and more recently to the prosperous tier of southern states, especially São Paulo and Paraná. But some prefer to stay and fight it out. In his fiery speeches the agrarian leader, Francisco Julião, has referred to Mao Tse-tung, and this has led some observers to conclude that the danger of communist-type upheaval today may come from the rural rather than the urban sector.[9]

In other countries, as in Mexico, land reform has been primarily political and nationalistic and has taken on a revolutionary character. A large part of the cultivated land in central Mexico is now owned by the community, in the form of *ejidos,* but generally the acreage is divided into inalienable family plots. In some cases the *ejidatarios* have been able to cooperate in a program of mechanization and modernization, with favorable results, but in the majority of communities the *ejido* yields are low. The high birth rate also presents a problem, as the plots are usually too small and too poor to accommodate more than one son with his family. Hence large numbers from the villages have been forced to seek work elsewhere. Many go to the cities; others join the movement of migratory labor (*braceros*) to the United States.

A vigorous commercial farming class has developed in northern Mexico and on the West Coast. This group has benefited directly from the credit policy of the Mexican government and indirectly from some of the official land policies, but the formation of this class was well under way before the Revolution, and its success has depended largely on the adoption of American agricultural technology, plus the availability of the United States market. The new element since the Revolution is that these farming communities are now definitely Mexican, whereas in earlier decades a large proportion of the landowners and settlers were gringos who doubtless took it for granted that sooner or later that part of Mexico would pass under the control of the Stars and Stripes. An important commercial farming element had also developed in Cuba, before Castro, but the revolutionary government has now brought all agriculture under government control.

The backwardness of agriculture is the chief reason for the low level of per capita income in Latin America. Over 50 per cent of the active population is engaged in agriculture, but it produces less than 25 per cent of the aggregate gross product. It is clear that higher output in the rural sectors would raise the general level of income and stimulate production in other sectors. Economic historians have pointed out that the industrialized countries of today had a well-developed and prosperous agriculture before the onset of industrialization. Professor Simon Kuznets of the Johns Hopkins University, a leading international authority, has estimated that per capita income in the United States may well have been higher than that of Great Britain even in the early nineteenth century, although industrialization was already well under way in Britain and had hardly begun in the United States.

It is also significant that the development of agriculture in the United States and other economically advanced countries involved comparatively little outside finance of any kind. In fact, a large part of the investment did not involve a cash outlay; it represented foresight and labor: clearing the land, building walls or fences, chopping wood for fuel or construction, improving roads, proper handling of livestock, selection of seeds. Recent theories of economic growth have tended to put great emphasis on needs for external capital but to disregard the fact that "the expenditure of time, effort and money in the creation, extension and upkeep of agricultural holdings" represent capital formation.[10] Professors P. T. Bauer and Basil S. Yamey illustrate their thesis by citing the cocoa acreage of the former Gold Coast, the rubber smallholdings of Sumatra, and the padi fields of Southwest Asia, which were developed by the natives themselves. Another authority on Africa has pointed out that "the expansion of the production of cocoa, palm oil, palm kernels, groundnuts, hides and skins to their present enormous dimensions was carried out by ordinary African peasants because they wanted to earn more money."[11] These developments were possible, however, only during the period when there was a favorable political framework.

Is it possible to change the panorama of rural society in the Americas without resort to revolution, as has happened in the past? Theoretically, it would be possible to bring about the subdivision of latifundia through taxation and to induce other changes by means of extension services and education. But the practical difficulty of obtaining progress by such means has led some observers to favor an active policy of industrialization as the only practical way of breaking through the crust of institutional rigidities in the rural sector.

THE PREBISCH THESIS

The case for industry has been presented by Dr. Raúl Prebisch, since 1950 Director General of the United Nations Economic Commission for Latin America. In the first of a series of essays on Latin

American economic problems Dr. Prebisch challenged the validity of part of the accepted body of economic doctrine, which he said reflects the points of view of the "great centers of world economy" and subordinates the interests of the countries at the "periphery." In particular, he reacted against the nineteenth century scheme of geographical specialization, which, in the hands of some economists, tended to assume that the pattern of international trade was fixed and immutable. In Dr. Prebisch's view, the periphery has not shared equally in the benefits of technical progress and increased productivity, the terms of trade have historically been unfavorable to the countries exporting primary materials, and the balance can only be redressed by a series of structural changes in the Latin American economies involving industrialization and a greater per capita investment per worker.[12]

Industrialization did, in fact, make rapid headway during the 1950's, stimulated by the prosperity of the export sector, aided by investments and technical participation by hundreds of foreign firms, and protected by tariffs and exchange restrictions as well as shortages during the Korean emergency. The larger countries have now reached the point where local manufacture supplies most of the demand for consumer goods and also some heavier items. Brazil has eleven plants producing twenty-four types of motor vehicles. Although some parts are still imported, hundreds of new factories supplying parts and accessories have sprung up. Brazil has also gone fairly intensively into the manufacture of machinery.

Dr. Prebisch has constantly stressed the importance of maintaining a high level of exports as a means of assuring the foreign exchange needed for imports of equipment and supplies required by industrialization. At one stage the thesis developed by ECLA apparently anticipated that sufficient exchange would be saved through the substitution of local manufactures for imported finished goods, but in practice the policy of import substitution has been counterproductive, and imports have increased as the result of the demand for the machinery, raw materials, and fuels required by industry, as well as for new "induced imports" of foodstuffs and luxuries arising from the enlarged consumer purchasing power.

The strong propensity to import has also been stimulated by the inflationary expansion of demand and by the conspicuous examples of consumption held up before the eyes of the people by modern communications and advertising media. One of the unfortunate by-products of economic development, especially very rapid economic development, in all climes and ages, has been the mushroom growth of materialism and love of costly display—larger and swankier residences and country estates, longer and wider motor cars, inflationary demand for works of art with prestige names, and costly caparisoned concubines, domestic and imported. Hence, despite numerous restrictions, imports have continued at a high level and would be higher if allowance were made for duty evasions through under-evaluation and contraband. Furthermore, the statistics do not show the "invisible imports" arising from expenditures of Latin American government officials and tourists abroad. These outlays inevitably result in considerable strain on the exchange reserves.

The problem of matching the heavy demand for imports with adequate capacity to import has been basic to all Economic Commission for Latin America analysis. The capacity to import is made up of the net receipts of exchange from all sources: exports, loans, credits, grants, investments, and the expenditures of foreign governments and tourists.

Receipts from exports are by far the chief source of exchange. Despite the very large gains from the extremely favorable terms of trade during the first half of the 1950's, this prosperity could not conceal the fact that the volume of exports of many items had declined from the peak (e.g., grains, meats, hides, flaxseed) and that the quantity of most other exports had risen very little. Only a few items showed a definitely upward trend: petroleum, copper, iron ore, and cotton. Latin America has been particularly pessimistic about the outlook for exports of foodstuffs (which comprise around 60 per cent of the total value of exports), owing to the relative inelasticity of demand for foodstuffs in the developed countries. This alleged inelasticity arises from the fact that, as income rises, a reduced proportion of the total income is spent on food, while a larger share is devoted to non-food items and to services. In addition to this theoretical argument, Latin American spokesmen have cited concrete actions by the industrialized countries tending to restrict the outlet for their raw materials and foodstuffs, such as quota restrictions imposed by the United States, development of synthetic substitutes for Latin American natural products, increased self-sufficiency in Europe and preference to Africa by the Common Market countries, internal taxes that tend to limit consumption of such products as coffee, and competition from exports subsidized by the United States.

Critics of the ECLA position admit that the quantity of most Latin American exports has been stagnant since the war, but they tend to put the blame on the policies of the Latin American governments themselves: undue protection of industry, distortions created by multiple exchange rates, price controls, inflation arising from expansion of currency issues, and nationalistic restrictions that have resulted in power, fuel, and transportation bottlenecks. It is clear that there are large opportunities for export expansion on the part of individual firms and countries, but, in the aggregate, it is hard to escape the conclusion that exports in sufficient volume to support a rising living standard on the part of a rapidly growing population are apt to force prices to a low level, especially in view of the network of restrictions and preferences in the postwar world.

STABILIZATION OF EXPORT RECEIPTS

Since the war the Latin American countries have looked hopefully to the possibility that the United States might undertake measures to support international prices of basic commodities. They were encouraged in this approach by their experience during the war and again during the Korean emergency, by the demonstration effect of our own price support measures, and by the example of our outpouring of grant aid to non-American countries. Furthermore, in 1941 the United States had taken the initiative in forming the Inter-American Coffee Agreement, which, by restricting the entry of coffee into the United States, doubled the cost of coffee to the American consumer and then more or less stabilized the price for the rest of the war. This agreement was terminated shortly after the end of the war on the initiative of the Latin Americans, who were more interested at that time in the prospects of further price rises.

Of course, interest in international price support schemes has not been confined to Latin America. The subject has been constantly on the agenda of the United Nations Economic and Social Council, as well as of other international agencies. Furthermore, effective measures dealing with prices of some commodities must take into account the cooperation of producers and consumers outside the Western Hemisphere. The United States became a member of the international wheat and sugar agreements, in response to the pressure of interested United States producers of those commodities, but prior to 1960 took a negative attitude regarding further participation in such agreements.

In the Charter of Punta del Este[13] the United States went all the way in agreeing to cooperate in the solution of commodity problems. The United States also took the initiative in working out an international coffee agreement, which was completed in August, 1962, subject to ratification. United States representatives have participated in study groups relating to commodities of interest to Latin America, and have expressed their readiness to discuss possible United States accession to the international tin agreement.

In addition to this commodity-by-commodity approach to the problem of severe fluctuations in the trade returns of primary producers, projects have been drafted both by the United Nations Commission on International Commodity Trade and by the Organization of American States designed to provide some type of compensatory financing to stabilize incomes. The report submitted to the United Nations Commission proposed the creation of a Development Insurance Fund which would compensate by loans or grants up to 50 per cent of any drop in receipts below a stipulated percentage of the previous three-year average of exports. The proposal drawn up by the OAS envisaged the granting of export stabilization loans on a virtually automatic basis. This scheme was estimated to involve an outlay of $1.8 billion to constitute a revolving fund, of which one-third would be contributed by the low-income countries. The United Nations plan placed the primary burden on the richer countries.

Despite the favorable disposition in the principal consuming countries to continue strenuous effort to find some way of avoiding catastrophic price declines of basic commodities, at the same time there is sober realization of the enormous practical difficulties of operating international price support schemes, especially when they depend upon the cooperation of governments lacking the will or the power to carry out decisions effectively. Experience has shown that high prices are not always helpful to producers, since they stimulate competition or encourage the development of substitutes. Furthermore, it is sometimes overlooked that most underdeveloped countries are importers as well as exporters of foodstuffs and raw materials.

PROBLEM OF CAPITAL FORMATION

Economists of both developed and underdeveloped countries are agreed that dynamic economic development requires a substantial increase in the rate of capital formation. Communist countries like Russia and China have succeeded in mobilizing capital required for the creation of heavy industry by keeping consumption by the masses down to the minimum. In some of the capitalist countries a regime of social austerity facilitated rapid economic growth. What is the solution feasible for Latin America? The ECLA analysis recognizes that the lack of savings for investment is partly the result of "certain types of consumption by high-income groups." At the same time the living standards of the masses are so low that it is considered desirable to avoid further cuts. The proposed solution, therefore, is to obtain sufficient foreign resources, both public and private, over a temporary period, until the coefficient of domestic saving rises to a satisfactory level. The principal argument has arisen over the respective roles of public and private investment, and the danger that detailed official plans of development might present to private enterprise. This subject will be discussed in the next chapter, but it may be pointed out here that the ECLA studies have emphasized the "burden placed on a country's capacity for external payments by the remittance of profits and interest," and have expressed a preference for public international loans over "more costly private investment."[14]

The Latin American countries also have what Dr. Prebisch has called "the inescapable need for economic programming," and ECLA has carried through a series of country studies designed to provide medium- and long-term aggregate and sectoral projections of economic growth. The national policy makers have not, in practice, given much more than lip service to these meticulously cal-

109

culated documents, but they have served as a training school for local economists and have influenced the rising generations in various ways.

Various attempts have been made to estimate the amount of external resources needed to assure a suitable rate of development in Latin America. A group of distinguished Latin Americans, working with the cooperation of the ECLA secretariat, in 1954 estimated that an increase of $1 billion a year, over a ten-year period, would be required to supplement domestic savings. This billion was conceived as an increase over the amount of foreign capital flowing into Latin America at that time. During the mid-1950's Latin America's net long-term capital inflow from the United States ranged between $500 and $750 million, and there was the beginning of a substantial inflow from Europe. This study estimated that private foreign investment would account for from $300 to $350 million annually, the balance to be furnished by international credit institutions.[15] Professors Max F. Millikan and W. W. Rostow of the Massachusetts Institute of Technology took this same estimate of $1 billion annually as the required additional foreign capital needed by Latin America.[16]

In a study prepared by the Secretariat of the Inter-American Economic and Social Council, a regional development institution is proposed, and the recommendation is made that it would need a capital of $2.5 to $3 billion provided that the entire amount would become available in convertible currencies over a period of ten years.[17] Since this report was prepared, the Inter-American Development Bank has begun operations, with comparatively modest capitalization, but since the Bank is to be "the primary mechanism" for the administration of the special inter-American fund, for which the United States Congress has authorized an initial amount of $500 million, it has received substantial financial resources to carry through an important social improvement and economic development program, provided the Latin American governments take effective action to put into effect the reforms envisaged by the Act of Bogotá of September 12, 1960.[18]

It should be kept in mind that practically all of the Latin American countries have enjoyed periods of great prosperity in the past, either because of a greatly expanded volume of exports on exceptionally favorable terms, or as the result of a large influx of foreign funds in the form of loans or business investment, or both. But the major benefits of these prosperous periods have been confined to a relatively small segment of the population, and have produced disappointing results from the standpoint of creating conditions for continuing and self-generating economic growth. The reasons for this failure are numerous and complex, but prominent among them may be counted the disproportionate outlays on showy public works and private sumptuary expenditures, much of it abroad. Particularly conspicuous has been the failure to provide the education and training necessary for the preparation of future generations of producers, or to afford adequate incentives and opportunities to enlist the support of all classes of society.

As mentioned earlier in this chapter, there are indications of important changes in attitudes in some of the principal commercial centers, and of a growing disposition on the part of governments to maintain the tempo of development set in motion during the last two decades. None of the countries has yet succeeded in creating the conditions such as will permit the mobilization of sufficient local private capital to undertake the investment needed under the circumstances, nor have the governmental mechanisms proved themselves able to do the job efficiently. It is this dilemma that has put so much heat into the pressures for additional foreign capital, especially public capital that will permit the countries to accelerate their growth without outcries against excessive foreign intervention in the economy. These demands create new dilemmas. Some Latin Americans welcome the restraints that international public lending agencies put on the disbursement of the funds furnished by them, since such guidance ensures more efficient use of the funds, but too many conditions, and too many advisers, also create problems and resentments. Some very large outlays on public works by governments during the 1940's were largely abortive as regards their effect in making additional production possible. It is not always recognized that neither public nor private investment leads automatically to economic development, although it may create a temporary wave of prosperity. Yet adequate supplies of capital are a necessary, if not sufficient, condition for economic growth.

There has also been inadequate recognition, especially in the United States, of the limitations on economic development in some areas. As the late James Bastor pointed out, there is the tacit assumption in most discussions of this problem "that all poor 'national' areas are capable of economic development to the point at which they can support themselves at a tolerable standard of living without some form of international noncommercial aid."[19] Of course, it is always possible, even in the poorest of countries, that some new resource of great value may be discovered that will make possible a fuller life, at least for a few insiders, but generations might be required to work out the social and economic adjustments necessary to raise noticeably the living standards of the majority of the people.

Economic Integration

It is, no doubt, partly in recognition of this problem, and partly as the result of a fuller understanding of the problem of developing heavy industry without broader markets than most of the countries provide that the Latin American countries have taken steps to follow the European lead in creating common markets or broader economic unions.

Two different projects have now been launched, one involving a complete customs union in Central America, and the other a looser but larger regional grouping open to all Latin American republics.

In Central America since mid-1958 a series of agreements have been signed and put into effect by the five historic Isthmian countries. Costa Rica, after some hesitation, finally took the plunge late in 1963 for participation in the common market program. Unlike the other countries in the Isthmus, Costa Rica is populated by people of largely European stock. It has enjoyed more political stability and a higher standard of living than the other Central American countries. Since Panama's prosperity depends primarily upon its position as an international crossroads of travel and trade, no basis has yet been found by which it could be brought into the Central American customs union, but discussions have been held looking toward its eventual incorporation into the union on an associated basis.

The General Treaty of Central American Economic Integration, providing for the establishment of a complete customs union within five years, went into effect in June, 1961, as regards Guatemala, El Salvador, and Nicaragua, and as regards Honduras about a year later. Except for a reserved list of commodities specified in an annex, the contracting parties granted one another immediate free trade for all natural and manufactured products originating in their respective territories. A standard customs nomenclature (NAUCA) has been adopted, and a common external tariff has been put into effect covering about half of the schedules. Upon ratification of a protocol signed in July, 1962, by all five countries, the common external tariff will cover 95 per cent of the classifications.

In the past, the international trade of the Central American countries has been overwhelmingly with nations outside the area: until recently, the intraregional trade did not comprise more than 3 per cent of the total, but this rose to about 8 per cent in 1961. The major exports of the region—coffee, bananas, cacao, fibers, lumber, and ores—have gone to the industrialized countries of Europe and North America, and in return the Central American countries have received not only a wide variety of manufactures but also foodstuffs, raw materials, and fuels not produced in the area. Since the war, as the economics have become more diversified, some of the countries have surplus productive capacity not only as regards a variety of agricultural and forest products, but also of manufactured goods such as textiles, cosmetics, glass containers, tires, and petroleum derivatives.

As there has been for some time a network of bilateral free trade agreements among the various Central American countries, the significance of the General Treaty lies less in its immediate effect on trade than in the expected stimulus to investment and in the impetus given to regional cooperation in a wide range of activities. Each of the countries has enacted an industrial incentives law; in July, 1962, a uniform investment incentives law for manufacturing industries was signed in the hope of avoiding ruinous fiscal competition among the various countries bidding for new industries. Discussions are still in progress as regards the implementation of the Convention on Central American Industries of Integration, signed in 1958, providing for a series of regional industries—one in each country as a starter—which

113

must be controlled by Central American capital. Preliminary approval has been given to a tire and tube plant in Guatemala, a copper wire plant in El Salvador, a caustic soda factory in Nicaragua, and a chemical plant in Honduras.

There has been set up a Central American Bank for Economic Integration, with a capital of $16 million, of which $10 million was provided by the United States government. It is located at Tegucigalpa, the capital of Honduras. The bank granted its first loan, the equivalent of $275,000, to a new firm which plans to produce pressed wood for use in the construction of housing and furniture. As several of the Central American countries have received housing loans on easy terms under the Social Progress Trust Fund contributed by the United States and administered by the Inter-American Development Bank, there is expected to be a large market for construction materials. Projects financed by the bank are supposed to be of a regional rather than of a purely national character, but some difference of opinion has developed regarding the financing of monopolies. Regular meetings of officials of the central banks of the five historic Central American states are now held, and studies have been made with reference to mechanisms to facilitate the movement of funds in the various national currencies, the unification of accounting nomenclature and monetary statistics, and the possibility of a Central American stock market.

A Central American Institute of Industrial Research and Technology, opened in 1956 at Guatemala City with the help of United Nations Technical Assistance funds, has become an important center for testing materials, investigating new industrial possibilities, and encouraging the adoption of standards. An Advanced School of Public Administration was opened at San José de Costa Rica in 1953. The Council of Central American Universities has drawn up a plan for integration of studies at the graduate level.

Economic integration in Central America has been facilitated by progress on the Inter-American Highway, financed largely by the United States government. Studies have been made of further coordination of transportation and communications in the area. A commercial television network, with stations in each of the five republics, was formed in 1960. The United States Agency for International Development has financed the preparation of a regional transportation plan, and the United Nations is developing a regional telecommunications program.

It was originally anticipated by officials of the United Nations Economic Commission for Latin America and others interested in the problem, that progress toward a Latin American common market would have to proceed, within a general regional framework, through a series of subregional customs unions or free trade areas, of which the Central American project would serve as a sort of guinea pig. Studies were made of the prospects in other regions, such as the Southern Zone of South America and Gran Colombia. The Southern Zone was of special importance, since nearly two-thirds of the entire intra-Latin American trade is normally between two countries, Argentina and Brazil. The problem was also becoming urgent for the southern countries as the time for resumption of convertibility of currencies approached. During the preceding two decades, trade had been conducted through bilateral clearing arrangements by means of which it was possible for the countries to grant preferential treatment to each other's products. Such exceptions to most-favored-nation treatment were permitted by the General Agreement on Tariffs and Trade (GATT) and by the International Monetary Fund so long as inconvertibility and balance-of-payments problems persisted. It was on the initiative of Argentina, Brazil, Uruguay, and Chile that a new regional trade formula was devised, which led to the signing of the Treaty of Montevideo on February 18, 1960, creating the Latin American Free Trade Zone, with seven original members (Paraguay, Peru, and Mexico, in addition to the four sponsors). Colombia and Ecuador have subsequently joined the Association (LAFTA) created by the treaty. Cuba's bid to join LAFTA was rejected at the second meeting of the contracting parties. It is open to adherence by all other Latin American republics, and has become the nucleus or "chosen instrument" for the achievement of closer Latin American economic integration.

The Latin American Free Trade Association follows the precedent of the European Free Trade Association ("Outer Seven"), in that each signatory will retain its own tariffs on imports from without the area, but one major difference is that the European agreement provides for automatic annual reductions of duties on nonagricultural trade between member countries, while in LAFTA the reductions must be negotiated periodically. The Treaty of Montevideo provides for two series of negotiations with a view to the gradual elimination of "duties, charges, and other restrictions" on practically all intra-area trade over a twelve-year period.

The flexibility of this procedure, combined with the large number of exceptions and escape clauses written into the agreement, has caused some observers to wonder whether or not effective solutions will be obtained on the really difficult problems before the expiration of the twelve-year period. The contracting parties are required to reduce duties and charges only on those items actually being traded in substantial volume, but other items may be included, and the member countries are encouraged to enter "mutual agreements on complementarity by industrial sectors." At present, intra-Latin American trade comprises less than 10 per cent of the area's total international trade, and consists largely of staple agricultural commodities and petroleum.

The treaty does not oblige any country to reduce barriers on any particular commodity, nor to make any substantial reduction of the average level of duties. Since most of the existing zonal trade is of a noncompetitive character, the periodic reductions called for in the treaty (annual reductions to be equivalent to not less than 8 per cent of the weighted average of duties and charges applicable to third countries, such reductions to comprise the national schedule, which may be renegotiated before the end of the treaty period; and a common schedule of irrevocable reductions to be negotiated at three-year intervals) need not touch any sensitive nerves, especially since the various escape clauses or safeguards confer wide latitude on the contracting parties. Furthermore, member countries are authorized to limit agricultural imports "to the amount required to meet the deficit in internal production." The first round of reductions in charges under the national schedules went into effect on January 1, 1962.

The possibilities for substantially expanded area trade are believed to lie chiefly in the negotiation of agreements providing for the mutual interchange of industrial products. So far, however, only two of these "complementarity" agreements have been concluded, one involving statistical machines, and the other electronic valves. Brazil was hopeful that Mexico would buy its automotive parts, rather than develop parts industries of its own, but late in 1962 Mexico decided to go ahead with her own plans for a completely Mexican automotive industry. Steel products and petrochemicals may offer some possibilities of a complementary character.

LAFTA has had a good press, on the whole, both within the participating countries and abroad, reflecting the fact that the regional solution to political and economic problems is now alamode. Spokesmen for some industrial groups have expressed doubts, but other industrialists, having excess capacity, are hopeful of expanding sales in preferential markets. Argentine opinion has been divided into two camps. On the one hand, there is a group that wants Argentina to recover its lost economic leadership in South America and expand its trade and financial relationship with adjacent states. Another group has misgivings on three counts: First, since during the last two decades Argentina has tended to fall behind Brazil and Mexico in industrial progress and technology, the country is not in a position to lead from strength in the bargaining over manufactured goods; second, as most agricultural products are excluded from the obligatory reductions, Argentina loses its chief advantage; and third, the feeling that a regional trade arrangement is, at best, marginal to Argentina's main economic problems: the revival of production, rehabilitation of transport, and restoration of its export trade in those basic products in which Argentina has its chief comparative advantage internationally.

A few voices have been raised among economists to express doubts about the alleged advantages of regional integration in general, and LAFTA in particular. The views of one critic may be summarized as follows: [20] The advantage of integration must come from (1) economies of scale resulting from optimum-scale operations in additional lines of economic activity; (2) improved terms of trade derived from enhanced bargaining power; and (3) improved allocation of resources arising out of the elimination of inefficient producers within the area. The studies of several economists (Joe S. Bain and J. Jewkes) are cited to show that an increase in the size of the market does not necessarily result in any significant economies of scale. Improved bargaining power depends upon a significantly greater share of control of some products, and the exercising of the power in concert. Much of the economic effectiveness of integration hinges on the advantages of competition, reducing domestic or import costs by eliminating inefficient producers, and forcing others to rationalize and to lower costs of production. Competitive forces operate most effectively when two or more countries are at about the same stage of economic development. Countries with a head start in industrialization will strengthen their position. (The Treaty of Montevideo contains special provisions relating to the less-developed countries. Paraguay and Ecuador have been classified as less developed, and hence entitled to receive special treatment.) The article concludes, "By itself integration does not necessarily improve investment prospects or promote growth."

Various students of customs unions and regional groupings have pointed out that great disparities in stages of economic growth or in the structure of the economies tends to keep the benefits to a minimum. Excessive state intervention in the economy may nullify the gains from economic unions through misallocation of resources.

Despite these dangers, many observers feel that the common market movement will justify itself by providing a new dynamism to the faltering Latin American economies. Furthermore, there are indirect gains resulting from closer attention on the part of the participating countries to some problems that have heretofore been neglected.

Economic integration of Latin America has received a strong endorsement in the Charter of Punta del Este establishing the Alliance for Progress.[21] In the application of financial resources under the Alliance for Progress, it is recommended that special attention be given to investment in multinational projects and the financing of industrial production. The agreement also bespeaks the cooperation of the Inter-American Development Bank and other international financial institutions.

LATIN AMERICA AND THE EUROPEAN COMMON MARKET

LAFTA, like the European Free Trade Association (The Outer Seven) is in some respects a reflex gesture occasioned by the organization of the European Economic Community (The Six), with strong United States backing. There has been widespread concern among Latin American producers of tropical products over the preferences accorded to former African colonies of The Six on such items as coffee, cacao, bananas, and sugar. Following protests by the Organization of American States, and pursuant to pressure from the United States, the common EEC tariff was reduced on some of these items when imported in crude form. However, the rates on simply processed materials are much higher. For example, the duty is 9.6 per cent on coffee beans but 24 per cent on soluble coffee. Likewise, the import duty is 5.4 per cent on cocoa beans but 20 per cent on cocoa butter and up to 80 per cent on chocolate products.

Increased self-sufficiency within the Common Market in such products as meat and grain could be serious for Argentina and Uruguay. Great Britain is an even more important market for these temperate zone products, and should it become associated with EEC and take larger amounts of these items from the Continent, the impact would be serious on South American suppliers. The EEC countries now take about one-fifth of Latin America's aggregate exports.

Six Latin American countries now have diplomatic missions accredited to the EEC in the hope of influencing decisions favorable to their interests. Late in 1962 the OAS also opened a regional office in Paris. In practice, the Latin American countries are as much concerned with internal fiscal measures of some of the members of the EEC, such as heavy excises on coffee levied by Germany and Italy, as they are worried about the tariff rates. The Latin Americans are also anxious to establish the principle that they should receive concessions on manufactured and semimanufactured products as well as on raw materials.

The interest of Latin Americans in the European Economic Community is political and psychological as well as economic, since they are worried as to just where they will fit into the Grand Design. Most of them feel that they are very much on the periphery. This feeling tends to strengthen the Latin American conviction that the countries of the area must hasten economic and political integration in order to maximize their influence in Atlantic councils. On several occasions, the President of the Inter-American Development Bank has expressed the conviction "that political complementation must be advanced as an indispensable requirement to the development of our countries, and to the assumption by Latin America of its own vigorous and independent role in the world in which we live."[22]

In conclusion, it may be noted that a Pan American Economic Union, to include the United States and Canada, has been proposed on numerous occasions. This was a favorite theme of the late Carlos Dávila, who held briefly such important positions as President of Chile and Secretary-General of the Organization of American States.[23] Possibly as the result of his association with Dávila during the course of his wartime experiences, Nelson Rockefeller has made similar proposals on various occasions. But there is no reason to believe that the Latin Americans would be disposed to open up their markets to unrestricted competition from American manufacturers, any more than The Six in Europe want the United States as a member. In 1889, at the first Inter-American Conference, the United States proposed a customs union of the Americas but it was rejected. Latin America (and other areas as well, for that matter) would, no doubt, like to see the United States provide an assured market at good prices for their export products, including processed goods, without any corresponding commitment on their part. Actually, this is virtually the deal the Associated Overseas States expect to receive from the European Economic Community, since the preferences extended to the former territories are in effect unilateral.

Notes to Chapter IV

1. Even in the United States between one-fourth and one-fifth of the population lives under conditions of squalor and misery. Despite the economic and technological dualism in Mexico and Brazil, the commercial sectors of these countries expanded rapidly during the last two decades. The rates of growth in these two countries have been among the highest in Latin America. Meanwhile, the growth rates in Argentina, Uruguay, and Chile (the three countries after Venezuela having the highest per capita income in Latin America) have slowed down.

2. Lecture by Dr. André Franco Montoro at Georgetown University, Washington, D.C., February 14, 1962. Dr. Franco is Secretary General of the Christian Democratic Party in Brazil.

3. United Nations, Economic Commission for Latin America, *Economic Survey of Latin America 1954*, p. 22 and footnote 22.

4. Ifigenia Martínez de Navarrete, "Notas sobre la distribución del ingreso nacional de México," *Investigación económica*, XIX (Primer trimestre de 1959), 31-39.

5. "Problemas económicas de Chile," *El Trimestre Económico*, XXVI (México, D. F., abril-junio de 1959), 170.

6. *Ibid.*, pp. 195-96.

7. International Bank for Reconstruction and Development, *The Economic Development of Nicaragua*. Report of a mission organized by the Bank at the request of the government of Nicaragua. (Baltimore: The Johns Hopkins Press, 1953), p. 99.

8. Frank Whitson Fetter, "The Need for Postwar Foreign Lending," *American Economic Review*, XXXIII, No. 1, Part 2, Supplement (March, 1943), 343.

9. Celso Furtado, "Reflexiones sobre la prerevolución brasileña," *El Trimestre Económico*, XXIX (México, D.F., 1962), 373-84.

10. *The Economics of Under-Developed Countries*. Cambridge Economic Handbooks (Chicago: University of Chicago Press, 1957), p. 29.

11. F. J. Pedler, *Economic Geography of West Africa* (London and Toronto: Longmans, Green & Co., 1955), p. 167.

12. United Nations, Department of Economic Affairs, *The Economic Development of Latin America and its Principal Problems* (New York, 1950).

13. See chapter IX.

14. United Nations, Economic Commission for Latin America, *The Economic Development of Latin America;* also, *Problemas teóricos y prácticos del crecimiento económico*, E/CN. 12/221 (Mexico, D.F., 1952); and *Analyses and Projections of Economic Development. I. An Introduction to the Technique of Programming*. Prepared by ECLA (New York, 1955).

15. ECLA, *International Cooperation in a Latin American Development Policy* (New York, 1954), pp. 18-19, 129.

16. *A Proposal: Key to an Effective Foreign Policy*, Appendix, Table 1 (1st ed., New York: Harper and Brothers, 1957), p. 155.

17. Pan American Union, *Financing of Economic Development in Latin America* (Washington, D.C., 1958), p. 290.

18. See chapter IX.

19. "Recent Literature on the Economic Development of Backward Areas," *Quarterly Journal of Economics*, LXVIII (November, 1954), 600.

20. Robert L. Allen, "Integration in Less Developed Areas," *Kyklos*, XIV (1961), Fasc. 3, 315-36.

21. See chapter IX.

22. Felipe Herrera, at the Conference of the Contracting Parties of the Latin American Free Trade Association, Second Period of Meetings, in Mexico City on August 28, 1962 (press release, p. 5). Three weeks earlier, at a Conference on Tensions of Development in the Western Hemisphere, held at Salvador, Bahia, Brazil, Sr. Herrera had stated that the area "must squarely face up to the need for political integration," and added: "Latin America is not a group of nations: it is one great disjointed nation" (IADB, press release).

23. See, for example, *We of the Americas* (New York: Ziff-Davis Publishing Co., 1949).

–V–

The Role of Private Foreign Investment

S ince the war the promotion of private investment abroad has been a cardinal principle of American foreign policy. Private enterprise and investment became, along with the expansion of trade and freedom of access to raw materials, part of the package of classic economic liberalism formulated during the war as the recipe for world reconstruction. Part of the doctrine was embodied in the Atlantic Charter, and other aspects were spelled out in the Master Lend-Lease Agreement between the United States and the United Kingdom in 1942. In the preparations for the postwar conferences on trade and finance it was assumed that all countries, including the Soviet Union, would accept these principles, the details of which would then be worked out through the new international organizations.

Private Investors and United States Protection

As early as 1943 the leading businessmen's associations, national and international, had begun pressing for "the active prosecution of a program of negotiating and concluding with foreign nations treaties that will establish and define generally the conditions under which foreign traders and enterprises may operate, and afford that reasonable security without which the expansion of trade and foreign investment cannot be fully realized."[1]* During the closing months of World War II, the Department of State, with the cooperation of the Department of Commerce, launched a program for the negotiation of up-to-date Treaties of Friendship, Commerce and Navigation (FCN) to provide a firm basis for the diplomatic and juridical protection of United States' interests abroad.

In practice this program encountered heavy going. From the end

*Notes to chapter V are on page 142.

of the war until the end of 1959, only one new FCN treaty had been put into force with a Latin American country (Nicaragua). Efforts have also been made to negotiate multilateral agreements favorable to private investment, in addition to the bilateral FCN treaties, but these attempts have been even less successful. The Charter for an International Trade Organization, adopted at Havana in 1948, contained some provisions that were considered unacceptable by businessmen in creditor countries, such as article 12, which recognized that members of the organization would have the right "to determine whether and to what extent and upon what terms it will allow future investments" and also to establish requirements as to the ownership and other matters affecting existing as well as future investments. Attempts to obtain ratification of the charter were abandoned. At the Ninth International Conference of American States at Bogotá in 1948, an economic agreement was concluded, but with reservations by most of the signatories, including the United States. The Latin American countries insisted that the provisions of the agreement "should be subordinated to the constitutional laws of each country." After unsuccessful efforts to reconcile differences, the project was dropped.

The attitude shown by many members of the United Nations Economic and Social Council has also been a disappointment to investors. A report issued in December, 1947, by a subcommittee of the Council set forth the views that have found frequent echo subsequently, that "experience has proved that direct private investments are accompanied by the dangers of harmful economic and political interference," going on to state that private or governmental loans or credits are preferable to direct private investments.

A larger volume of international public investment (i.e., by the World Bank, the Export-Import Bank and similar institutions) was urged in a report submitted to the Economic Conference at Quintandinha, Brazil, 1954, by the secretariat of the United Nations Economic Commission for Latin America. Although recognizing an important place for foreign private investment in a wide range of activities, and disclaiming any "ideological considerations" against private capital, the report argued, first, that in view of the urgency of the developmental needs Latin America could not depend upon private capital to come in the required amounts; secondly, that foreign private capital, especially when it occupies a monopoly position such as control of public utilities, has "at times given rise to feelings of mistrust" (adding, "There is no reason to suppose that the attitude of the Latin American public in this respect is any different from that of the public in the United States"); and thirdly, that the yields on private capital are much larger than interest on public money and hence create additional transfer difficulties.[2]

Neither Democratic nor Republican administrations in the United States have been disposed to accept the Latin American point of view, and the United States' delegations at numerous inter-American conferences have returned to the charge over and over again to argue the superior merits of private enterprise and to warn against the danger of "socialistic" state enterprises. The statements made on this subject by Secretary George Humphrey at Quintandinha in November, 1954, and by Secretary Robert Anderson at the Economic Conference of Buenos Aires in August, 1957, were essentially the same as those made by General Marshall and Secretary Averell Harriman at the ill-fated Bogotá Conference in April, 1948. It may also be noted that Point IV of President Truman's Inaugural Address of January 20, 1949, linked guarantees to the investor with guarantees to the people providing the resources and labor, and in his subsequent message to Congress he recommended the enactment of programs of technical assistance and the encouragement of private investment outflow.

Our Counterproductive Tactics

Whatever the merits of private enterprise, which most Latin Americans recognize, there can hardly be any doubt now that our tactics in handling this issue, although achieving some minor successes, have on balance harmed rather than helped the cause of foreign investment. Our tactics have convinced Latin Americans that we are much more interested in promoting private investment than they are in accepting it, and in some cases have created alarm as to our real intentions and hence brought about new restrictions against American companies in their countries.

Our spokesmen have often stated that we have no desire to force capital on any country and that it is indeed up to each nation to attract it in competition with other possible fields for investment, both at home and abroad. This position is clearly stated in the International Code of Fair Treatment for Foreign Investments, approved by the Quebec Congress of the International Chamber of Commerce in 1949, as follows: "But if there is to be a revival of private international investment on a scale sufficient to meet present-day needs, there must first be created a climate of confidence and stability encouraging to the potential investor. The private investor is free to invest or not, as he pleases. If the conditions surrounding the investment are unattractive, he will simply refrain from putting up his money."

Unfortunately, the problem is not one "simply" of putting up or not putting up the money. In the first place, there is the problem of already existing investment. Some very large American firms are almost entirely dependent on their Latin American operations, or depend upon the profits of their Latin American operations for a large part of the sums distributed to the stockholders as dividends. Large utility enterprises have discovered that if they fail to expand to meet growing power needs they will either wither on the vine or be nationalized. In fact, some of the governments have deliberately refused permission to public utility enterprises to charge viable rates as a means of forcing them to sell out or withdraw and leave the field to national concerns.

The statement is frequently made that, in a private enterprise economy, e.g., the United States, investment is a matter for individual or company decision. This is, of course, true but it is not quite the whole truth. Not only have there been, and now are, restraints of both an obligatory and of an advisory character on investment in some areas and under certain conditions, there are also important incentives, such as tax credits, guarantees, loans at favorable rates, diplomatic and consular assistance, and other direct and indirect facilities. Also of great importance is the "climate of opinion" in the United States favorable to foreign investment that has been fostered by both Democratic and Republican administrations since the war. Furthermore, international operations have acquired great social prestige among businessmen and their families.

At any given time a nation's attitude toward foreign trade and investment is institutionally biased. The United States is a world power center, to use the language of the late Professor Erich W. Zimmermann.[3] The United States is one of the active and organizing elements in the world economy, and as a highly industrialized country needs imports of raw materials. United States' petroleum and mining companies have seldom "simply" waited for a country having rich mineral resources to create favorable conditions for investment; on the contrary, with the active aid of the United States government they have steadily pursued opportunities, and have vigorously opposed any alternative methods of developing such resources. We not only demand the "open door" (i.e., most-favored-nation treatment) but also insist that other countries create conditions favorable to outside investment. This preoccupation is reflected in the study, *Resources for Freedom,* prepared by the President's Materials Policy Committee,[4] in which the conclusion is reached that "a tremendous expansion in foreign investment is necessary if the needs of the future are to be met."[5]

There is undoubtedly a continuing need for foreign capital in Latin America and perhaps even more for foreign initiative and technology in many fields, if economic growth is to be maintained or accelerated. The problem is to find a modus vivendi that will permit the transfer of these factors of production under conditions that are mutually acceptable. One could argue endlessly about mistakes on both sides in the past, and some of these will be mentioned hereafter as throwing light on present-day issues, but it is more important to consider calmly and objectively the structural and psychological changes that have occurred in Latin America and in the world, and how these relate to the present situation.

Latin America's Continuing Dependence upon Foreign Capital

Historically, the economic development of Latin America has been passive and derivative to a far greater degree than was the case in the United States or in some of the other developed countries. Before the word "underdeveloped" was coined to describe the poorer nations, the Latin Americans frequently referred to their economies as colonial. One of the characteristics of such an economy is that it is a net debtor on international account and depends in large measure on foreign capital and enterprise, as well as for most of its technology.[6]

The failure of this region to develop a higher rate of saving and investment was clearly not due to lack of natural resources, but rather to the political and institutional structures of the countries, reflecting the scale of values inherited from the Hispanic peninsula. The Spanish and Portuguese conquerors and adventurers who established themselves in the Americas were certainly not lacking in zeal or enterprise, but their value systems were not conducive to saving nor to scientific research and technology. When the Spanish colonies and Brazil became independent they did not turn for assistance to their mother countries, which were in any case impoverished and technologically backward, despite, or perhaps on account of, the enormous inflow of treasure from their colonies during the preceding three centuries.

The achievement of political independence did not automatically bring any accretion of personal liberty or prosperity to the peoples of South and Middle America; in fact, the first half century of independence was one of penury and political upheaval in most of the region. During the last quarter of the nineteenth century, however, there was an economic renaissance, and Latin America shared in the world-wide expansion of trade and economic growth.

The sixty years from about 1870 to 1929 might be called the classic period of economic development. There was a great outpouring of migrants and capital, chiefly from Europe, improvement of transportation and communications, and a huge expansion of international trade. The movements of capital, people, and goods were closely interrelated and in many respects mutually interdependent.

On the eve of World War I total foreign investment in Latin America was estimated at $8.5 billion, of which 43 per cent was British and 20 per cent American. The latter was concentrated chiefly in Mexico and Cuba, while over 80 per cent of the British investment was in South America, with 47 per cent of the total in the River Plate. French investments of $1.2 billion shrank heavily during and after the war, and nonresident German investments of nearly $1 billion were largely wiped out. Despite some losses, the British investment in 1938 was approximately the same as in 1914, but by the 1950's had been reduced more than two-thirds through debt readjustments, expropriations in Mexico, sale of some securities, and repatriation of the large railway and utility holdings in Argentina and Brazil. United States investments rose rapidly during the first World War and during the 1920's, and then declined (expropriations in Mexico, readjustment of government bonds, reduced earning capacity during the depression) until mid-World War II, when another period of expansion began. At the end of 1959 United States private direct or business investments had a book value of $8.2 billion, after substantial writedowns of assets to take account of currency depreciation in some countries.

Data for European investments in Latin America at this time are not strictly comparable with our own figures. A large part of the old investment in railways, port works, utilities and the like has been liquidated, and most of the government bonds have been paid off. Most of the new investment in Latin America has been American, oil production (chiefly in Venezuela and more recently in Argentina), oil distribution in most of the countries, manufacturing plants, mining (iron ore in Venezuela, Peru, Chile; manganese in Brazil; copper in Peru and Chile), merchandising (e.g., Sears), aviation, hotels, and expansion of utility operations in some countries. British investments in government securities, lands, manufacturing plants, mining and oil, department stores, railways, meat packing, shipping, airlines, cables and telegraph, and miscellaneous activities, are perhaps in the neighborhood of $500 million. Canadian investments were placed at $322 million in 1955, but there has since been some reduction as the result of the purchase by the Mexican government of the controlling shares in the Mexican Light and Power Company (a Toronto corporation until recently controlled by Sofina of Belgium).

Since the war, German firms have invested $170 million in Latin America (over half of which is in Brazil), and have gotten back most of the patents and trademarks that were taken over by local governments during the war. It is difficult to make a reliable estimate of the investments of other continental European countries. These governments refrain, wisely no doubt, from bragging about the amount of their investments, and the companies operating in Latin America tend to take on local color. Many Europeans take advantage of what amounts to dual citizenship. French firms have been active since the war, especially in construction and trading operations. One of the largest European investments is in the Shell Oil Company, and Philips of Eindhaven has electronics plants in several countries. The big utility holding company, Sofina, is Belgian-controlled but other nationalities are represented. Its major property, CADE in Argentina, has recently been reorganized and is being nationalized. There are Belgians active in a wide variety of fields in Latin America, and the Luxemburg combine, ARBED, has an interest in the Belgo-Mineira steel works in Brazil. Several large Italian firms (Fiat, Montecatini, Pirelli, Lepetit) have branches in Latin America, and Innocenti has taken over a big contract in Venezuela. Of course, Italian immigrants are well represented among the successful businessmen of every South American country. There are many prosperous Portuguese in Brazil. Swiss have holdings in various large concerns active in Latin America. Japan's investments may be estimated at from $25 to $30 million.

Misgivings about One Country's Outsized Investments

It is precisely the size of the American investment, several times as large as that of all other nationals combined, that is cause for concern and one of the chief factors in the growing anti-Americanism in Latin America. How can that be, the shocked American asks, when the Latin Americans complain of the lack of capital and of our neglect of them as compared to other areas of the world? The answer is, they want and need capital, but are not prepared to accept it on terms that will result in what they consider to be an undue amount of foreign influence in the economy. Now there was a time when foreign help was needed so badly that some political leaders were willing to accept it along with the risks of political or military intervention, but even then there were protests and exceptions. General Juan Vicente Gómez, dictator of Venezuela from 1908 to his death in 1935, was careful to pay off the foreign debt that had caused international complications for his predecessors. Even General Porfirio

Díaz, whose government was called "the mother of foreigners and the stepmother of Mexicans," became concerned about undue foreign influence and took steps to reduce foreign insurance and banking operations and brought under control of the Mexican government the principal rail lines of the country. International lawyers and ministers of foreign affairs were also busy fashioning legal weapons against intervention, such as the Drago Doctrine (that armed force should not be used to collect debts against a sovereign state) and the Calvo Doctrine (that states owe no greater duties or obligations to foreigners than they owe to their own citizens).

The military interventions by the United States in the Caribbean from the turn of the century until the mid-1920's have not been forgotten and undoubtedly have sharpened the misgivings regarding disproportionate foreign holdings. But the present-day attitude reflects chiefly the changes that have occurred during recent decades. The strong currents of nationalism have stimulated pride and the desire for national (and individual) power and prestige. These psychological factors are even more important than the economic motivations on which our policy has placed so much emphasis. During the course of a visit to the Amazon Valley in 1947 the author made enquiry as to why the Brazilian authorities had not encouraged the Ford organization to continue its rubber plantation on the Tapajós River, and was told that "we cannot afford to have the best operation in the Amazon Valley controlled by foreigners." At the time of our visit the plantation was managed by an American agronomist who had become naturalized through marriage with the daughter of the Brazilian in charge of agricultural research operations in the north.

Until recently the Latin American governments were so anxious to encourage new industries that they tended to ignore the protests of rising local industrialists who found it difficult to compete against foreign firms disposing of superior technical and financial resources, but more recently several governments (Brazil and Mexico, for example) have been more selective in granting permits to operate in the country. In 1960 the President of the São Paulo Federation of Industries frankly stated that they "were not especially eager to encourage any further competition" in the form of additional American investment. Many American firms have sought a way out of this dilemma through joint ventures, licensing, or royalty arrangements.

This changing attitude is indicative of the growth of the spirit of industrial and business enterprise that has taken place. Important groups of entrepreneurs have appeared not only in São Paulo but also in Buenos Aires, Santiago de Chile, Lima, Bogotá and Medellín, Mexico City and Monterrey, and in Havana before Castro. The older group of bankers, merchants, and industrialists tend to retain their international ties and to look askance at the pushing "new men" aflame with nationalism. But the new men are winning the battle. Actually, this increasing interest in business and machines is indicative that real grass roots economic development is taking hold. The very fact that Latin Americans want business opportunities for their sons and nephews and brothers-in-law makes life complicated for the foreign investor, but it is at the same time an encouraging sign for those who put their faith in economic development.

We have been inclined to blame all criticism of foreign investment on the communists, but in fact the real forces back of the harassment are the wealthy, the rising industrialists, the military, traditional conservative forces like the Church and the Hispanicists, and, of course, leftists and politicians seeking a patriotic and popular issue. The nationalization of the petroleum industry in Brazil found strong backing among the military and among some of the most powerful financial groups in the country, but the communists were the ones who got out in the streets and painted signs *O petroleo e nosso* ("the petroleum is ours") on walls and billboards.

Incidentally, the fact that the Soviet bloc countries do not have investments in Latin America has been one of the reasons why Latin Americans have not been inclined to take the communist menace too seriously. This parallels the prewar attitude of many Latin Americans toward Nazi Germany. A friend of the writer, a very influential Mexican, once argued seriously that it would be a good thing if Germany had some colonies in the Caribbean; this would provide protection to the Latin American countries by setting up a counterweight to the United States.

VALUABLE CONTRIBUTIONS OF AMERICAN FIRMS

It is important to keep in mind that the real problem arises where the total volume of foreign investment appears disproportionate in relation to the aggregate national economy, or is unduly conspicuous, rather than as the result of the shortcomings of particular individuals or companies (although the latter may be a contributing factor). In practice, most of the American companies have done a superb job and have made an outstanding contribution to the economies of the countries in which they operate, and furthermore have contributed generously to local civic, cultural, and charitable undertakings. In fact, in some countries their very virtues have been the chief cause of complaint, since local concerns consider their competition unfair. (One is reminded of the complaints of Californians against Japanese settlers some decades ago; the Japanese were wicked enough to work for low wages or small profits.)

The United States Department of Commerce recently published a study of the economic impact of United States' investment in Latin America.[7] This survey brings out that the operations of American companies in Latin America in 1959 gave employment to about one million Latin Americans, involving a disbursement of $1.4 billion in wages and salaries, paid in taxes an amount equal to one-fifth of the aggregate Latin American revenues, and accounted for one-third of the total Latin American exports. These figures are certainly impressive and provide evidence of the notable service American interests have rendered in laying the indispensable foundations for economic growth, including the training of many thousands of Latin Americans. At the same time it is likely that many Latin Americans will be even more impressed by another aspect of this statistical analysis, namely, the formidable size of the foreign slice of the economy. If we assume that foreign companies other than American account for 10 per cent of Latin American exports, then nearly half of the total is in foreign hands.

One of the mistakes that is sometimes made is to assume that the contribution made by foreign investment (or foreign aid, for that matter) varies directly with the volume. In fact, an undue amount of foreign investment not only inevitably raises political problems,

132

but also can be a positive drag on real economic development. A large influx of funds from any source, whether it be investment or aid, can bring about a temporary flush of prosperity, and make a few insiders rich, as has happened frequently in the past, but, as history shows, real self-generating economic development does not necessarily follow. An area can ingest only modest proportions of outside factors at a time, and larger doses are apt to produce pathological symptoms. Isn't it a *reductio ad absurdum* to insist, as we have done, that in countries like Guatemala, where foreign-controlled activities are ubiquitous, the one thing needed for development is more foreign capital?

The history of the United States has frequently been cited as demonstrating the advantages to be gained from foreign capital. It is no doubt true that our traditional hospitality to foreign peoples, capital, ideas, and, within limits, goods, did much to accelerate our expansion. But the differences between our experience and that of Latin America are such that the analogy is apt to be more irritating than convincing. Many persons of European birth, and some of Asian origin, have played important roles in our economic development, but in most cases they became American citizens and ceased to be a foreign element. We do not think of Andrew Carnegie as a foreigner. The fact that sociopolitical conditions in Latin America did not encourage foreign investors there to identify themselves more intimately with the country of domicile throws light on some of the circumstances that have retarded development in that area. But in recent decades Latin American countries have become increasingly sensitive on this point, and for better or for worse have enacted numerous restrictions on the activities of foreign nationals and of companies of foreign registry.

In the United States foreign long-term capital was never more than a small fraction of the total economy, and it never took over control or management of basic industries. Students of our economic history have pointed out that our borrowing and imports of capital before World War I reflected the underdeveloped state of our banking system and capital markets, rather than our inability to match current domestic investment with current savings. Even during the periods when the United States was borrowing heavily abroad it was remitting huge sums to Europe, as interest and amortization of debts, tourist expenditures, and immigrant remittances.

Americans early showed a decided aptitude for business and mechanics. As indicated above, we did not hesitate to borrow ideas wherever we could find them, but it was chiefly Americans who took the initiative in developing domestic resources. The large amounts of European capital invested in American railways undoubtedly accelerated railway construction, including the construction of many parallel and competing lines, but it may be questioned whether a smaller foreign investment would not have been more advantageous.

During most of its history the United States has had a stable political system. As a large country with important military potential, there have been no military interventions, although Professor Leland Hamilton Jenks reports that "it was embarrassing for an American to be in London in the winter of 1842-43," owing to resentment at default of various states of the Union.[8]

Although the United States has followed a fairly liberal policy toward foreigners, there have been, and are, numerous restrictions on immigration, employment, and investment. In the United States a large portion of the jurisdiction over doing business belongs to the several states, all of which have some restrictions on foreign activity. There are also important federal restrictions.

PRIVATE ENTERPRISE VS. STATE INTERVENTION

As indicated above, our support of private investment has been turned into a crusade for the cause of private enterprise. Our position was laid down by General Marshall at Bogotá on April 1, 1948, in the following words: "My Government is prepared to increase the scale of assistance it has been giving to the economic develoment of the American Republics. But it is beyond the capacity of the United States Government to finance more than a small portion of the vast development needed. The capital required through the years must come from private sources, both domestic and foreign. As the experience of the United States has shown, progress can be achieved best through individual effort and the use of private resources. Encouragement should therefore be given to the increase of investment capital from internal as well as external sources. It is obvious that foreign capital will naturally gravitate most readily to countries where it is accorded fair and equitable treatment." This position has been repeated, in almost identical words, at every inter-American conference since 1948.

Unfortunately, we have at no time been willing to recognize the real nub of the issue, and have merely repeated the shibboleth of private enterprise. In view of the long tradition of highly centralized government in Latin America as well as in Spain and Portugal, it would be surprising if there were not more sympathy for state intervention than there has been historically in the United States or other English-speaking countries. But at the present time Latin America is in roughly what might be called the Grant era in the United States. A friend of the writer who has spent most of his life in Latin America is authority for the statement that "there are more robber barons in Latin America than there were in the United States in the 1870's and 1880's." Neither American nor Latin American businessmen object to government intervention when it is favorable to them or is considered necessary for national defense. Private investors are not as a rule prepared to put their money in railways, utilities, or pioneer industrial ventures, because they can make larger profits elsewhere, but they prefer government control of these activities rather than leave them in foreign hands. Most of the Latin American governments have shown a disposition to bring in local private capital in such enterprises as far as possible, and in some cases (e.g., the Huachipato steel works in Chile) ownership has passed into private hands. But there are some forces making for continued government control. Among these are bureaucratic empire builders and the military. Representatives of these groups make frequent trips to the United States, where they have learned some useful lessons in the bureaucratic arts, as well as other types of technical assistance.

Now it is unfortunately true that many, perhaps most, of the large state enterprises in Latin America are poorly managed, heavily overloaded with personnel, and that deficits from state enterprises are among the chief causes of the continuing inflation in several important countries. The late Dwight Morrow, when he was Ambassador to Mexico, tried to persuade the Mexican government to divest itself of control of the National Railways (and other state enterprises) and pointed out that there was little hope of getting satisfactory financial or economic results out of the system until it was freed from political influences. Mr. Morrow was not successful in this endeavor, nor is it likely that any general turnover of state enterprises will occur on a significant scale in any Latin American country (or elsewhere, for that matter) in the foreseeable future.

Our determination to turn promotion of private investment into an ideological struggle has been a boon not only to European competitors and Canada, but also to the Soviet bloc, which has thus received an unearned increment of popularity in Latin America. There are, of course, some large American companies which are not happy with our policy. They made huge profits out of ECA-financed sales to government enterprises in Europe, and would not be averse to repeating the process in Latin America. In fact, much of the Latin American insistence on larger aid programs for that area has been inspired by Americans having an interest in larger expenditures.

Our basic dilemma arises from our mistake in assuming what amounts to a moral commitment to provide all nations with the capital and know-how required for economic development. We are only now slowly and painfully coming around to a realization that economic development involves a lot more than capital, much more indeed than capital plus the initiative and technology that goes along frequently with private investment.

The fact is that through our foreign investments we have given hostages to fortune. At the Tenth Inter-American Conference in 1954, during the course of committee discussion which involved criticism by several delegates of what they considered to be the excessive influence of United States' investment and the drain on exchange reserves created by profit remittances, the Bolivian representative spoke up to justify American investments in his country on the ground that United States grant aid *exceeded* profit remittances from Bolivia. This point was not lost on the other delegates, as is shown by the fact that we have since that time had to put increasing amounts of United States government funds into Latin America in order to ransom our existing investments. Furthermore, the ransom price is steadily rising. Castro put it at $30 billion in a speech at

Buenos Aires in 1959, and at Bogotá, Brazilian spokesmen raised the ante to $40 billion.

What of the future? Is the day of foreign investment over? By no means. There is still an important place for private investment, although we are probably in for a period of readjustment and consolidation in some areas. Our high-pressure salesmanship of private investment in the fifties had some of the get-rich-quick attitude of investment bankers in the twenties.

As real self-generating economic development takes hold in countries like Mexico and Brazil, and the dimensions of the home-grown sector become larger, foreign investment will be less conspicuous and less objectionable, especially if the foreign sector is not concentrated in the hands of any one country. Hence we should adopt the soft sell on United States participation and welcome investments from other countries. The Latin American Free Trade Association and the Central American treaties of economic integration may create new opportunities for foreign investment, but on terms yet to be worked out.

Mexico's Recent Policies

It is not likely that the solution will be exactly the same in all countries, but an interesting example is provided by the evolution of Mexican attitudes. One of the avowed purposes of the Mexican Revolution, embodied in the Constitution of 1917, was the reduction of foreign economic influence, especially in connection with lands, subsoil ownership, and basic industries. This has involved, at various stages, a considerable amount of expropriation, particularly in connection with lands and petroleum properties. Railways and utilities were bought out after they had been softened up by refusing rate increases necessary to keep them out of the red. Recently the tempo of nationalization or domestication has been stepped up. The Mexican government bought the properties of the American and Foreign Power Company and of the California Electric Power Company. It also purchased the Belgian Sofina 40 per cent holdings of the Mexican Light and Power Company, long the principal utility operation in Mexico. In May, 1960, the government announced its plan to redeem, several years ahead of schedule, the outstanding balance of its old bonded foreign debt, totaling $37 million. Control of the formerly American-owned Consolidada steel company was purchased by Altos Hornos, an official enterprise. Most significant of all was the mining law effective April, 1961, providing for the eventual Mexicanization of the huge mining industry (of which about 85 per cent has been under the control of United States investors and most of the remainder held in Europe), to be achieved by means of penalty taxation against companies having less than 51 per cent Mexican ownership. The law did not call for state ownership, but owing to the difficulty of finding private capitalists able and willing to buy the stock of the mining companies, the government has been considering a plan to buy control of the companies and then offer stock to Mexicans. The Mexican government also has bought out several airlines.

Mexican private interests, aided by liberal government financing in some cases, have acquired control of a number of the country's largest and oldest manufacturing industries, in steel, textiles, paper, and tobacco, as well as the principal telephone systems.

Mexico has received substantial financial assistance from the Export-Import Bank of Washington, the World Bank, and the International Finance Corporation, but is beginning to look primarily to private capital markets. Stock of the Industria Eléctrica de México has been listed on the New York Stock Exchange since 1945. Later, steps were taken to obtain the permission of the Securities and Exchange Commission of Washington to list securities of the telephone company and of the steel tubing plant known as TAMSA. Banking credits were obtained in New York and Paris for PEMEX, the government oil company, and a French loan was received for an electric plant on the Balsas River. But Mexico's biggest coup was the loan of $100 million obtained from the Prudential Life Insurance Company of America early in 1960.

Mexico has also recently shown a disposition to restrict foreign investment in certain industries to minority holdings. Du Pont was required to accept 51 per cent Mexican capital participation in its titanium dioxide plant before receiving permission to proceed with construction. Production of basic petrochemical products has been reserved to PEMEX.

Despite heavy disinvestments, direct investments of United States individuals and companies in Mexico rose from $286 million in 1943 to $759 million at the close of 1959, and there are also substantial investments by Canada, the United Kingdom, Germany, Sweden, Italy, and other countries. Mexico has officially encouraged trade with, and investment from, countries other than the United States but has met with only moderate success. Many Mexican economists have had a large dose of Marxism, but in most cases the Marxian dialectic has been used as a weapon against foreign economic control rather than as an ideological argument against private property or private enterprise. The Mexican government has supplied the capital to ensure the Mexicanization of formerly foreign-owned activities, where private Mexican capital is not available, and to establish or assist in establishing, mixed companies to undertake new industries in their experimental stages. At the same time Mexico has some of the most flourishing groups of hard-headed and successful private entrepreneurs in the Americas.[8]

During recent decades the policy of successive Mexican administrations has been to hold down the income of the workers, thus restricting consumption and permitting large profits to management. The managerial class spends liberally on consumption, both conspicuous and otherwise, but at the same time it reinvests a substantial proportion of its income. A study issued by the International Bank for Reconstruction and Development in 1953 showed that Mexico was spending comparatively little on housing (other than private luxury housing in Mexico City), education and public buildings, and that there had been a shift in the distribution of income in favor of profits and against wages and salaries. The 1954 annual *Economic Survey* of the United Nations Economic Commission for Latin America estimated that the share of profits, interest, and rentals in the net national income rose from 34.5 per cent to 51 per cent between 1939 and 1952, but that the proportion which the propertied sector invested rose only from 19 to 22.6 per cent.

Unlike Mexico, which undertook maneuvers and established restrictions against foreign investment even before the onset of the 1910 revolution, Brazil has traditionally followed a hospitable policy as regards foreign capital. But in recent years Brazil has in some fields shown an aggressively antiforeign attitude at a time when some of the

Central and South American countries were taking a more conciliatory, or even propitiatory, stand. In addition to expropriation of one of the telephone companies, moves to buy out the American-owned utilities, and cancellation of mining concessions, Brazil enacted a law in September, 1962, limiting annual remittances on foreign investment to 10 per cent and refusing to permit reinvested profits to be added to the capitalization base of an enterprise.

The Mexican and Brazilian experiences, as well as developments in other countries, would appear to indicate that in the future a larger proportion of the needs for capital will be supplied through both public and private loans and through portfolio investments than through direct private investments involving foreign control. There has also been considerable spread of joint ventures in which one or more foreign companies provide part of the capital and most of the production techniques in a given enterprise. This is not to say that joint ventures or minority participation by an American company is always the solution. Sears, Roebuck & Company, for example, takes the position that at this stage, at least, its contribution can be made best by complete ownership and control. Nelson Rockefeller discovered that his Venezuelan stockholders had a different view of business than he had, so he sold his hotel enterprise to local investors. On the other hand, some companies (e.g., tire manufacturers) have long preferred a minority equity position, and others have in recent years actively sought to dispose of stock to nationals of the country in which they operate. For example, the American and Foreign Power Company has since World War II sold upwards of $54 million in bonds, debentures, and common stocks to local investors in seven Latin American countries in which their subsidiaries operate.

American public lending agencies like the Export-Import Bank have generally refrained from lending to certain types of publicly owned enterprises, like petroleum companies,[10] and international lending agencies have followed suit. This has been, in a sense, a special exception, since loans have been made for power, transportation, manufacturing industries, and other sectors. It is not without interest to note that even in the heyday of laissez-faire over three-fourths of the large British investment in Latin America was in government securities or in government-guaranteed railway paper. The bulk of the United States investment has always been in direct or business investments, but during the 1920's some $2.2 billion in bonds of Latin American official entities were sold in the United States.

CHANGING UNITED STATES POLICIES

In recent years, American firms and their affiliates in Latin America have received special consideration at the hands of the public lending agencies, such as the Export-Import Bank and the Development Loan Fund, and have been eligible, under the Cooley Amendment [Section 104 (e)] of Public Law No. 480 (the Agricultural Trade Development and Assistance Act), for loans up to 25 per cent of the local currencies received from sales of farm products. In view of the high interest rates prevailing in the Latin American countries, these loan facilities have been a real boon to American firms operating in countries where such arrangements have been put into effect, but they have sometimes been resented by national firms in the country. Brazil has objected strongly to further Cooley Amendment set-aside of currencies for United States firms on the grounds that such loans provide an unfair advantage to such firms, which already possess greater financial and technical resources than their Brazilian competitors, and furthermore, that the Cooley funds permit United States firms to increase their net worth without additional dollar imports and thus increase profit remittances in dollars, driving up the cost of exchange and decreasing Brazil's capacity to import. Another drawback of the official loans of all types is that they tend to identify the borrowing firm closely with the United States government and thus destroy the image of private risk capital we have been at such pains to build up. One by-product of this agitation was the enactment of Brazilian legislation, mentioned above, restricting profit remittances to 10 per cent.

New Latin American undertakings have also received extensive financial support from both United States and international financing institutions. Nevertheless the feeling persisted that credit facilities were inadequate, especially for small new enterprises, and that a special Inter-American Fund could perform a valuable service in stimulating private enterprises and promoting economic develop-

141

ment. A proposal along these lines made to the Economic Conference at Quintandinha in 1954 did not receive the support of the United States, but four years later we changed our mind, and set in motion discussions which resulted in the creation of the Inter-American Development Bank, one of whose functions is to aid the smaller private enterprises that cannot qualify for World Bank loans. It will thus be seen that a number of new investment channels are being opened up, and that the details of their operations are still in the formative stage.

NOTES TO CHAPTER V

1. Excerpt from resolutions adopted by the National Foreign Trade Council at its annual convention, 1943.

2. ECLA, *International Cooperation in a Latin American Development Policy,* pp. 6-19, 28, 29, and 39.

3. *World Resources and Industries* (rev. ed., New York: Harper and Brothers, 1951), especially chapter X.

4. (5 vols., Washington, D.C.: Government Printing Office, 1952), known as the Paley Report.

5. *Ibid., Summary of Volume I* (published separately), p. 61.

6. See chapter IV.

7. Samuel Pizer and Frederick Cutler, "United States Foreign Investment; Measures of Growth and Economic Effects," *Survey of Current Business,* XL (September, 1960), 15-24.

8. *The Migration of British Capital to 1875* (New York: Alfred A. Knopf, 1927), p. 104.

9. For a useful recent summary of the situation in Mexico, see Frank Brandenburg, "A Contribution to the Theory of Entrepreneurship and Economic Development: The Case of Mexico," *Inter-American Economic Affairs,* XVI (Winter, 1962), 3-23.

10. Early in the Kennedy administration, the Export-Import Bank announced that it would finance or provide guarantees for equipment sold to government-owned as well as to privately owned oil companies. In practice, this change does not appear to have made any appreciable difference.

–VI–

The New Dollar Diplomacy

Whatever the merits of the Marshall Plan—and they were impressive—it had several unfortunate by-products: it gave a fatal cash bias to our foreign policy, and it created a network of vested interests that are the twentieth century counterpart of the nineteenth century tariff lobby.

The granting of massive aid to Europe also inevitably produced reactions in other areas. As regards Latin America, it was the starting point of a divergence of points of view that has become increasingly difficult to bridge. Most Americans, conscious of the nobility and generosity of their motives, have been outraged by the greed and shortsightedness of the Latins, and their failure to appreciate what we had done and were doing not only for Latin America but for the free world. But the charge of neglect of our friends and neighbors has continued to plague us to the present day.

LATIN AMERICANS CHARGE NEGLECT

It would not be difficult to show that, in economic terms, this neglect has been grossly overstated; that both during and after the war the United States took steps to support the prices of Latin America's major exports and to take troublesome surpluses off their hands; that Latin America benefited more than any other area from the rise in commodity prices during the 1950's; that during the period of shortages lasting up to about 1952, Latin America received special consideration in the allocation of supplies; that the Marshall Plan itself helped Latin America by reviving the European market and creating a more abundant and varied source of imports; that Latin America received favored treatment at the hands of the United States and international public lending institutions; that, despite the

143

war and the Korean emergency, the United States aided Latin America's industrial expansion through loans, grants, technical assistance, and allocation of scarce equipment and materials, as well as through the encouragement of private investors in establishing branch plants or in participation with local groups; and, finally, that Latin American receipts of foreign exchange from all sources other than purely military transactions, increased more in relation to 1940 than the receipts of any other area. This is all true, but regardless of the number of times it is repeated, it has not changed the climate of opinion. Why?

The following is offered as a partial explanation: It should be noted at the outset that Latin America receives most of its foreign news through American news media and more than any other area has received the full force of the Gospel of Plenty that has poured forth in a constant stream since the time of the Atlantic Charter and the Four Freedoms. It is difficult for a person without knowledge of the languages and without access to the Latin American press to realize the extent to which our official and unofficial pronouncements have been played up in the lands to the south, and the scope of the expectations aroused thereby.

It is inherent in the very nature of foreign aid that it involves the emotions more than commercial or financial transactions. In Europe the intangible benefits of the Marshall Plan probably outweighed the tangible ones. The other side of this coin is that failure to receive largesse that is being distributed rather bountifully in other directions becomes a stigma that is difficult to wipe out by other means.

PREWAR COOPERATIVE PROGRAM IN LATIN AMERICA

No doubt part of Latin America's disillusionment was inevitable, given the shift in the United States position away from a hemisphere-centered policy, and coming as it did on the heels of a vast outpouring of effusive good will and neighborliness before and during the war. Before the war our "good neighbors" had occupied a special position from the standpoint of financial and technical cooperation. The first regular official program of technical and scientific cooperation began in 1939, when Congress enacted two laws to authorize the implementation of the various resolutions adopted by inter-American conferences relating to cultural and technical interchanges. An inter-departmental committee, meeting originally under the chairmanship of Sumner Welles, established the pattern for subsequently expanded operations in this field. At this time the Export-Import Bank was becoming an important instrument for providing credit on relatively easy terms, and in 1940 Congress increased the Bank's lending authority to $700 million specifically to meet Latin American needs.

Of course, it was in large measure this record of favorable and even preferential treatment that produced the later charges of neglect.

Although the two 1939 acts of Congress, one authorizing the temporary detail of United States government employees to governments of the American republics (and the Philippines), and the other authorizing "the President to render closer and more effective the relationship between the American republics," may be considered the starting point of the present technical aid programs, there had been earlier instances of official foreign aid. In 1812 Congress voted a grant of $50,000 for relief of the stricken people of Venezuela following a catastrophic earthquake in March of that year. Curiously enough, this act of God affected only the areas held by the revolutionary patriots; the towns loyal to Spain were untouched. Apparently the motives prompting this gift were mixed. Altruism was a factor and so was the desire to aid the revolution, but most important was the commercial motive. In any case, this gesture missed the mark, since the Royalists triumphed and seized most of the gift flour as well as some of the ships that brought the donation. The vessels were later released, but all United States residents were ordered to leave the country.[1]*

The United States also provided extensive assistance in connection with education, highways, agriculture, health, and sanitation as a part of its military and fiscal interventions in the Philippines, Cuba, Haiti, and the Dominican Republic. In 1900 some 1,400 Cuban teachers came to the United States aboard Army transports to be guests of Harvard University in a special summer session.

One of the best-known instances of official cultural exchanges was the bringing to the United States of many Chinese students with

*Notes to chapter VI are on page 164.

145

the funds from the remission in 1908 of the Boxer indemnities. In addition, aid was provided China in other fields by church missions, foundations, and commercial establishments. In fact, China was the first instance of foreign aid on a really impressive scale. Private foreign investment was also very substantial. In a penetrating article in *Foreign Affairs* (January, 1958), Y. Chu Wang, Associate Professor of Economics and Far Eastern History at Pennsylvania Teachers College, points out that these returning students came to monopolize all top posts in Chinese higher education and also other important positions. He suggests that it was this cleavage between the foreign-trained officials in the large cities, on the one hand, and the peasants and provincial officials, on the other hand, that prepared the way for the success of communism. It is possibly not without significance that Mao Tse-tung, a man of rural origin who gave up an opportunity to study abroad, developed an aptitude for traditional Chinese poetry.

In their general outlines, our technical assistance programs have not changed basically from the categories established by the original Interdepartmental Committee on Cooperation with the American Republics in the late 1930's and early 1940's, but emphasis has shifted from time to time, and the annual appropriations are many times larger than in the earlier years. During the war the emphasis was on training aviation personnel to replace Axis pilots and administrators, in providing health and sanitation facilities of interest to our civilian and military personnel operating in the area, and in augmenting the output of food and agricultural raw materials. After the war there was a large expansion in the various exchange-of-persons programs, under which thousands of Latin Americans were brought to the United States for special studies, to visit factories and power installations, consult labor leaders, or make a tour of principal American cities. In recent years emphasis has been placed on public administration, productivity and management, and cultural types of exchanges.

Early in 1948 Congress passed the Smith-Mundt Act, which authorized the extension of scientific, technical, and cultural interchange to areas of the world outside the Western Hemisphere and the Philippines, to which the programs had previously been limited.

In practice, by that time emergency aid had been extended to many countries, either under the United Nations Relief and Rehabilitation Administration, through the American military forces, or by virtue of special acts (or from the President's Emergency Fund) relating to China, Finland, Near Eastern, and African countries.

In his inaugural address of January 20, 1949, President Truman spoke of the large outlays the United States had made "to restore peace, stability, and freedom" and outlined the four major courses of action for the coming years. The first three covered support of the United Nations, continuation of the European Recovery Program, and defense pacts in the North Atlantic and the Western Hemisphere. Point Four involved his "bold new program" of providing technical assistance and promoting private investment.

President Truman's Point Four did not arouse any enthusiasm in Latin America, where it has generally been considered as a sop to areas not receiving massive grant aid, and as an entering wedge for more foreign investment and control of their economies than is compatible with present-day nationalisms. American technical cooperation has been mentioned very rarely in the numerous inter-American conferences since 1949, and even those few references were of the type that damned with faint praise. It is not unusual for Latin American spokesmen, both in international conferences and in official reports, to claim exclusive credit for operations which owed their initiative, financing, and technology almost entirely to the United States. Such episodes do not, in themselves, prove anything about the usefulness of the projects in question, since it is desirable that each government should assume responsibility for the welfare of the country. They do, however, reflect a widespread feeling that the United States, in promoting technical assistance, is serving its own interests, or the interests of special groups, and that therefore there is no reason to thank us for it. These feelings have been strengthened by the fact that our aid agreements or projects have seldom represented a genuine desire or request on the part of the host government. It is our aid officials themselves who are constantly trying to think up new ways to enlarge their operation. They are usually able to get the strong support of our embassy officials, since a large program adds to the feeling of personal and official importance. Furthermore, it is not healthy for

147

an officer to raise questions; in at least one case an ambassador was removed because he did not give unstinted support to efforts to enlarge the local program.

TYPES OF AID

Aid is a generic term that covers a wide variety of activities and is effected through many different channels. It would require several pages of fine type merely to list all of them. But for our purposes it will be sufficient to distinguish two principal types: one, the provision of capital or goods, and two, cooperation in training and indoctrination in scientific, industrial, educational, administrative, and cultural fields. Grants to Latin America have been modest in comparison with those to Europe, Asia, and the Near East, but in a few countries they have been large in relation to the country's annual budget. Bolivia and Guatemala provide the two leading examples. In Central America the United States supplies two-thirds of the cost of the Inter-American Highway and has loaned the countries the remaining third. Most of the technical assistance programs have some element of investment or grant, for example, model low-cost houses. In recent years some countries have done very well out of our Public Law 480 programs, receiving some shipments of agricultural products for free, buying others on easy terms, and obtaining long-term loans from a large part of the counterpart funds. But here again it is the United States Department of Agriculture and the farmers' lobby that are pushing these programs. Furthermore, they are bitterly resented by countries producing competitive products, and they destroy any moral influence we might otherwise have in persuading the Latin Americans to follow orthodox policies.

Private long-term investment in Latin America from the United States averaged around $500 million during the 1950's, of which about 40 per cent was reinvested profits. During recent years there has been a sizeable inflow from Europe. Although the marketing of dollar bonds of the Latin American governments has been negligible since 1930, there has been an increase in medium-term credits by exporters and banks.

Latin America has fared comparatively well at the hands of the international public lending institutions, but funds have not been adequate in the judgment of the Latin Americans, and there have been constant complaints as to the delays, costs, and difficulties involved in obtaining loans. There is also the feeling that the operations of the large financial institutions involve a measure of tutelage which, however wholesome, does become a bit irksome at times.

Despite the loud protests of the Latin Americans that they are not seeking gifts, most, and probably all, of the countries have accepted some grant aid, and most of them would quickly accept more if it did not have too many strings attached to it. It is nevertheless true that the official spokesman for Latin America, the Economic Commission for Latin America, has consistently urged a more liberal loan policy on the part of the United States, but has at no time asked for a little Marshall Plan. Its directors have been wise enough to know that a large grant program inevitably raises difficult political problems, and, however generous the program may be, would end by whetting appetites for more. Furthermore, it is realized that in Latin America it would be difficult to get agreement as to the distribution among the countries of a lump sum of cash. Hence the Commission proposed an Inter-American Fund for Industrial, Agricultural, and Mining Development, which we opposed in 1954 but later endorsed in a different form, the Inter-American Development Bank.

TECHNICAL ASSISTANCE

In the majority of countries the cooperative programs in the technical, scientific, and cultural fields have been the most conspicuous and characteristic features of our aid programs. It is extremely difficult to judge the effects of these programs on any of the various levels they are intended to operate, such as increasing the pool of technical skills and scientific knowledge, improving administrative procedures, accelerating economic growth, creating good will for the United States, combating communism and *étatisme,* and promoting democratic government. Undoubtedly the attempt to introduce American technology and standards into an alien environment results in many mistakes. Much publicity has been given to our agricultural programs, but in some cases, after large expenditures, they have been a fiasco, and in others it appears likely that we have introduced methods which will be a disservice in the long run.

149

The programs have come in for criticism from Congressional and other investigators on the grounds of poor administration, waste, personal misconduct, and use by administrators of funds and facilities for their personal advantage. No doubt part of the difficulty arises from the complications of the appropriation process. It is difficult to carry out really worthwhile foreign operations on the basis of yearly appropriations. Unfortunately Congress has misgivings in view of the empire-building tendencies of most of the operators. It is easy to understand how enthusiastic and patriotic officials are carried away by the vision of what they think needs to be done in the country where they are working, but in most cases they lack the specific knowledge of the country and the historical perspective to judge properly all aspects of the situation. All too frequently a technical triumph becomes a Pyrrhic victory.

The projects have been justified on the basis that once the feasibility and advantages of the operation have been demonstrated to the host government, and key personnel have received training, there will be a solid and enduring achievement. In practice, the governments have shown little disposition to continue the operation once American money and personnel are withdrawn. Not infrequently our officials convince themselves that there is a real desire for a program because a few local authorities who stand to benefit officially or personally from it show an interest. Even in those cases where the officials are convinced of the value of a project to the country, it is difficult publicly to acknowledge help from a foreign government. Motivations here are very complex: in most cases there is some residue of jealousy and resentment; they see an opportunity to obtain credit easily and it is not difficult for them to convince themselves that it was their collaboration that made the operation a success. In other cases the host country goes along with the project because they want to humor us. Possibly the project will add to their prestige and bring money into the country. Some Latin American officials, including their ambassadors in Washington, are constantly trying to enlist new technical assistance operations in the hope that one of them, or their combined effect, may result in larger financial support. Examples could be cited where the same problems have been studied within a few years by three or four different agencies without any real attempt by the government to implement any of the recommendations. Some countries that have received large amounts of American aid may deliberately drag their feet on implementation in order to show their spiritual independence.

The exchange-of-persons programs appear to have been enormously overdone. In many cases they are nothing more than a free ride at the taxpayers expense. At one time the chief interest of some of the visitors was to make an extra profit on smuggled goods, or to be able to enter automobiles, TV sets, and electrical apparatus as the personal effects of returned travellers, thus evading the exchange restrictions. Recently several highly competent and experienced observers have reported that the official student exchange program, far from promoting international understanding and friendship, often only arouses or strengthens dislike and prejudice.

Regardless of the conscientious and useful work of many of the technicians, there is widespread suspicion and resentment against our intervention. Most of the people simply do not believe that the United States is spending so much money without ulterior motives. To many the projects are a new kind of imperialism and brain washing that may prove to be more dangerous than the old-fashioned type. The communists criticize the programs, yes, but they criticize them because they understand the misgivings, doubts, and irritations that inevitably grow up about the programs. Latin American officials are not averse to using the gap between per capita income in the United States and in Latin America as an argument to obtain more financing from the United States, but these same persons do not like for us to remind them of the gap between the status of the elite and the poverty and ignorance and underdevelopment of the rest of the country. Some countries have laws designed to prevent foreigners from taking photographs of their beggars or poor people. Mexico has on at least two occasions refused Red Cross aid, partly because Mexico has come to realize that it will not progress as long as it is morally and materially dependent on foreigners, and partly because it is not willing to have its misery exploited to raise money abroad. It is doubtful if many Latin Americans are acquainted with Thoreau's writings, but most of them would agree with his statement that if he knew someone was coming to do him good he would flee as though for his life.

151

In attempting to assess the effect of our programs on Latin American attitudes it must be kept in mind that these operations are part of a larger complex involving our aggregate official and private performances in the country. In the larger countries there are several hundred Americans in official capacity regularly stationed there (not including thousands of private American citizens), and in addition there are almost daily arrivals and departures of experts, inspectors, politicians, the Vice President, the President's aides, the President himself, cabinet members, assistant secretaries, Congressional delegations, trade missions, goodwill missions, military personnel, FBI and CIA agents, Export-Import Bank and AID officials, and other lesser lights too numerous to mention. This does not include the personnel of technical assistance teams and advisers from international agencies, part of whom may be Americans. For every project there are two or three Congressional committees and an equal number of Senate ones, some of whom feel their responsibility to inspect the operations on the grounds. Most of these delegations must see the president and other high officials of the host country and take advantage of the opportunity to lecture them on their shortcomings. It is not surprising that some local officials feel the point made by a British wag that the International Cooperation Administration[2] is the American Colonial Office.

Assumptions Underlying Aid Programs

Our aid programs have been based on a number of assumptions that have never been adequately examined. Some high officials, however, have come to recognize the pernicious effect of these "false beliefs," outlined at the 1958 meeting of the American Economic Association by C. Tyler Wood out of his experience as a Deputy Administrator of the International Cooperation Administration and as field administrator in Europe and Asia, as follows:

1. The belief that economic development and rising standards of living produce political stability and guarantee rapid progress toward democratic institutions;

2. Exaggerated expectations of the extent of influence the United States can exert on the course of events in a given country;

3. The belief that we can accomplish our objective in a relatively short time, if we use sufficient vigor and resources; and

4. The belief that people are motivated largely by a desire for a better life and will behave in a rational manner.

President Truman in his inaugural message stated that material progress will further "the secure growth of democratic ways of life," and this point of view has been echoed in Congressional reports and thousands of speeches and articles. This argument that our aid programs bring prosperity, and that prosperity is a prophylactic against communism, has been very effective in selling the programs to Congress and the public. The danger of this thesis is that it has encouraged policies and actions that are counterproductive from the standpoint of our major objectives. In practice, rapid economic development has widened the gap between the rich and the poor, and has created flagrant examples of vulgarity and luxury. Unfortunately it has been precisely such types of development with which the United States has been most closely associated. In Guatemala, the communist crisis arose at a time when very high coffee prices had brought exceptional prosperity to many; furthermore, decisive support for communism did not come from the bottom but from the top. Cuba was one of the four or five Latin American countries having the highest per capita income. In his *Review of U.S. Government Agencies in Latin America,* submitted to the Senate on February 2, 1958, Senator Allen Ellender stated that our aid programs had fostered discontent, instead of allaying it, since, under existing economic and institutional patterns, our expenditures have "further enriched the well-to-do, with only a pittance trickling down to those who need help the most."

The Senator's generalization may be a bit too broad, but it is undoubtedly correct in many instances. In so far as our aid program has been successful in reaching the underprivileged, it has created social ferment and dissatisfaction with the old ways. Such ferment may be a necessary prelude to progress, but in its early stages it is not a force for either political or economic stability. And in the Latin American institutional and ideological setting, it can have revolutionary implications. It would certainly be naive to assume that Latin American political evolution will necessarily follow along British and American lines.

Original communism, like primitive Christianity, did not promise prosperity, it promised revolution or a complete change of society, which is quite a different thing. It is not poverty that is humiliating, but injustice and discrimination. Perhaps later "all these things shall be added unto you."

Is it possible for a foreign country to provide substantial aid on a continuing basis without incurring a large measure of responsibility for the government and its actions, or at least having responsibility attributed to it? Some of the programs are like an inclined plane on which we slide further and further into intervention in internal affairs. Bolivia provides an outstanding example. The United States provides a large share, doubtless in some years a major share, of the national revenues, and in addition has furnished food, equipment, technology and advice in large amounts. At the same time the United States has very limited power or control over the government or its operations. It is well known that there have been serious abuses, such as the smuggling out of the country of food provided free by the American taxpayers for "the hungry people of Bolivia." What is the answer? One way of stating the dilemma is that we may have to decide either to shape our policies so that they will involve less direct involvement, or else recognize that our responsibilities must be accompanied by some corresponding degree of power or authority.

The Latin American situation as regards foreign aid may, then, be summarized, as follows:

Latin America was deeply perturbed and vexed after World War II when it not only did not share in the provision of massive grant aid to certain areas but was rebuffed on several important occasions on its applications for loans. The Latin Americans will continue to consider as preferential and discriminatory failure to treat them on the most-favored-nation basis as far as grants and loans are concerned.

The immense amount of propaganda in the United States in favor of foreign aid—most of which is transmitted southward by radio, cable, telephone, letter, or by word of mouth—has convinced many Latin Americans that they should and will be included in the bounty. Naturally this point of view is encouraged by those American firms and individuals who would benefit from such outlays.

Nevertheless, some important Latin American countries like Mexico have long been averse to gifts, and some Latin American spokesmen, like Dr. Prebisch of the Economic Commission for Latin America, have clearly indicated their preference for other types of support, such as a more liberal loan policy, favorable treatment for Latin American exports, and cooperation in the establishment of a Latin American Free Trade Association. A similar position has been taken by Dr. Eugenio Gudin, a leading Brazilian economist and former Minister of Finance, who feels that the United States has not lived up to its role as the leading creditor nation and has missed numerous opportunities to meet the legitimate needs of Latin America while at the same time creating an atmosphere of mutual confidence.

There has been some ambivalence in the Latin American attitude towards technical cooperation. In the beginning the projects were well received, and undoubtedly many persons have profited from them, but as they have reached unmanageable proportions they have become increasingly a political symbol and, alas, in some cases a symbol of American waste and inefficiency. The very size and conspicuousness of our operations—and operators—inevitably creates irritations, such as parking privileges, competition for housing and servants, favoritism to particular groups or individuals, and the jealousy and resentment of those not included in the free trips and handouts.

Unfortunately the foreign aid propaganda in the United States has given the impression that these programs offer the only way by which the underdeveloped countries can obtain the benefits of advanced technology. In fact, the transfer of techniques from the more advanced countries to Latin America has been going on for a long time, not only through the normal channels of individuals and firms anxious to increase their knowledge or improve their business, but also through the contracting of foreign experts by the various governments and innumerable business establishments. For example, Brazil developed its rice and cotton industries with the help of United States agronomists. In Argentina, the fruit industries were developed by the British-owned railways with the aid of American technicians. American and European machinery exporting firms have long made important contributions in the introduction of new methods and in the

155

establishment of new industries. Large American firms having operations in the countries have trained many thousands in their offices
and plants, both in the countries and in the United States. During
the years 1890 to 1912 the Mexican National Railway, originally
under American control and management, established apprentice
schools to train Mexicans in various crafts and offices. Over 15,000
Mexicans were given training in this way, while on the payroll. In
Latin America, as elsewhere, many of the leading industrial establishments got their start with the efforts of a modest craftsman to improve
his position. In some cases known personally to the author they saved
sufficient money to send their sons to the United States or Europe to
enable them to learn advanced methods. With this additional know-
how more advanced operations were undertaken.

Despite the generosity of the American government, some countries have preferred to hire their own advisers and technicians. The
record would appear to suggest that the officials heed the advice of
such advisers more frequently than in the case of those supplied by
outside governments or agencies without charge.

Substantial aid and technical assistance have been provided by
international organizations, such as the United Nations agencies, the
World Bank, the International Monetary Fund, and the Organization of American States. In some fields European technicians have
been preferred, since they have less prejudice against state enterprise
in such fields as utilities and transportation. It is expected that the
recently organized Inter-American Development Bank will devote
major attention to technical assistance, but its role has not yet been
clarified. One problem faced by all agencies is that many of the more
promising technicians seek jobs with the international agencies or
with large foreign interests instead of taking their chances in their
own countries. It was reported at the end of 1959 that five thousand
Argentine technicians and professionals had gone to the United
States and remained in that country. It is estimated that 20 per cent
of the 43,500 scientists and engineers who moved to the United
States between 1949 and 1961 came from Asia and Latin America.[3]

It is the practice of some countries to shop around among all of
the agencies offering assistance, both United States and international,
and then to pick the one that appears most likely to support the

government's point of view and to be able to obtain financial backing for its recommendations. Some countries have been brutally frank
in making it clear that what they want is the money and not either
technicians or reports. Back in 1952, when the author was in Quito,
Ecuador, one of the leading newspapers published a cartoon illus-
trating this point. It showed a huge, voracious eagle, with a head like
Uncle Sam, flying over the country, dropping leaflets and reports that
fluttered in the air. The caption read: *Mas vale dinero en mano que
peritos volando,* which may be translated roughly as "cash in hand
is worth more than a hundred transient technicians." In Spanish,
it may be noted, one says, "A bird in hand is worth one hundred
flying" rather than "A bird in the hand is worth two in the bush."
Certainly Ecuador has had no shortage of *peritos* ("experts": another
cartoon in the same newspaper reported that Ecuador had a case of
perito-nitis). During his last period as President of Ecuador, José
María Velasco Ibarra demanded American financing for "a vast
plan of public works" and made it clear he did not want a lot of
studies by high-salaried experts involving endless delays.

It is difficult to assess the achievements and mistakes of our foreign
aid programs because our objectives have never been clearly established. Some of the stated objectives, such as the creation of
democratic governments, are, as has been shown, untenable and
counterproductive. Some of the other purposes may now be examined briefly.

1. Reduce the gap between the developed and underdeveloped
countries: Are the Latin Americans who make this argument prepared to go in for a share-the-wealth program in their own countries?
The real social problem is not the difference between the average
incomes in Latin America and those in the so-called more developed
countries, but the gap between the privileged and underprivileged
within each Latin American country itself. Before Americans go in
for international leveling wouldn't it be well to consider first the
differences in income level among different groups and regions in
the United States? It is estimated that over one-fifth of our population still lives miserably, however affluent Harvard professors may be.
Our large cities have become disgraceful tangles of slums, garish
advertising, traffic jams, used car lots, unsightly dumps, and streets

157

littered with newspapers and trash. Perhaps that is one reason why so many Americans now want foreign jobs, but wouldn't our advice carry more weight abroad if we could show a better record at home? The levelers also show a lack of historical perspective and a misunderstanding of the principles of economic development. Some countries simply do not have the resource endowment to make possible higher per capita income with a constantly expanding population; furthermore, larger populations, greater power, and a place in the world are stronger motivations in most of the countries than reducing poverty. Any attempt to level out national incomes would result in a policy of nondevelopment. Different levels of development, both within a country and as between countries, have always been an important element in stimulating activity and growth. Historically, nations rise and decline, as trade routes shift, resources are exhausted, new technologies appear, or human energies and initiative become dulled by prosperity and moral decay. Spain was once the richest and most powerful nation in Europe. Some of the poor countries of Asia, Africa, or South America may become dominant powers when the United States has gone the way of Ninevah and Tyre.

2. Holding support of the Latin American bloc: Since the war the United States has had to make many promises and concessions to Latin American countries and individuals in order to obtain their vote or support in the United Nations or other forums. With the organization of the United Nations and the formation of a Latin American bloc the United States has become more isolated in the inter-American organizations. Pursuant to the suggestion of President Kubitschek for a hemispheric plan of development known as Operation Pan America, the Council of the Organization of American States set up a Special Committee to Study the Formulation of New Measures for Economic Cooperation. This committee was generally known as the Committee of Twenty-one (that is, one representative for each American republic), but the irreverent called it the Committee of Twenty against One. To some Americans the aid programs are a sort of permanent income-sharing device designed to assure Latin American support in international and inter-American organizations, not unlike the subsidies Rome paid out for centuries to minor potentates. Experience would appear to indicate that in

such arrangements the cost of alliance tends to rise. In the days of the Roman Empire, or even of the Pax Britannica, most client states were ruled by absolute monarchs, which considerably simplified the subsidy technique. In any case, it is already clear that we cannot count indefinitely on sure majorities in the United Nations or the OAS, regardless of the amount of the *quid pro quo*.

3. Humanitarianism: The strong support given by the American public to our foreign aid programs reflects a widespread feeling of generosity and international good will. Unfortunately the public is not in a position to evaluate all of the elements in a continuing aid program. It is always dangerous to apply to governments the moral categories that are pertinent in the case of individual morality. Charity may be a case in point. The United States has on various occasions, usually through a combination of public and private measures, made effective gestures of sympathy to nations in cases of great national disaster from earthquake, famine, flood, or war destruction. Even these gestures have, at times, been spoiled by excessive emphasis on political or commercial considerations. It is one thing for an individual or a foundation to undertake charitable operations abroad, but it is quite a different thing for a government to tax its citizens for continuing programs. Foreigners naturally tend to look upon such actions as political, as indeed they must be.

Various writers have recently pointed out that the high standard of living in the United States is one of our most serious handicaps in gaining the sympathy and support of other peoples. However well intended our Point Four activities may be, and however conscientious most of the personnel, there is almost inevitably a barrier between them and those it is desired to aid. One is forced to conclude sorrowfully that if we are to make friends and influence people our aid programs will have to be put on a different basis of operation. Those jobs requiring social and diplomatic status for negotiating purposes might well be turned over to the regular staffs. Missions that are advertised as humanitarian can probably succeed only if they are handled on what might be called a missionary basis. Otherwise the spokesmen will have no real moral weight. Our planners are constantly seeking the magic formula that will put the world to rights, mostly by spending more money. There is a magic formula, but it is not the one they seek: it is the road followed by the world's great religions, the road of humility and sacrifice, the road of Gandhi, the road even of the communists when they have been successful.

ENTER THE KENNEDY ADMINISTRATION

Some shift of emphasis in the aid programs, and also considerable administrative reshuffling, were introduced by the Kennedy administration. In September, 1961, it merged the principal aid organizations into a new Agency for International Development, with an Assistant Administrator responsible for Latin American operations and serving as coordinator of U.S. activities relating to the Alliance for Progress.[4] Another innovation of the Kennedy administration was the establishment of the Peace Corps on March 1, 1961. Originally focused primarily on Africa, by the end of 1962 the emphasis had shifted to Latin America. At that time there were 1,100 volunteers in thirteen countries, and a total of 4,000 was anticipated for the end of 1963. In view of the limited experience to date, any judgment on its operations would be premature, but the care shown in selecting the volunteers, the rigorous training to which they are subjected before taking up an assignment, and the absence of conspicuous prosperity on the part of the corpsmen, have been important factors in the apparently favorable reception with which most groups have been received by local communities. Of course, the essential idea of the Peace Corps is not new. Various religious and private organizations have long carried on similar activities. The American Friends initiated overseas service activities during the first World War, and have subsequently remained in the field. Likewise, the Volunteer Service Overseas Movement in England helped to provide a pattern for official ventures of the United States.

The Alliance for Progress envisages a substantially enlarged American aid program for Latin America, both in the form of loans and of grants. It also commits us to the support of various other Latin American objectives, such as commodity price stabilization, diversification and industrialization, and assistance to the Latin American common market movement.

Under the Alliance for Progress the grant component of foreign aid has been reduced. This is a step in the right direction, although some of the public loans made in the name of the Alliance have been based on dubious political and economic concepts. A good case can be made for some grant assistance for technical training, whether handled on a bilateral basis or through international organizations.

There is still a tendency to interpret assistance to backward countries largely in terms of monetary outlays, rather than as part of the whole of our economic policies. Trade policy is still one of the major elements in growth, even though it may not now occupy the almost exclusive position it held during the nineteenth century. Owing to the political opposition to trade concessions, some have turned to grant aid as a substitute. But we cannot escape the effects of unwise trade policies, whether we give aid or not.

Supporters of aid programs have continued to be overimpressed by the virtues of large outlays of funds, while at the same time acting in a very niggardly fashion in allocating small sums where they could achieve maximum results from the standpoint of policy and goodwill. It would be advisable, for example, to strengthen the position of United States ambassadors and provide them with some emergency funds to take care of special situations. Carefully and discreetly used by our regular and responsible officials, useful results can be obtained by modest expenditures. One of the main difficulties in the past has been the tendency to assume that if $50,000 can be used to advantage, $5 million will do one hundred times as much good. Actually, the expenditure of the larger sum, instead of achieving a political breakthrough or economic takeoff, may well end by creating no end of headaches and tensions.

President Kennedy continued the efforts initiated by President Eisenhower to induce the prosperous European countries to take over a larger share of the total expenditures on foreign aid. The principal European countries have long followed the policy of guaranteeing or facilitating commercial credits as a form of export promotion. As a matter of fact, U.S. policies in this field, such as the organization of the Export-Import Bank of Washington, were largely inspired by European practices. In recent years the European governments have enlarged the sums available for such purposes, and have created modest funds under the rubric "technical assistance" which can be used to facilitate their exports and investments,[5] but they

161

have consistently refused to accept our concepts of aid. For example, a leading German spokesman has stated that the Federal Republic "grants capital aid as a matter of principle under the form of credits," and that his government "is convinced that credits are best suited to promote the concept of partnership and strengthen the recipient country's own feeling of responsibility."[6] There has been some revival of direct investment in Latin America by European nationals, chiefly Germans.

The European countries also contribute their pro rata to the various international organizations operating in Latin America, but the only organizations involving substantial sums are the credit institutions like the International Bank for Reconstruction and Development and the International Monetary Fund, and their affiliates. The United Nations and the Food and Agricultural Organization carry on technical assistance activities throughout the area, and many Latin Americans have found employment in their ranks, including in the top brackets. A Venezuelan, for example, was recently designated Deputy General of the United Nations in charge of matters relating to industrialization. The United States contributes one-third or more to the budget of each of these activities. The larger part of United States public funds going to Latin America is still handled on a bilateral basis, but with the launching of the Alliance for Progress a big chunk of United States financial aid has been turned over to inter-American organizations, such as the Inter-American Development Bank and the Central American Development Bank. The technical assistance activities of the Organization of American States have also been expanded greatly in recent years.

During the annual debate in Washington over foreign aid legislation and appropriation, it is inevitable that the chief struggle should be among those having a definite interest in attempting to get the best possible deal for their clients and *coreligionnaires,* and to exclude those they do not favor from receiving anything. As a result, some countries and some types of activity have received more funds than could be spent without inflation and waste, while on the other hand some types of aid have been prohibited or severely restricted. For example, there are restrictions on aid to communist countries as well as on aid to countries furnishing assistance to communist countries.

The Foreign Assistance Act of 1962 directed the President to suspend assistance to the government of any country that has nationalized the property of United States citizens or corporations, or imposed discriminatory taxes or other exactions, unless said government takes steps within six months to indemnify the owner or to remove discriminations.[7] This provision may be said to represent a victory for those who have long insisted that foreign aid should be used as an instrument to promote United States interests, including the protection and promotion of private investment abroad. In practice, of course, virtually every important opinion-forming group in the United States has been cut in on the benefits of foreign aid outlays (including senators and congressmen, to be sure), and, as was pointed out in the preceding chapter, foreign investors also have come in for various types of aid. There are many experienced observers, however, who feel that the decision to tie foreign aid to private investment is apt to prove to be a boomerang. One possible effect is that foreign public officials faced with this threat will be all the more determined to get rid of possibly troublesome foreign investors. As a matter of fact, Mexico provides an excellent case history. Back in the mid 1920's the United States was carrying on an acrimonious exchange of diplomatic notes with Mexico regarding subsoil rights. President Calles was not anti-American and by no means a radical; there were many indications that he would have welcomed a reasonable compromise. But at this point United States Secretary of State Frank B. Kellogg, after consultation with Ambassador James R. Sheffield, then in Washington, on June 12, 1925, issued a statement that Mexico was "now on trial before the world." This action infuriated President Calles, who instructed his lawyers to draw up legislation implementing the 1917 Constitution so as to eliminate foreign control.[8]

Another aspect of this question has been cogently expressed by Secretary of State Dean Rusk: "If we are going to tie American policy by law to the private investor overseas . . . then I think that we must of necessity reassure ourselves as to the operations, the conduct, the financial structure, and the other aspects of these private investors."[9] A former under-secretary of commerce has also made a proposal to put foreign investment on a new basis:[10] The United

States government would insure its investors in Latin America and other underdeveloped areas, but in order to qualify for political-risk insurance an individual or firm investor would be required to conform to certain requirements: namely, adopt specific measures to widen ownership and modernize employee practices as regards profit sharing and training; and commit itself to offer to sell to the people of the host country a substantial percentage of its common shares.

American aid in relation to education and cultural activities is discussed in chapters VII and VIII.

NOTES TO CHAPTER VI

1. Harold A. Bierck, Jr., "The First Instance of U.S. Foreign Aid: Venezuelan Relief in 1812," *Inter-American Economic Affairs,* IX (Summer, 1955), 47-59. Authorities claim that the first instance of foreign aid was in 1794, when Congress voted an appropriation for the relief of refugees in Santo Domingo.

2. Now merged with the Agency for International Development (AID).

3. Report to technology conference at Geneva by associate training director of the National Institutes of Health, Bethesda, Md. At the same conference the director of UNESCO's Department of Natural Science reported that 25 per cent of newly trained scientists emigrate from developing countries. *Washington Post,* February 12, 1963.

4. Established by the Charter of Punta del Este, signed August 17, 1961. See chapter IX.

5. During the years 1960 and 1961 German grants for technical assistance to Latin America averaged only slightly more than one million marks. Hans Georg Sachs, Executive Director, Foreign Office, Federal Republic of Germany, "European Public Financing of Latin American Development," *Europe's Role in Latin American Economic Development,* Inter-American Development Bank, Third Meeting of the Board of Governors, April 24, 1962, Buenos Aires, p. 51.

6. *Ibid.,* pp. 38-39.

7. Public Law 87-565, 87th Congress, S. 2996, August 1, 1962, Section 301.

8. L. Ethan Ellis, *Frank B. Kellogg and American Foreign Relations 1925-1929* (New Brunswick, N.J.: Rutgers University Press, 1961), pp. 28-29; also on Kellogg, Norman A. Graebner (ed.), *An Uncertain Tradition: American Secretaries of State in the Twentieth Century* (New York: McGraw- Hill Book Co., 1961), chapter 8.

9. Hearings on S. 2996, p. 32, cited by John Hickey, "The Alliance for Progress —the First Year: Business," *Inter-American Economic Affairs,* XVI (Summer, 1962), 56.

10. Philip Alexander Ray, *South Wind Red: Our Hemispheric Crisis* (Chicago: Henry Regnery Co., 1962).

–VII–

Mutual Cultural Relations: Education

Widespread interest by Americans in Latin American history, literature, and languages first developed during World War I. Earlier there had been a long-standing interest on the part of certain groups, and, indeed, during the late colonial and early independence periods, multiple considerations, evangelical, military, commercial, and political, conspired to attract general attention to the Hispanic areas. During the last years of the seventeenth century, for example, Cotton Mather, the great New England clergyman, studied Spanish and prepared a religious appeal to South Americans. American recruits provided an important contingent of the British forces involved in the conquest of Jamaica and the siege of Havana. There were active trade relations with the Caribbean, the Spanish Main, and the Iberian peninsula, despite the Spanish monopoly and British restrictions.[1]*

EARLY HISPANIC STUDIES IN UNITED STATES

Out of these contacts developed cultural activities of a practical, literary, and philosophical character. Historians report that the Spanish language was taught at New York as early as 1735. John Adams, Thomas Jefferson, and Benjamin Franklin were among the prominent patriots who learned Spanish. Franklin arranged for instruction in Spanish at the Philadelphia Academy in 1749, and Jefferson insisted that Spanish be studied at the College of William and Mary. Nor was interest confined to the practical aspects of knowledge of the language. Libraries in leading cities formed collections of historical and economic works. The American Philosophical Society at Philadelphia and other learned societies nominated Spaniards and Spanish Americans as corresponding members. Newspapers serialized

*Notes to chapter VII begin on page 193.

articles on travel and history. Leading magazine editors like William Tudor and Jared Sparks were in correspondence with scholarly Latin Americans.[2]

Interest in the Spanish-speaking countries dwindled after the 1820's, but a few leading educational institutions continued work in the field.[3] The Smith Professorship of French and Spanish Languages and Literature was established at Harvard University in 1816, George Ticknor being the first to hold the chair. Portuguese was also taught at Harvard for a time. During the last three quarters of the century Spain received more attention than Spanish America. The names of Irving, Longfellow, and Howells occur at once in this connection. At the same time, Latin America was not entirely neglected: William Hickling Prescott's historical studies began with the period of Ferdinand and Isabella in Spain but included his much better known accounts of the conquest of Mexico and Peru.

Toward the end of the nineteenth century the spotlight shifted back across the Atlantic. Archaeologists, ethnologists, historians, and professors of language and literature began to cultivate the field actively. Studies of the ancient Mexicans were published as early as 1879 by the Peabody Museum of American Archaeology and Ethnology at Cambridge, Massachusetts. Other institutions participating in the work were the Bureau of American Ethnology at Washington, D. C., the American Museum of Natural History at New York, the Field Columbian Museum at Chicago, and the Carnegie Institution of Washington. The International School of Archaeology and Ethnography at Mexico City received strong U. S. financial and technical support. On the eve of World War I, the Hispanic Society of America, founded in 1904 by Archer M. Huntington, sponsored an exhibition of Mexican majolica ware, and gave financial support to the Yale-Peruvian Expedition, which rediscovered and made known the ruins of Machu Picchu, the Inca stronghold high in the Peruvian Andes.

Following the revival of political and commercial interest in Latin America, historians also began to give special attention to the area. Already before the first World War five universities—Columbia, Chicago, California, Texas, and Illinois—were offering courses in Latin American history, and in 1915 Harvard entered the list. Others followed suit, and in 1918 the Hispanic American Historical Review, organ of the Hispanic American Historical Association, began to appear. By 1925 courses in Latin American (or Hispanic American, as many prefer) history were offered in 135 colleges and universities, not to speak of numerous junior colleges and normal schools.

World War I also ushered in a huge expansion in the teaching of Spanish, which benefited from the expulsion of German from the classroom. Before the war less than 1 per cent of the students in public high schools were enrolled in Spanish language courses. By 1922 this had risen to over 11 per cent, making Spanish a close second to French among the modern languages, although at that time there were still more students enrolled in Latin classes than in French and Spanish combined.

Quantitatively the growth of Latin American studies in the United States during the 1920's and 1930's cannot compare with the huge expansion during the years 1938-45, but developments during the interwar period were of much significance and deserve special mention. Elihu Root, who as Secretary of State had been one of our ablest exponents of the Good Neighbor Policy, also had an important influence in promoting mutual cultural relations both as Secretary of State and as president of the Carnegie Endowment for International Peace. Through the patronage of the Carnegie Endowment, the American Institute of International Law was founded in 1912. Beginning during the war years with the inauguration of the review *Inter-America* and the publication of various scholarly works, the Endowment pioneered in practically all the fields that later came to be revived and expanded under such names as cultural cooperation and Point Four: granting travel fellowships, financing visiting Carnegie professors from the United States and from Latin America, sponsoring group visits; providing collections of books on United States history, institutions, and culture to leading Latin American libraries; distributing news digests in Spanish; financing the translation into South American languages of important works written in English, and their distribution to more than seven thousand selected individuals and institutions in the other American Republics, and cooperating with bilateral cultural centers.

The service of Dwight Morrow as United States Ambassador to

167

Mexico in the late 1920's, and the influence of Mrs. Morrow, were also of great importance in establishing United States-Latin American cultural relations on a new basis. The Morrows made Mexican, and indirectly Latin American, art, handicrafts, music, not only respectable but chic in the United States. During their tour of duty at Mexico City the Morrows brought down as their guests numerous American artists, critics, museum and foundation directors, and also assisted local artists and dealers. Ambassador Morrow paid Diego Rivera $50,000 for a mural on the wall of the upper loggia of the Governor's Palace at Cuernavaca. Several leading Mexican painters and muralists exhibited or executed commissions in the United States during the 1920's and 1930's.

During this period the Guggenheim Foundation began the award of fellowships to Latin Americans for study in the United States, and various large American firms active in Latin America adopted the policy of sending promising local employees for study or training north of the border. Archer M. Huntington, who through the Hispanic Society of America had from the beginning of the century promoted American interest in the Hispanic world, in 1927 provided funds to build up the Hispanic collections of the Library of Congress, and subsequently gave support to the creation of the Hispanic Foundation in the Library of Congress. The walls of the vestibule of the Hispanic Room at the library were decorated with murals by Cândido Portinari, the Brazilian painter.

Mention may also be made of the work of the Rockefeller Foundation, which supported Latin American activities through such organizations as the American Council of Learned Societies, which in turn set up a Committee on Latin American Studies.

On the broader international basis, both the League of Nations and the Pan American Union were active during the interwar years in developing international cultural cooperation. The Pan American Union arranged a series of concerts by composers of the Americas. In 1929 the educational work of the Union was expanded into a Division of Intellectual Cooperation, and in this year there was also established the Pan American Institute of Geography and History. Beginning in 1908, a series of so-called Scientific Congresses[4] brought together leaders from many fields including the natural and social sciences as well as finance and trade. An official inter-American program for the exchange of students and professors was launched at the Conference for the Maintenance of Peace held at Buenos Aires in 1936 at which a convention for the Promotion of Inter-American Cultural Relations was approved.

The work of the League of Nations in the realm of intellectual cooperation enlisted the enthusiastic support of the Latin American countries, and most of them established National Committees of Intellectual Cooperation. This zeal was later transferred to UNESCO: all but one of the republics were represented at the First Session of the General Conference of UNESCO held at Paris at the end of 1946. Latin Americans have been strongly represented on the Executive Board of UNESCO, as they were on the League's Committee on Intellectual Cooperation, and a Mexican served as the second Director General of UNESCO.

COOPERATIVE PROGRAM LAUNCHED IN 1938

The year 1938 marked a significant turning point in our cultural relations with the other American republics: it signalized, first, the acceptance of the principle of a large-scale program directed by the government and supported by public funds, and, secondly, the implementation of a cooperative Inter-American plan of interchange of persons. In that year an Interdepartmental Committee on Cooperation with the other American Republics was set up under the chairmanship of Sumner Welles, and this committee prepared detailed plans for increasing the interchange of scientific, technical, cultural, and educational knowledge and skills with the other republics; Congress enacted a law (Public Law 63, 76th Congress) authorizing the temporary detail of United States employees possessing special qualifications to governments of the American republics and the Philippines, and providing for the reimbursement of travel expenses; and the Department of State created a Division of Cultural Relations, having as its immediate responsibility the administration of grants to students and professors provided for in the Buenos Aires Convention for the Promotion of Inter-American Cultural Relations.

There was, of course, no lack of precedent for United States government action in promoting exchanges of both persons and knowledge. From an early period Congress authorized acceptance of Latin Americans as students in our military and naval academies, and in 1892 the National Bureau of Standards was authorized to receive qualified foreign scientists and technicians as guest workers. In 1849 the Smithsonian Institution set up an International Exchange Service (which is still in operation) to handle exchanges of official publications with other countries. In 1908 there was created the Boxer Indemnity Fund, which financed study by many Chinese in the United States. Facilities had been granted for the service of United States personnel in Liberia and the Philippines. And, of course, some foreign governments, notably France and Germany, had long subsidized foreign activities designed to encourage the use of their national languages and appreciation of their cultural contributions to the world.

In 1939 Congress enacted additional legislation (Public Law 355, 76th Congress) authorizing the President to utilize the services of government departments in carrying out the reciprocal undertakings and cooperative programs established in the treaties, resolutions, declarations, and recommendations signed by the American republics at the Buenos Aires Conference in 1936 and the Eighth Inter-American Conference held at Lima in 1938. In 1939 and annually thereafter Congress appropriated funds to carry out the programs formulated by the Interdepartmental Committee.[5]

During the war years this cooperative program was expanded but it was to some extent subordinated and overshadowed by the operations of the Office of the Coordinator of Inter-American Affairs, under the vigorous leadership of Nelson Rockefeller. Some of the problems arising from this administrative confusion have been described in the report of the Committee on Educational Interchange Policy, established by the Institute of International Education, as follows: "The history of CIAA provides an early example of difficulties encountered in attempting to combine activities having widely different objectives. Although CIAA was set up to meet emergency wartime needs in the economic, cultural and information spheres, it was also charged with long-term activities aimed at 'strengthening bonds' between nations. This meant that unilateral information activities such as short-wave broadcasting to counteract hostile Axis propaganda, were combined with long-term reciprocal activities such as exchange of persons. It also meant that CIAA programs cut directly across those of the Cultural Relations Division. The inevitable result was a confusion of both basic principles and lines of administration."[6]

The Coordinator's activities, backed by ample funds, yielded many useful and enduring results in the cultural field, but the shot-gun wedding of scholarship and war information begot some dubious progeny: the mongrel mixture of culture and propaganda, with the propaganda traits most in evidence. Of course, the wartime atmosphere of exaggeration and distortion was not confined to any one agency,[7] but our relations with Latin America are still suffering from some of the ill effects of the overdose of official good will during this period. The very phrases "Latin America," "Good Neighbor," and "Good Will" still call up visions of propaganda in the minds of many Americans both of the North and of the South.

As a prelude to an examination of present-day programs in the cultural and informational fields, it is well to note that these operations, like Janus, have two faces, one looking in and the other outward. It can be argued that the former have been relatively more successful and more appreciated in Latin America than the outwardly directed programs. The effect of combining official interest with public and private funds has resulted in a substantial expansion and strengthening of Latin American studies in the United States, not only in established fields like archaeology, language, history, political science, and geography, but also in anthropology, sociology, philosophy, labor relations, and economics. Library resources have been increased, and numerous scholars and professors in Latin American fields of study have had an opportunity to obtain firsthand acquaintance with the area. Spanish has gained in favor as a foreign language in our schools, and holds first place in both our elementary and our secondary schools. In many graduate schools language requirements for the Ph.D. degree are no longer confined to French and German, as was long the case, since Spanish and other languages are now acceptable. The literature of Hispanic America, as well as that of the Peninsula, is now taught in secondary schools and in the universities.

171

These developments have been a matter of great satisfaction to Latin Americans, who, like the rest of us, want to be understood and appreciated. The fact that their countries are relatively weak economically and militarily has made them all the more anxious to receive recognition and compensation elsewhere. Furthermore, the receptivity in the United States of Latin American cultural products —painting, sculpture, literature, music, movies, dances, architecture, city planning—is a matter of vital dollars-and-cents concern to many Latin Americans. Not a few Latin Americans have found teaching positions and professorial chairs in our schools and colleges, or well-paying jobs with inter-American and international organizations. The United States has provided a major market for Latin American art. Literature has had harder going, but there have been some striking successes. Gabriela Mistral, the only Latin American to receive the Nobel prize in literature, won her first important recognition in the United States.

Our cultural programs in Latin America now involve four or five major types of activities: education, provision of books and magazines in English or in translation, encouraging the translation and publication in the United States of Latin American literary and scholarly productions, lecture tours, operation of reading rooms and libraries, lessons in English, and cultural presentations involving tours by jazz bands, symphony orchestras, singers, actors, and athletes.

EDUCATION

For the sake of clarity, our work in the educational field may be examined under seven headings.

1. *American Schools in Latin America.* Prior to the war American educational efforts in Latin America were almost entirely private. The church mission schools are the oldest and most important. In 1956 there were 1,363 schools (not including nursing schools) in Latin America supported by American missionary agencies. Of this total over a thousand were primary schools, some in every Latin American country but one. The Instituto Mackenzie at São Paulo, Brazil, which started as a small Presbyterian mission school in 1870, has grown into one of the largest and most important educational institutions in Latin America. The development of primary education

172

in a number of countries has been greatly influenced by American practices.[8]

American business concerns also have established and operated a considerable number of schools. In 1955, for example, the United Fruit Company operated two hundred and fifty schools in Middle America, all staffed and maintained at company expense. The company also has endowed the Pan American Agricultural School in Honduras, and provides scholarships enabling outstanding students to go to the United States or Canada for further study. The petroleum companies in Venezuela also long operated schools in that country. In 1956 the Creole Foundation was established to work primarily in the educational field in Venezuela. Mining and other large enterprises also have constructed school buildings, and provided financial assistance for education, although in some countries the government has taken over the operation of the schools. In recent years many of the countries have enacted legislation requiring employers of large groups to maintain schools for the children of the workers. This legislation is sometimes drafted so as to make the educational requirements obligatory only as regards foreign companies.

Since the first World War, and in some cases earlier, American schools have been established in the capitals and some of the chief cities of most of the Latin American countries.[9] Although designed originally to prepare the children of resident Americans for college entrance examinations in the United States, in most cases the children of nationals of the host country outnumber the offspring of Americans in attendance, and courses are also offered in line with the requirements of local secondary and higher educational institutions. Some of these American schools have become elite institutions that attract applicants from many nationalities. At one time the American schools had to depend upon the support of the local American community, but since World War II community-type, nonsectarian, nonprofit schools have been eligible for assistance out of an appropriation of the United States Congress administered by the Inter-American Schools Service of the American Council on Education. In 1961 there were fifty-three such schools with an enrollment of 18,000 students, of whom two-thirds were Latin Americans or of other than American nationality.[10]

173

2. *Latin American Students in the United States.* Since the war popular attention has come to be centered on bringing Latin Americans to the United States for study, and this interest has been reflected not only in federal and state legislation but also in grants of scholarships and fellowships by universities, foundations, business enterprises, communities, and professional groups. Meanwhile, United States educational institutions have been growing in favor with Latin Americans over recent decades. Back in 1930 only about one thousand Latin Americans were studying in the United States as compared to ten times that number today. The growing prestige of the United States as a world power, its expanding trade and investment, and the comparative blackout of Europe during the war years, influenced the choice, as did the growing interest in technology and industrialization. Traditionally Latin Americans have not rated United States schools and colleges very highly in the intellectual and humanistic fields, but have recognized our standing in science and technology. In an investigation of the programs of American universities in Latin America, two American professors discovered that in one Latin American university 90 per cent of the students receiving grants for foreign study in the scientific and technical fields opted for the United States, whereas "only a minute proportion of those receiving grants in the humanities or social sciences come to the United States."[11]

Be that as it may, an increasing number of Latin American students are coming to the United States, either as a matter of personal or family choice or as the result of inducements held out in the way of scholarships and travel grants. During the scholastic year 1960-61, the number of Latin Americans in the United States for study or training was as follows: students 9,626, faculty members 231, physicians training in the United States 1,975, and industrial trainees 765. Furthermore, the number of students enrolled in the humanities (2,378) and social sciences (963) exceeded those following courses in engineering (2,316) and the physical and natural sciences (914). Other fields of major interest were agriculture (522), business administration (882), education (446), medical sciences (786), and unknown (419).[12]

Data compiled by the Institute of International Education show

174

that one-third of all Latin American students in the United States were self-supporting, 5 per cent were supported by foreign governments, organizations, or individuals, 6 per cent received support from the United States government, and one-third obtained support from United States private organizations or individuals. The Institute reported that the number of self-supporting students is declining, while the number of government grants has increased. It will be noted that those receiving official financial aid comprise a comparatively small proportion of the total. At the same time action by the United States government has been important, not only in stimulating larger programs by private agencies but also directly in providing facilities in a variety of ways, such as language instruction, orientation courses, assistance in connection with immigration formalities, and encouragement to local American groups to provide hospitality and aid to the students living in their communities.

It appears likely that the number of Latin American students in the United States now exceeds the number of Latin Americans in Europe, but the available data are not conclusive. Data compiled by UNESCO[13] showed a total of approximately 3,500 students from the twenty Latin American republics in Europe, of whom the largest number (1,774) were in Spain, followed by the Vatican (587), France (507), Italy (152), Switzerland (127), United Kingdom (114), Germany (80), Austria (57), Belgium (51), and the Netherlands (10). It is possible that these figures are incomplete, since an official report of the British Council showed 382 Latin American students in the United Kingdom at the beginning of the scholastic year 1959-60 (not including 4,230 students from the West Indies).[14]

Apparently the UNESCO figures cover only those students receiving aid from national or international bodies and do not include students in Europe at their own expense. It is difficult to estimate the number of the latter, but they probably equal the number receiving aid, in which case the total would be around 7,000.

Russia's oneupmanship in rocketry has aroused some interest among Latin Americans to find out what is going on behind the Iron Curtain, but Soviet Bloc universities attract very few Latin American students other than Cubans. Estimates of Latin American students enrolled in Soviet Bloc institutions in 1960 were as follows: In the Soviet Union 200 (of whom 100 were Cubans), in Czechoslovakia 199 (110 Cubans), in the German Democratic Republic 71 (30 Cubans), and in other Soviet Bloc countries 26 (10 Cubans); total 496 (250 Cubans).[15]

3. *American Students in Latin America.* As has been indicated earlier, official activity in connection with "exchange of persons" may be said to have originated with the Convention for the Promotion of Inter-American Cultural Relations approved at the Buenos Aires Conference in 1936. The United States ratified this convention and has subsequently enacted a number of measures under which expanded programs of student-professor exchanges have been developed: the Fulbright Act (Public Law 584, 79th Congress), the Smith-Mundt Act (Public Law 402, 80th Congress), the Agricultural Trade Development and Assistance Act of 1954 (Public Law 480, 83rd Congress), and the Mutual Educational and Cultural Exchange Act of 1961 (Public Law 87-256, 87th Congress). All of these measures provide for a two-way exchange between the United States and the particular foreign countries where funds are available (the Buenos Aires Convention laid the basis for exchanges among any two of the twenty-one American republics), but in practice the number of students going to Latin America from the United States has been much less than the flow northward: 1,683 American students in Latin America as against 9,626 Latin American students in the United States. Furthermore, the Americans are largely concentrated in Mexico. Europe remains a big favorite with American students going overseas. During the academic year 1959-60, 69 per cent of American students reported abroad were in Europe, 13 per cent in Canada, 11 per cent in Latin America, and 4 per cent in the Far East. Of United States faculty members abroad in 1960-61, only 10 per cent were in Latin America. The number of American faculty members in Latin America (230) was, however, almost identical with the number of Latin American faculty members in the United States (231).[16]

4. *American Assistance to Latin American Schools.* In addition to the maintenance of schools in Latin America and the provision of numerous grants for study in the United States, the United States, both officially and privately, has participated in the educational ad-

176

vance of Latin America through financial and technical cooperation with Latin American educational authorities and institutions. This type of help from official sources first became significant during World War II.[17] Beginning in 1943, the United States worked out a series of agreements with thirteen Latin American countries providing for bilateral cooperative educational programs handled through a so-called *servicio* jointly administered by United States and local educational experts. In addition to personnel, the United States has supplied funds to cover part or total costs of equipment and supplies, and also has met the cost of training teachers abroad. Between 1944 and 1960, approximately 2,000 Latin American educators were given training in the United States, Puerto Rico, or a third country. During the year 1960, such training was given to 344 Latin American educators.[18]

In most of the countries, priority attention under these programs has been given to primary education, especially in the rural areas. Vocational education also has received considerable attention.

In the field of higher education, the United States aid agencies have adopted the practice of contracting with a United States university to undertake an assistance program vis-à-vis the Latin American university requesting help. Requests for help have fallen mainly in the areas of science and technology, economics, preservice training of teachers, and university administration. Other fields are public administration and agricultural extension and research.

Examples of the university-to-university type of arrangement are the University of Michigan and the Brazilian School of Business Administration, the University of Tennessee and the University of San Andrés of Bolivia, the University of North Carolina and the School of Sanitary Engineering, University of Engineering, Peru, the University of Pittsburgh and the Universidad Técnica Federico Santa María of Chile, and Stanford University and the School of Geology, University of Chile. Some observers feel that this type of direct contact between universities offers one of the best ways by which educators from the United States can assist in the improvement of higher education of Latin America,[19] but others are inclined to emphasize the difficulties and problems involved in such arrangements.[20] In addition to university cooperation involving technical

177

assistance and perhaps the provision of equipment and materials, there are a substantial number of interuniversity programs, such as junior-year programs, which involve primarily an exchange of students and perhaps some faculty members. During the academic year 1957-58, American universities took part in sixty-two programs of interuniversity cooperation with Latin American institutions.[21]

New types of assistance are constantly being introduced. Recently there has been considerable emphasis on scientific programs. In 1960 and 1961, for example, the Pan American Union Division of Science Development, in cooperation with the National Science Foundation, helped to bring Latin American secondary school teachers of science and mathematics to the United States to study at the National Science Foundation summer institutes. Following this initiative, several similar institutes have been held in Latin America.

The National Academy of Sciences of the National Research Council at Washington has also undertaken missions to survey the needs of Latin American universities in the scientific field. The Academy's Committee on Inter-American Scientific Cooperation also has undertaken to give specific assistance in certain cases.[22]

5. *Growing Interest in Education.* Until recently, education has been assigned a very low priority in most of the Hispanic countries. Practically all of the constitutions call for universal and free primary education, but there has been lacking the willingness to pay the taxes necessary to support it, and in most cases the dominant classes have been opposed to mass education on principle. Only in those countries of predominantly European stock—Argentina, Uruguay, Chile, and Costa Rica—has the literacy of the adult population been raised to 80 per cent or more.

Traditionally the argument in favor of education has been primarily political, that the achievement of democracy assumes the broadening of the educational base. And it is, of course, not merely a coincidence that the four countries mentioned above as having the least illiteracy have also been among the countries having the more stable and democratic governments. Recently the cause of education has received powerful reinforcement from two new factors: the emotional forces of nationalism and the drive for industrialization. One hears less of democracy these days but more of the pride that insists on stronger nation-states that can play a role on the world stage. Through their participation in international organizations the leaders have become ashamed of their low standing in comparative world educational statistics. Even more important, there has come to be increasing realization that the foundations of the industrial state require the cement of technical training and that this in turn presupposes a minimum level of general education. The expansion of the public services has also created acute shortages of personnel having the necessary training in economics, diplomacy, languages, and other fields.

The net result of these trends has been a substantial increase in the attention and financial support given to education, but it would be a mistake to jump to the conclusion that all Latin Americans have adopted our educational philosophy. For one thing, they do not necessarily equate education and democracy. Furthermore, they specifically reject the "myth" that "education, and especially the basic learning of the abc's, is indispensable to economic progress."[23] This point of view is important since it reflects a widespread sentiment in Latin America that the assumptions of nineteenth century liberalism are out of date. In their view these assumptions have been disproved not only by the experience of Russia but also by the examples of prewar Germany and Japan. Likewise, Mexican anthropologists like Manuel Gamio, and educators like Moisés Sáenz, long ago pointed out that the establishment of a school in an Indian village did not result in any important change in the way of life of the inhabitants. These observations have recently been confirmed by an American anthropologist as the result of his investigations in southern Sonora.[24]

One manifestation of the new interest in education has been the launching of alphabetization or adult education campaigns. Mexico in 1944 enacted a law requiring every literate Mexican from eighteen to sixty either to teach an illiterate to read and write or to pay for such training. Regional and local centers were established, and millions of readers were printed and distributed. In practice, most of the instruction was provided by teachers in their spare time. The Defense Department also tackled the illiteracy problem among recruits.

After the war anti-illiteracy campaigns had a great vogue. Part of the interest came from UNESCO, which, in looking for something to please the Latin Americans, hit upon fundamental education as its major objective in this area. The Regional Fundamental Education Center for Latin America (CREFAL) was opened at Pátzcuaro, Mexico, in May, 1951. The campaign against illiteracy also received strong support from the Pan American Union. At that time the Division of Education of the Union was headed by a Colombian who was a director of UNESCO. During the early 1950's the Union prepared and published a series of illustrated *cartillas* or booklets designed to provide enticing reading matter for beginners, and some millions of copies were distributed. The Tenth Inter-American Conference at Caracas in 1954 approved a resolution declaring "that the eradication of illiteracy is of extraordinary importance," and recommending to the Council of the OAS that it give priority in the cultural field to the campaign against illiteracy.

This whole subject of fundamental education has aroused such strong differences of opinion among the experts that the layman is inclined to tread warily. One positive achievement of the drive has been the dramatization of educational needs. Partly, at least, as the result of the campaigns the official illiteracy figures have declined. This outcome has been the cause of considerable self-satisfaction, but since the literacy test is very lax, it is not certain that the enormous expenditure of money and effort has resulted in any significant contribution to the real problem of education. In Mexico, for example, some observers feel that the campaign against illiteracy is an educational fraud, on a par with the ventures of the early revolutionary governments in distributing translations of the ancient classics and in launching "ambulatory missionaries" who became more involved with politics and personal intrigue than with education. Despite all this misdirected enthusiasm, ten million Mexicans (nearly one-third of the population) remain without the most rudimentary educational techniques.[25] Nevertheless, in the cities and in the industrial communities where the big companies are required to provide schools, there has been considerable increase in educational facilities, and more students are remaining in school long enough to acquire some effective educational foundation.

In Brazil in 1960 there were reported 20,700,000 illiterates ten years of age or over, or not far from one-third of the population. Owing to the high rate of population growth, the absolute number of illiterates is increasing and is expected to continue to increase until 1975, despite the rapid expansion in the number of children in the schools. In 1959 about 77 per cent of the population between seven and eleven years of age was reported enrolled in primary schools. The increased enrollment has in large part resulted from the rapid urbanization of the country, since school enrollment in the rural districts is low.[26]

In Venezuela, a World Bank study reports two million illiterates out of a total population of 6.8 million. In 1958 43 per cent of the total schoolage children were not attending school, but since the change in government in that year strenuous efforts are being made to improve the educational situation.

Progress in secondary education has been more rapid proportionately than in the primary field. For example, Brazil in 1957 had almost five times as many secondary schools as in 1933 and over eight times as many students attending them.[27] In most of the countries there have existed two parallel systems of education, one for the lower classes, the other for the elite. As regards the former, after a few years of primary schooling, some go on to vocational or normal schools. On the other hand, the sons of the upper middle class and aristocracy go to a *liceo* or *colegio* having a curriculum based on the French *lycée*. Most of the secondary schools have traditionally been private, operated by church groups, by individuals for profit, or by foreigners, although some of the countries have maintained a model secondary school at the national capital. The growth of the middle class has been in large measure responsible for this tremendous demand for secondary education. Not only the middle class but some of the more successful or ambitious members of the lower classes are also demanding an opportunity for secondary education for their children when they finish the primary school.

Changes affecting higher education have been the most spectacular of all: the swarming of students from all classes of society into the universities in the chief urban centers, and the establishment of new research and teaching institutes, especially in the fields of the social and natural sciences. At the end of 1960 the University of Buenos Aires was reported to have 63,000 enrolled students.[28] Of the total enrollment, 30 per cent were women—evidence of another significant change in the educational situation, although a large part of these were doubtless preparing for positions as teachers. Other large Latin American universities are the National University of Mexico, with over 60,000 students, and the University of Chile with 14,000. Enrollment at the University of Havana at the time Castro came into power was about 22,000. During the two years following the revolution of 1958 in Venezuela, enrollment in the five already established universities doubled, and two new universities were opened. Of the national total of 21,800 university students, 60 per cent were in the Central University at Caracas. Registration at San Marcos University in Lima, Peru, in 1960 was 15,000.

The first university in Brazil was organized in 1920 through the merger of the law, medicine, and polytechnic schools at Rio de Janeiro. Official 1960 data showed a matriculation of over 61,000 in Brazil's twenty-one universities, the largest being the University of São Paulo with over 10,000, and the second largest the University of Brazil at Rio de Janeiro with more than 8,000. Plans are now being made for an imposing new university at Brasília, the new capital of Brazil.

Historically the universities of Hispanic America have differed from those in the United States not only in organization, curricula, and teaching methods, but also as regards the social role of the university. Until recently, the universities of the Hispanic republics were state controlled and supported and alone were competent to grant degrees or certificates that enabled the graduates to exercise the professions of law, medicine, dentistry, engineering, etc.[29] The reform movement of 1918, originating with a manifesto by the students of the University of Córdoba, Argentina, and soon spreading throughout Spanish America, resulted in a number of changes that in some respects represented a return to colonial practices: the granting of administrative autonomy to the universities and the admittance of representatives of the students (including, in some cases, graduates) to the governing council of the universities. One unexpected by-product of autonomy was the proliferation of private universities, owing their creation and support primarily to specific pressure groups—the church, banks, industrialists—although in most cases the private universities also receive some financial aid from the government.

Most Latin American universities are a loose aggregation of quasi-independent professional schools, reflecting the historic position of the various faculties, the entrenched position of the *cátedras* or professorships, and the concept that the role of the instructor is to prepare the students for a career rather than to conduct research or undertake investigations. The fact that most of the faculty members are professional men who devote only a small fraction of their time to their university lectures renders impracticable any original investigation or experimental work in connection with the course. As the result of this situation, there has been a tendency to create separate schools or institutes, having at least some full-time staff, to undertake research or introduce new branches of study.

Although Latin American universities are much closer to the European concepts and organization than to those of the United States, the economic and political changes of recent decades, together with the availability of official and private American funds, have resulted in the adoption of some American methods and points of view. The growth of domestic industry and the rise of the middle class of engineers, managers, and government administrators, have created a demand for more technical, scientific, and economic training. The strong emotional drive for economic development since World War II has accentuated this trend.

Since the 1920's the universities in Middle and South America have been receiving increasing numbers of students from the middle and lower classes. Although university fees are very moderate, and there are various types of scholarships, many of the students are able to attend only because they live with their families and perhaps have part-time work. This tends to restrict university education, in the case of the less-favored classes, to those living in the cities where a university is located. In an attempt to meet this situation, a considerable number of municipal, state, or regional universities have been created, although most of these lack the revenues or facilities to maintain very high standards.

183

Traditionally the Spanish American university has not had a liberal arts college, or college of arts and sciences, since it has been considered that the cultural requirements of the professional man are met by the secondary school program, which, in the better schools, covers a broader range than the American high school. Some of the universities, however, have faculties of humanities, philosophy, letters, or education; and some have inaugurated a "common basic year" as prerequisite to admission to the professional faculties. The National University of Mexico operates preparatory schools which offer preuniversity instruction and provide a basis for admission to the university proper.

Contrary to the popular impression in the United States, most university instruction in Hispanic American universities "tends to be almost entirely of a narrow, professional and utilitarian bent."[30] Yet it is also true that the universities have usually managed to attract at least one outstanding scholar or personality, like Jorge Mañach in Cuba, Antonio Caso in Mexico, Ricardo Rojas in Argentina, José Enrique Rodó in Uruguay, or, going further back, Andrés Bello in Chile, who influenced not only a generation of students but an important segment of the public as well. The careers of some of these distinguished scholars also illustrate the essentially political character of the Spanish American university. The late Jorge Mañach, who died in exile on June 26, 1961, had taken an active part in the political activity which led to the overthrow of Machado in 1933. In 1940 he became professor of the history of philosophy as the result of a competition, and in the same year he was elected to the senate. In 1956 Mañach again went into voluntary exile.

The respective roles of the students illustrate dramatically some of the differences between the universities of the United States and those in Spanish America.[31] Since the generalization of the 1918 Córdoba reforms, the Spanish American student bodies have come to have an important voice in university administration, including academic policy, choice of faculty, teaching methods, and even course content. The extent of this influence varies greatly in different countries, being most extensive in Argentina, Uruguay, and Bolivia, and least in Colombia. In the United States, the influence of student bodies on such matters is slight, although alumni associations like to throw their weight around and, in the absence of conscientious and worldly-wise department and university heads, may succeed in making it difficult for faculty members who have indiscreetly criticized football or big business.

In Spanish America the students are not averse to harassing a professor who offends them or unwisely insists on attendance at class (many of the students have full- or part-time jobs), but they are usually out for higher stakes. The fact that student associations tend to intervene actively in current political matters results in the frequent closing of the universities in some countries, either by student strikes or by action of the authorities. On various occasions students have spearheaded successful movements to overthrow dictators, and on other occasions have paid the supreme penalty for failure to topple the tyrant. Various superficial reasons have recently been adduced as explanations of student agitation in Hispanic America, while overlooking the extent to which it is deeply rooted in the Spanish tradition. Julián Marías, the distinguished Spanish philosopher, has recently pointed out that the Spaniard "has always been . . . one of the readiest of men to stake his life for something" but that "he has a certain indolence in staking anything less than his life."[32] It is important to note that such attitudes are not a matter either of class or of economics. Sons of well-to-do families are just as likely to be found on the barricades as the *sans-culottes*.

The rough treatment accorded Vice-President Richard Nixon by student groups during the course of his South American trip in 1958 was attributed to the communists by some official United States spokesmen, no doubt with considerable justification. Yet it is useful to recall that back before World War I Chilean students gave President Theodore Roosevelt and a visiting papal nuncio much the same sort of reception. Whatever the explanation, on his return Vice-President Nixon induced the Department of State to take steps to court student leaders south of the border. During 1959 ten special seminars were held for 165 Latin American student leaders on various campuses in the United States. All of these groups except the one from Mexico also visited Puerto Rico—all expenses paid, of course. In three cases, return trips to the Latin American university were also made by students from Rutgers, Texas, and California.

185

These seminars were repeated with other student groups during the summer of 1960.[33]

Since the underlying philosophy of Latin American universities reflects the political, social, and economic systems of the countries, there are limitations on the effect of these exchanges on students and teachers. Nevertheless, a number of circumstances have conspired to bring about some greater approximation of American and Latin American universities, superficially, at least. For example, the construction of university cities in several Latin American capitals has helped to create an atmosphere reminiscent of American campuses.[34] Likewise, some of the newer universities and institutes, aided by public and private funds from the United States, have been organized along lines suggested by our experience. In southern Chile, two new institutions, the University of Concepción and the Austral University at Valdivia, are built around central campuses and provide for a union of teaching and research. Both institutions are located in developing industrial areas, and give special attention to physics, chemistry, biology, and mathematics. In Mexico, the Monterrey Institute of Technology, with an endowment from the city's prosperous industrialists, aspires to be the local M.I.T., and in Mexico City the National Institute of Cardiology has acquired an international reputation. In Colombia, the University of the Andes, at Bogotá, and the University del Valle at Cali, both of which have received Rockefeller Foundation grants, employ chiefly full-time professors and restrict their students to the number that can be handled adequately. The University of the Andes has a study-abroad program under which qualifying engineering students are sent to a university in the United States for their last two years of undergraduate work.

It would be misleading, however, to assume that all of the ideas in the technological field come from the United States. The Polytechnic School of the University of São Paulo, founded in 1894, and the affiliated Institute of Technological Research, which conducts tests and undertakes materials research, have been strongly influenced by European practices, especially Swiss.

Interest in economic development at the official level, as well as the growing private demand for trained personnel, have spawned new courses in economics as well as the creation of research institutions. Traditionally, instruction in economics has been confined to the law schools, which included chairs of economics and public finance. In most countries there have also been commercial schools for the training of accountants, but these rated distinctly lower in the social scale than the universities. Gradually graduate work in economics and research activities has been organized in separate schools or institutes, although some of the universities, especially the newer ones, have economic departments or faculties separate from the law school (although the latter may also continue its courses as well).

Important centers of economic studies have been developed in connection with the central banks established in the 1920's or subsequently. The Bank of Mexico, for example, in 1925 organized a Department of Economic Studies, and in 1941 a Department of Industrial Research. La Escuela Superior de Economía was set up in the 1930's as a part of the National Polytechnic Institute, and in 1941 the School of Economics of the National University of Mexico founded the Institute of Economic Research.

The Institute of Economics of the University of Chile, founded in 1949 and reorganized in 1955, is perhaps the largest non-governmental organization for economic research in South America. It has had significant financial aid from the Rockefeller Foundation, and also has received special grants from the Chilean government and its dependencies to enable it to undertake particular projects. There are also several other centers for economics studies at Santiago, Chile. The Economic Research Center of the Catholic University of Chile was created in 1956 as the outcome of a contract between the United States' International Cooperation Administration and the University of Chicago, and an agreement between the latter and Catholic University. Several international organizations also are engaged in both research and training. The Inter-American Training Center for Economic and Financial Statistics was established in 1952 by the Inter-American Statistical Institute. The United Nations Economic Commission for Latin America, with headquarters in Santiago, is not only one of the major research organizations in the area, but also operates an economic development training program in conjunction with the United Nations Technical Assistance Administration. The ninth course was inaugurated in July, 1961, with fifty students from twelve countries in attendance. Plans are now being made for a more ambitious Institute for Development Planning to be conducted by the Economic Commission for Latin America with funds from the United Nations Special Fund and other agencies. It has received a grant of $1 million from the Inter-American Development Bank, of which sum 70 per cent came from the Social Progress Trust Fund set up by the United States.

Two conferences of Latin American faculties of economics have been held, the first at Santiago, Chile, in 1953, and the second at Rosario, Argentina, in 1961. Interest in economics also resulted in the preparation of a special report on the subject by a team of three economists designated by ECLA, OAS, and UNESCO.[35] Latin Americans have been in attendance at the annual Economics Institute for Foreign Students held during the summer months at the University of Colorado.

6. *Inter-American and International Agencies.* Over the past decade, the United Nations, the Organization of American States, and their specialized agencies have undertaken a number of projects in the educational and training field. Mention has been made of the Fundamental Education Center (CREFAL) of UNESCO in Mexico. The OAS also maintains an Inter-American Rural Education Center (CIER) at Rubio, Venezuela, open annually to fifty teachers and school directors or administrators. This project, like CREFAL, has been judged by some to be "more sentimental than brilliant" and also as probably being too expensive in relation to possible achievements.[36]

Since 1951 the OAS has inaugurated a number of technical assistance projects involving training and research and also has built up an extensive program of fellowships involving both education and job training. The most impressive of these is the Fellowship Program, under which 1,079 fellowships had been awarded from the inauguration at mid-1958 up to the beginning of November, 1961. Under this program the prospective student is permitted the choice of institution for study, subject to the understanding that the student can qualify and can show adequate facility in the language in which instruction is given. Fellowships are granted for a minimum period of three months and a maximum of two years. Most of the grants are made for advanced study at universities. A considerable proportion of the grants made for one year are extended.

Under this program students must agree that, on the expiration of the fellowship, they will return to the country in which they maintain permanent residence. This proviso was made necessary by the feeling that an excessive proportion of the foreign students coming to the United States under exchange programs were actually immigrants rather than exchangees.

During the scholastic year 1959-60, 57 per cent of the awards were for study in the United States, involving universities in all parts of the country. The most favored institutions outside the United States were the National Institute for Heart Diseases in Mexico, the Obstetrical Service at Montevideo, the graduate economics institutes in Brazil and Chile, the Inter-American Institute of Agricultural Sciences at Turrialba, Costa Rica, and the Caro y Cuervo linguistic and teaching institute in Colombia.

From the beginning of the program up to November, 1961, only eighty-three students from the United States had received fellowships, although this country was entitled to twice that number under the quotas. The reason for this lies in the fact that the Latin American educational and training institutions have proved attractive to American students only in such fields as anthropology and ethnology, language, geography, and history.

Medicine has been the favorite field of study under the Fellowship Program, followed by engineering and education.

A Professorship Program was launched in 1960. So far the few grants made under this program have been at a high level. For example, the noted Brazilian architect and urban planner, Lucio Costa, gave some lectures at Yale University. Dov Tamari of the Institute of Higher Studies at Princeton lectured at the Mathematics Institute of the University of Ceará, Fortaleza, Brazil, and Dr. J. Robert Oppenheimer of the same institution lectured at scientific research centers in Argentina, Brazil, Chile, Mexico, and Uruguay.

The OAS also has established training or study centers in a number of Latin American capitals to take advantage of specialized courses already being offered in existing universities or institutes.

Some of these (with the number of grants available to citizens of member countries of the OAS) may be mentioned:

Primarily social

Advanced training in applied social sciences; 72 grants over a period of five years, beginning in 1959, for advanced study and training in application of techniques at the Escuela Nacional de Antropología e Historia at Mexico City.

Planning and administration of social welfare programs; 26 grants annually for three years, administered by the Ministry of Social Welfare and Public Health at Buenos Aires.

Technical education for the improvement of agriculture and rural life; conducted by the Inter-American Institute of Agricultural Sciences in Costa Rica, but with courses and demonstrations organized by zones: north, Andean, and south. From 600 to 900 are enrolled annually in the general and national courses.

Urban and regional planning; to be offered by the Pan American Union at the Planning Institute of the National University of Engineering, Lima, Peru, with 105 grants available over a period of five years beginning 1962.

Primarily economic development

Evaluation of natural resources; grants available each academic year for two students from each member country, offered by the Pan American Institute of Geography and History at the Pan American Training Center for the Evaluation of Natural Resources at Rio de Janeiro.

Training in business administration; offered at the School of Business Administration in São Paulo, with 40 grants available annually (20 for each course of four months each).

Economic and financial statistics; offered by the Inter-American Statistical Institute at Santiago, Chile, open to one candidate from each member country of the OAS.

The Leo S. Rowe Pan American Fund makes no-interest loans to Latin Americans in need of supplementary help to finish their studies at postsecondary institutions in the United States. In thirteen years, beginning in 1948, the Fund granted 1,023 loans averaging $600 each.

This list does not exhaust the educational and training opportunity provided through the inter-American organization, since a number of the specialized organizations not previously mentioned, such as the Pan American Sanitary Bureau and the Inter-American Indian and Children's Institutes, also maintain training and research centers. Sixteen fellowships are offered by the OAS annually for postgraduate training in the social sciences at the Institute of Caribbean Studies of the University of Puerto Rico. Mention may also be made of the Librarians' School of the University of Antioquia, at Medellín, Colombia, which has received Rockefeller Foundation support over a period of eight years. Likewise Rockefeller money has aided the Center for Inter-American Monetary Studies at Mexico City.

The United Nations and its specialized agencies also have been active in the educational and training field. UNESCO has been active in scientific matters, in addition to its work in the field of fundamental education, mentioned earlier. It has an Office for Scientific Cooperation at Montevideo, which has sponsored numerous seminars and symposiums, and also a Regional Mathematics Center at Buenos Aires. From 1947 until mid-1961, UNESCO awarded more than 2,000 fellowships to Latin Americans for study and training.[87]

The United Nations Special Fund has given financial support for the establishment of research laboratories and training institutes. It promoted an International Center for Higher Studies in Journalism at Quito, Ecuador, and a Latin American Institute for Educational Films in Mexico.

The International Bank for Reconstruction and Development since the early 1950's has operated an Economic Development Institute, which annually enrolls a number of Latin Americans.

7. *Recent Developments.* Education is given a high priority both in the Act of Bogotá (1960) and in the Alliance for Progress (1961). Among the objectives of the Alliance are: "To eliminate adult illiteracy and by 1970 to assure, as a minimum, access to six years of primary education for each school-age child in Latin America; to modernize and expand vocational, secondary and higher educational and training facilities, to strengthen the capacity for basic and applied research, and to provide the competent personnel required in rapidly-growing societies." However skeptical one may be as to the prospects of achieving 100 per cent of this goal, there is no gainsaying the significant increase in the support being given education in most of the countries. It is interesting to recall in this connection that a bare decade ago, at the inter-American seminar on elementary

191

education at Montevideo in 1950, the delegates voted down a resolution to assure three years of elementary education on the grounds that the proposal was visionary. This episode illustrates, among other things, the danger of regional generalizations in a field like education, where both ideology and practice vary greatly in the different countries.

The Charter of Punta del Este recognized that the training of teachers, technicians, and specialists should receive attention in the early stages of the plan in order to lay the foundation for constructive work in the various sectors of production. The United States promptly made available funds for self-help educational projects in Chile, Nicaragua, and Paraguay. Subsequently the United States, acting through the Agency for International Development (AID), contributed $100,000 and provided experts to assist Ecuador in the construction of 5,000 classrooms, and furthermore provided aid in the training of 19,000 teachers. Under another agreement with Ecuador, AID contracted with the University of Pittsburgh to provide technical assistance to Ecuador's two leading universities in such fields as basic sciences, education, English, and physics. In Bolivia, AID cooperated in providing in-service training to rural school teachers. In Central America AID launched a program to provide text books and teacher manuals for the six grades of the elementary schools of the five countries. Furthermore, financial assistance was given for the construction of new classrooms and for developing courses in basic science instruction. Support was also given for a massive three-year education program in the Northeast of Brazil. Other AID projects included contracts with thirty-five American universities to carry out educational programs in fifteen Latin American countries; and likewise cooperation in teacher training programs in fifteen countries as well as in five centers in the United States. (In addition, it may be noted that in 1961 over a thousand Latin Americans received grants through the Bureau of Educational and Cultural Affairs of the Department of State, and that a large part of these were related to various phases of education.) Fellowships were also provided by the National Institutes of Health and other official organizations. In his State of the Union Message delivered to Congress on January 14, 1963, President Kennedy stated that the United

States is "feeding one out of every four school-age children in Latin America an extra food ration from our farm surplus."[38]

The Inter-American Development Bank has drawn on its Social Progress Trust Fund donated by the United States to provide assistance to universities in Argentina, Chile, and Peru. Practically all of the Bank's loans may be said to include some educational content, since in most cases provision must be made for special training.

The Department of State has given moral and financial support to programs for bringing from Latin America young people of high school age, who live with American families and attend high school. Provision is also made at the end of the school year for a bus tour of the United States, ending in Washington with a reception at the White House. Other programs to assist selected Latin American communities are carried out by individuals and groups, such as cities and schools.

In conclusion, it should be noted that several of the Latin American countries have launched vigorous educational programs under their own steam. In Mexico, education has received special attention since 1959, when an eleven-year plan was started.

NOTES TO CHAPTER VII

1. Harry Bernstein, *Origins of Inter-American Interest 1700-1812* (Philadelphia: University of Pennsylvania Press, 1945), chapters I, II, and V.

2. The factual data in this paragraph are taken chiefly from the Bernstein, and from Stanley T. Williams, *The Spanish Background of American Literature* (2 vols., New Haven: Yale University Press, 1955), I, 25; and 325, note 5.

3. That this period was not entirely barren is made plain by Bernstein, *Making an Inter-American Mind* (Gainesville: University of Florida Press, 1961).

4. It is interesting to reflect that the word "science" was at that time still used in its generic sense of "knowledge."

5. This Committee, in 1944 renamed the Interdepartmental Committee on Scientific and Cultural Cooperation, continued in operation until 1950, following the enactment of the Smith-Mundt Act (International Information and Educational Exchange Act of 1948, Public Law 402, 80th Congress, June 27, 1948), which authorized the extension of the cooperative programs to other areas of the world.

6. *Twenty Years of United States Government Programs in Cultural Relations* (New York, January, 1959), p. 11.

7. Secretary of Agriculture Henry Wallace frequently referred to Latin America as a "new Frontier," yet his Director of the United States Soil Conservation Service has estimated that one-fourth of the cultivated land, past and present, in South America has either been ruined or seriously damaged for further potential cultivation. See Hugh H. Bennett, "Soil Conservation," *Proceedings of the Inter-*

American Conference on Conservation of Renewable Resources (Denver, Colorado, September, 1948), p. 353.

8. James G. Maddox, *Technical Assistance by Religious Agencies in Latin America* (Chicago: University of Chicago Press, 1956), and Manoel Bergström Lourenço Filho, in *Brazil,* Lawrence F. Hill (ed.), The United Nations Series (Berkeley and Los Angeles: University of California Press, 1947), pp. 143-44. It is beyond the scope of this study to evaluate the work of other nationalities, such as the English, French, Spanish, German, etc., in Latin America, but at least passing mention must be made of Joseph Lancaster, whose monitorial system, first introduced into Nueva Granada (now Colombia) by Simón Bolívar, spread to all the countries of the New World.

9. The American School at Mexico City was established in 1894. Two American schools were started in Monterrey in the 1880's.

10. It is estimated that around 118,000 students are enrolled in all American-supported schools in Latin America.

11. Richard N. Adams and Charles C. Cumberland, *United States University Cooperation in Latin America* (East Lansing: Michigan State University Press, 1960), p. 166.

12. Institute of International Education, *Open Doors 1961* (New York, 1961).

13. *Study Abroad XI, 1959-10* (Paris, 1959).

14. *Overseas Students in Britain.* A handbook for all who are interested in the welfare of overseas students. Issued by the Standing Committee of the London Conference on Overseas Students (London, 1960).

15. "Sino-Soviet Bloc Exchanges with the Free World in 1960," Intelligence Report No. 8401, Department of State, Feb. 1, 1961, in *Mutual Educational and Cultural Exchange Act,* Hearings before the Committee on Foreign Relations, U. S. Senate, 87th Congress, 1st session, on S. 1154, March 29 and April 27, 1961 (Washington, D.C.: Government Printing Office, 1961).

16. IIE, *op. cit.*

17. Of course, various Latin American countries had earlier borrowed educational ideas from the United States and Europe, and, on occasion, had contracted American teachers and educational administrators. President Sarmiento of Argentina became a close personal friend of Mr. and Mrs. Horace Mann, and, inspired by their ideas, employed many American teachers, who laid the foundation for the educational system in that country. The relatively high percentage of literacy in Cuba goes back to the support to education given by the American authorities during the period of occupation at the end of the nineteenth century. Some of the American mission schools also have had a profound effect on educational ideals and methods. Private American philanthropists also have made contributions in a number of countries.

18. These totals relate only to training under the International Cooperation Administration, as the United States aid agency was then called. It does not include teachers, professors, or educational administrators coming to the United States under other programs or those who paid their own way.

19. John P. Harrison, "The Confrontation with the Political University," *The Annals of the American Academy of Political and Social Sciences,* CCCXXXIV (March, 1961). Mr. Harrison is an official of the Rockefeller Foundation.

20. Richard N. Adams and Charles C. Cumberland, *United States University Cooperation in Latin America: A Study Based on Selected Programs in Bolivia, Chile, Peru, and Mexico* (East Lansing: Michigan State University Press, 1960).

21. OAS, 11th Inter-American Conference, *The Organization of American States and the Exchange of Persons for Study, Training, Research, and Teaching Abroad.* OEA/Ser. E/XI.I, Doc. 6 (Washington, D.C.: Pan American Union, 1959), p. 12.

22. National Academy of Sciences—National Research Council, *Report of the Mission to the Seven Universities of Chile,* prepared for the International Cooperation Administration (Washington, D.C., 1960).

23. Victor Alba, in Hirschman, *op. cit.,* p. 45.

24. Charles J. Erasmus, *Man Takes Control: Cultural Development and American Aid* (Minneapolis: University of Minnesota Press, 1961).

25. Stanley R. Ross, "Mexico: Government Control of Education," *Current History,* XL (June, 1961), 352.

26. J. Roberto Moreira, "Perspectiva do Desenvolvimento Educacional no Brasil e em Alguns Paises Latino-Americanos," *Boletim do Centro Latino-Americano de Pesquisas em Ciências Sociais,* ano III (Rio de Janeiro, agosto, 1960).

27. Charles Wagley, "The Brazilian Revolution: Social Changes since 1930," *Social Changes in Latin America Today,* p. 201.

28. This figure is somewhat misleading, since it includes a large number of mature students who are not candidates for degrees. The student body includes a substantial number of political exiles from other South American countries and from Europe. By a reciprocal treaty of 1889, six South American countries recognize diplomas of the University of Buenos Aires as automatically constituting license to practice their professions.

29. At the beginning of the nineteenth century (i.e., at the end of the colonial era), San Marcos University at Lima, Peru, was open only during the examination periods, and no organized classroom or other academic work was performed. Carlos Cueto Fernandini, *Higher Education in Latin America: A Symposium* (Washington, D.C.: The Catholic University of America Press, 1961), p. 24.

30. Frank Bonilla, "The Student Federation of Chile: 50 Years of Political Activity," *Journal of Inter-American Studies,* II (1960), 313.

31. Brazil and Haiti may be omitted in this connection, Brazil because the students have only a minor role politically or in university administration, Haiti because it receives its chief cultural influences from France.

32. *Atlantic Monthly,* CCVII (January, 1961), Supplement, 74.

33. Adlai Stevenson had the benefit of more adequate police and army protection during his good will trip to Latin America in June, 1961, but the press reported that his visit provoked riots in Chile and resulted in two deaths and four wounded at La Paz.

34. In some cases the Spanish Americans were doubtless influenced by the examples of the University City at Madrid and the Cité Universitaire at Paris. The Madrid colleges reflected strong English influence.

35. *The Teaching of Economics in Latin America* (Washington, D.C.: Pan American Union, 1961).

36. *Informe de la comisión de evaluación del programa educativo de la Unión Panamericana, presentado al Secretario General de la Organización de los Estados Americanos* (Washington, D.C.: Pan American Union, December, 1958), pp. 19, 20.

37. "UNESCO'S Main Projects in Latin America," *UNESCO Chronicle,* VII (1961), 222-27.

38. Cited in the Department of State Bulletin, XLVIII, No. 1232 (1963), 161.

–VIII–

Mutual Cultural Relations: Books and Information Services

The providing of American books and periodicals to Latin America, and the aiding of the reverse flow by making available to American readers in translation the books and articles of Latin American authors, have been important aspects of our cultural programs. Various channels have been used to achieve these purposes: (1) outright gifts of books and periodicals from the United States to individuals, institutions, and libraries, (2) operation of reading rooms and libraries in the principal Latin American cities, (3) translation and distribution of works of American writers, (4) granting financial aid and moral support to encourage translation into English and publication in the United States of books and articles by Latin Americans, and (5) action by inter-American and international agencies in handling exchanges of publications and in undertaking translations.

DISTRIBUTION OF BOOKS

Some of the private foundations have, over a considerable period, as noted in the preceding chapter, made grants of American publications to Latin American libraries, and similar gifts have been made by numerous individuals and organizations. In 1940, for example, three libraries of three thousand volumes each, donated by American publishers, were sent to the public libraries of Rio de Janeiro, Buenos Aires, and Montevideo. Similar gifts have been made to libraries in other cities.

During the war years, when United States government purse strings were loosened, substantial official presentations of books were carried out. From 1943 to 1947, more than 100,000 volumes were distributed to 986 libraries in Latin America through the intermediary of the American Library Association.[1]* In addition, inexpensive editions of American classics, as well as of some recent writers, and also reference works, were distributed through our embassies (the number per post varied from fifty to four thousand). Our embassies were also provided with some funds for the purchase of American publications, either in English or in translation, to be used as presentation copies to local individuals or institutions or for use as prizes in English classes or essay contests.[2]

The presentation of American books and periodicals to key individuals and groups continues to be a part of the regular activities of the United States Information Agency, which was established in 1953 to handle promotion of the United States abroad. For example, a selected library on atomic energy was presented to one Latin American government. In addition to gifts, the United States has promoted the distribution of American publications in various ways: (1) under the Informational Media Guarantee Program, USIA assists publishers to convert into dollars local currency receipts for book sales in countries where dollar shortages exist; (2) in 1941, agreements were negotiated for reduction by one-half of postal rates on books going to other American republics; (3) for the benefit of readers with a limited English vocabulary, the United States assists publishers abridging and simplifying standard American works; (4) with the aid of funds provided by the official United States aid agency, the United States Book Exchange, Inc., has enabled many Latin American libraries and institutions to obtain a wide variety of books, especially in the scientific field; and (5) the Library of Congress has distributed pamphlets, photographs, library cards, microfilms, and other materials, as well as providing assistance to scholars throughout the hemisphere.

Access to American publications has also been facilitated by the establishment of reading rooms and cultural centers in Latin America. The initiative in this work was taken by local nationals, aided by resident Americans, beginning in the 1920's. The Instituto Cultural Argentino-Norteamericano opened in Buenos Aires in 1927, and similar institutes were established at Córdoba, Argentina, in 1931,

*Notes to chapter VIII begin on page 214.

at Rio de Janeiro in 1935, and at Santiago, Chile, and Lima, Peru, during the late 1930's. These types of operations, which came to be known as binational centers since they are supported and operated by nationals of the country in which they are located although also receiving United States assistance, now exist in eighty-nine communities and in all of the republics except Uruguay. In addition, USIA operates seven cultural centers in Latin America that are supported and operated by the United States. One of the main activities of these centers is providing instruction in English, which attracts thousands of individuals. English classes are also offered by the British Council.

TRANSLATION AND PUBLICATION IN LATIN AMERICA

Possibly of even more significance than the providing of books in English has been the program of translations into Spanish, Portuguese, and French. In the early days of the official program, at the end of the 1930's, this work was handled through a central translation office in the Department of State, and the focus was on foreign-language editions of United States government publications having wide popular appeal, such as health and infant care. Eventually, most of the translations came to be handled through contracts, and a wide range of publications was covered. An official report issued by the Department of State early in 1948 gave the following summary: "Major grants are given for publication in translation of books which would probably not otherwise be translated. Grants are also given for books that might possibly be translated but at a price so high that the number of readers would be very small. Many translations in Spanish and Portuguese are now appearing in the other republics at prices equivalent to those of the original editions published in the United States. Books representative of United States culture, published commercially by Latin American publishers, are often purchased for distribution through the American Embassies to libraries and institutions in the other American republics. A wide field of publication is covered . . . Because of the demand which exists in the other American republics for scientific, technical, and medical information, major emphasis has been placed on books in these fields. Texts for medical schools have received major attention."[3]

It may be noted that this program coincided with several important developments in the Latin American scene: the expansion of the reading public as the result of the growth of the middle-income group; increased need for textbooks created by rising enrollment in the schools and universities; the shifting of the publishing centers for the Spanish language to Spanish America, chiefly Buenos Aires and Mexico City, as the consequence of the Spanish Civil War; and the eclipse of Europe, as one nation after another was drawn into the vortex of World War II. Brazil had long had its own publishing industry. In 1959, some five thousand titles were published in Brazil as compared to an aggregate of about seven thousand in Spanish America.

The Fondo de Cultura Económica, originally established at Mexico City in 1934 with a government subsidy to translate and publish textbooks on economics, has developed into a major publishing house, with a long list of titles in economics, sociology, history, philosophy, political science, law, anthropology, psychology, science, technology, art, and fiction. Despite the large and growing list of Mexican authors, 25 per cent of all titles published in Mexico annually are translations. Mexico has become a sizeable exporter of books, chiefly to the other Spanish American countries, but with some shipments to the United States and Spain.[4]

PUBLICATION IN THE UNITED STATES OF LATIN AMERICAN WORKS

The United States has not confined its interest to the propagation of its own publications. It has also sponsored the presentation of Latin American literary, artistic, and scholarly works in the United States. In order to encourage publishers to issue in English books originally published in the other American republics, grants have been made either by the government or by private foundations to cover the cost of translating and editing. In the spring of 1960 the Rockefeller Foundation made a grant of $225,000 to the Association of American University Presses to cover part of the cost of issuing in translation works of scholarly or literary importance, the selection of titles to be made by a panel of four specialists. Facilities have also been provided to assure the publication in English of scientific and scholarly articles by Latin Americans. In 1959, for example, the National Science Foundation made a grant to support a scientific translation center in the John Crerar Library of Chicago.

Publication in translation of representative works of the Latin American countries is underway through the collaboration of the Organization of American States and UNESCO.

Generally speaking, the subsidy programs have been confined to learned works or to literary classics rather than to the current output of belles-lettres. Creations of Latin American writers have never achieved a mass audience in the United States, although works of merit have found favor with the *cognoscenti*. Prior to World War I most of the translations appearing in the United States were of poetry, the medium in which Latin Americans have made their maximum literary contribution in the past. As early as the 1820's William Cullen Bryant became interested in Cuban and Mexican poets and translated a number of their works. Quite likely at that time a larger proportion of educated Americans were seriously interested in poetry than at any subsequent period.

Despite the emphasis on poetry, two of the most popular translations from South American writings during the nineteenth century were in prose: Sarmiento's *Facundo,* translated by Mrs. Horace Mann and published in New York in 1868 under the title *Life in the Argentine Republic in the Days of the Tyrants,* and Jorge Isaacs' *María,* a highly romantic novel set in the Cauca valley of Colombia, published in English translation at New York in 1890 and reprinted in 1918. Annotated editions of *María* in Spanish have also been published in the United States for classroom use. *María* is said to have had the widest circulation of any Spanish American novel. Up to World War II, it had also "attained the greatest success so far achieved by any Latin American work translated into English."[5]

Also worthy of note were the translations of the early chroniclers and colonial histories published in England, especially the series issued by the Hakluyt Society.

During the nineteenth century Middle and South America provided inspiration for numerous historians, travellers, scientists, and fiction writers of other regions, and some of their productions have become classics, such as Humboldt's accounts of his travels in South

America, Mexico, and the Caribbean, Darwin's *Voyage of the Beagle*, Agassiz's *Journal in Brazil*, Stephens' *Incidents of Travel in Central America, Chiapas and Yucatan*, Dana's *Two Years Before the Mast*, Prescott's volumes on the conquest of Mexico and Peru, Wallace's *The Fair God*, Flandrau's *Viva Mexico!*, and Hudson's sensitive impressions of the regions bordering the Río de la Plata and the Orinoco.

The United States' interest in Spanish American literature and arts began to take root around the turn of the century and came into flower during World War I, along with the huge expansion in the enrollment in Spanish classes. By the 1890's articles on Spanish American and Brazilian literature began to appear in encyclopedias and in literary magazines. In 1916 there appeared the first major study in any language of Spanish American literature as a whole (Alfred Coester, *A Literary History of Spanish America*, New York, 1916. A Spanish edition was published in Madrid in 1929). In 1917 the American Association of Teachers of Spanish was organized, the first of six separate national modern language associations, in addition to the Modern Language Association of America, organized in 1883. The journal of the Spanish and Portuguese teachers' association, *Hispania*, as well as others in this field, helped to give a considerable stimulus to research and literary criticism. Several important anthologies of Spanish American poetry and short stories were published, and special courses in Spanish American literature began to be offered in American universities.[6]

The attention given in the United States to Spanish American or Latin American literature as a whole did much to promote the concept of a distinct Latin American literature, although various forces were working in the same direction. Among the latter were the meteoric career of Rubén Darío, the continental perspective developed by Latin American writers and critics living in Paris, Madrid, and New York, and the fact that many Latin American writers found it healthier at times to live temporarily beyond the reach of the authorities in their own country and hence were forced to earn a living in another Spanish-speaking nation.

In poetry, Darío not only added new lustre to American letters but had a profound influence in Spain itself. Latin America has pro-

201

duced many other fine poets both before and since Darío, including the aforementioned Nobel prize winner, Gabriela Mistral, of Chile. Spanish American poets have had an enthusiastic, if limited, audience in the United States. More than one Spanish American poet was first published in the United States or first obtained serious recognition in this country. As a matter of fact, Gabriela's first book, *Desolación,* not only was published in the United States by the Instituto de las Españas en los Estados Unidos (New York, 1922), but the initiative in collecting the poems and publishing them was taken by American teachers and students. American presses have brought out excellent anthologies of Spanish American poets, some including both the original text as well as the translation in English. Unfortunately, poetry in translation inevitably loses much of its flavor along with any special qualities or associations that it may have in the original tongue. Robert Frost has defined poetry as "what disappears in translation."

LATIN AMERICAN NOVELISTS

Spanish America has produced some fine novels, but very few have revealed the originality, depth, and technical skill necessary to win international recognition. A leading Peruvian critic wrote in 1940 that a Spanish American prefers to live his novel rather than write it,[7] and an outstanding American scholar in 1951 expressed doubt "whether there is yet a Spanish American novel of universal importance."[8]

It is to Brazil that one must look for the finest contributions of the area in the novel form. There appears to be general agreement that the novels of Machado de Assís, published at the end of the nineteenth century, represent the best to come out of South America. The Brazilian Generation of the 1930's also produced some works that must take high rank in any over-all assessment. Although most of these carry overtones of regionalism (the cane and cacao cycles of the Northeast, the tragedy of drought in the *sertãos* or backlands, crossed lives in Pôrto Alegre and the *gaucho* state) and are not lacking in cries of anguish or social protest, the Brazilians not only have shown great vitality and penetration, but have avoided for the most part the striving for effect, the lack of selectivity in use of local color, and the general weakness of aim that have marred many promising Spanish American novels.

A representative selection of Latin American novels has been published in English translation. Novels by Alencar and Taunay appeared in London in the 1880's, and some Spanish American short stories and novels were published in whole or in part during the nineteenth century. In the United States, with the exception of *María*, no novels, strictly speaking, appeared in translation until after World War I. In 1919, a translation of José Marmol's *Amalia*, a romantic historical novel from the time of Rosas in Argentina, appeared, to be followed during the 1920's and 1930's by one or more selections from Manuel Gálvez, Hugo Wast, Enrique Rodríguez Larreta, Carlos Reyles, Ricardo Güiraldes, Horacio Quiroga, Alberto Blest Gana, José Eustacio Rivera, Rómulo Gallegos, Gregorio López y Fuentes, Mariano Azuela, and Martín Luis Guzmán, from the Spanish, and Aloísio Tancredo Gonçalves de Azevedo's *A Brazilian Tenement* and Paulo de Oliveira Setúbal's *Domitila*, from the Portuguese. During the 1940's and 1950's the chief works of Machado de Assís and of contemporary Brazilian novelists were added to the list, as well as those of Spanish Americans, such as Ciro Alegría and Eduardo Barrios. In 1960 three Mexican novels appeared in translation: Carlos Fuentes' *Where the Air is Clear*, Luis Spota's *The Enemy Blood*, and Rosario Castellanos' *The Nine Guardians*. Subsequently there have appeared in translation Fuentes' *The Good Conscience*, Spota's *The Time of Wrath*, Juan Rulfo's *Pedro Paramo* (all three by Mexicans), and Jorge Amado's *Gabriela, Clove and Cinnamon*. The last mentioned, primarily a sex thriller, received a tremendous advertising build-up.

The novel has been gaining in popularity as a literary form of expression in Latin America, and in a few countries, such as Brazil and Mexico, a popular work may have impressive sales. None of these has, however, in translation become a best seller in the United States. Painters, sculptors, architects, musicians, moviestars—not a few Latin Americans in these categories have had phenomenal success. The financial rewards obtained by writers have been less, although well-known authors, critics, and professors of literature can

203

usually count on an expense-paid trip to the United States, and, if their English is adequate, on some lecture fees. Foreign recognition also augments their standing at home. Not a few have obtained temporary or permanent appointments as lecturers or professors of literature in American universities.

A considerable number of Latin American short stories have been published in English translation, and some have appeared in Spanish in collections of Hispanic *cuentos*. There are critics who insist that Spanish Americans are better suited by temperament to poetry, essays, short stories, and polemical historical writings than to novels or more extensive pieces of work, since the former are the product of impulsive *élans*.[9] Most compilers of short stories for text books still use a considerably larger proportion of stories from Spain than from the Americas. This is understandable and proper, since in most types the writers of the Peninsula are superior. What the Spanish Americans do best of all, perhaps, are short essays or sketches, but these make a limited appeal to readers in the United States without personal experience in the region.

A few Spanish American plays have been published in English. In 1927 an annotated edition of *La Gringa* by Florencio Sánchez was issued. Representative plays by Sánchez have recently been published in English under the UNESCO-OAS program of translations. A collection of one-act plays by Elena Garro were published in English translation in the *Evergreen Review*.

As regards prose nonfiction, this realm is obviously so large that most of it must be left to the specialist, but some outstanding works have appeared complete in English, and excerpts from others have been included in anthologies or selections of readings. In this century there have been published translations of Rodó's principal books, Manuel Ugarte's severe indictment of the United States in *Destiny of a Continent*, selections from the Cuban patriot, José Martí, Francisco García Calderón's *Latin America, its Rise and Progress*, and some outstanding Brazilian studies, such as Graça Aranha's *Canaan*, Euclides da Cunha's *Rebellion in the Backlands*, Arthur Ramos' *The Negro in Brazil*, and Gilberto Freyre's *The Masters and the Slaves*.

Recent contributions to the anti-American literature that have appeared in English translation in the United States are *The Shark and the Sardines* (1961), by Juan José Arévalo, former President of Guatemala; various products of Fidel Castro's propaganda machine, and a translation of Vicente Sáenz's *Hispanoamerica contra el coloniaje.* ("Latin America Against the Colonial System," 1949). Articles by Latin Americans have appeared in United States journals devoted to literature and to the natural and social sciences. The points of view of our neighbors have found frequent expression in the published proceedings of conferences and seminars. A series of lectures at Harvard University by the Dominican scholar and critic, Pedro Henríquez Ureña were published under the title, *Literary Currents in Hispanic America,* and recently a series of lectures at the University of Nebraska by the Mexican historian, Daniel Cosío Villegas, were issued with the title, *Change in Latin America: The Mexican and Cuban Revolutions* (1961). Two Latin Americans state their views in a recent volume published by the Twentieth Century Fund, *Latin American Issues,* Albert O. Hirschman, editor (1961). Selected writings of Latin American philosophers are given, with introduction and notes, in Aníbal Sánchez Reulet, *Contemporary Latin American Philosophy* (1954). During the 1940's a series of histories of the principal Latin American countries, written by nationals, were translated and published by the University of North Carolina Press.

The channels for the distribution of Latin American literature are constantly broadening. The *Odyssey Review,* established in 1961, publishes poetry, short stories and articles in translation. The recently organized William Faulkner Foundation will award prizes and facilitate the publication in translation. In Washington the Pan American Union and the Institute of Contemporary Arts provide forums for Latin American writers.

QUALITY VS. NUMBERS

From the above sketch it is clear that the United States has long been engaged in cultural interchanges with Latin America and that these activities have been greatly intensified in recent decades. From the end of the 1930's the United States has given substantial financial support, both officially and privately, in educational matters, in cultural presentations, and in promoting in the United States a wider knowledge and appreciation of hemisphere languages, literatures, arts, music, and philosophy. On the whole, these activities have been more successful and less controversial than our activities in some other fields. Furthermore, the sums of money involved have been more modest. And, most amazing of all, many of the principal backers of the programs have, until recently at least, realized the dangers of inflation in cultural coinage[10] and have insisted that our cultural exchanges be "strengthened rather than expanded."[11]

Secretary of State Dean Rusk also has insisted that "federal and private aid to education of foreign students in this country should stress quality rather than numbers."[12] Members of the House Committee on Education and Labor, reporting on a trip to South America, emphasized that the Latin Americans want only the best professors and are sensitive on this point. They quoted the Argentine Minister of Education and also Dr. Bernardo Houssay, the Nobel prize-winning scientist, to the effect that only graduate students should be sent to the United States under exchange programs and that a guarantee should be required that the students will return to Argentina.[13] This Argentine attitude may be said to reflect the general Latin American view. At a symposium held in Washington, D. C., Dr. Vasco Mariz, Cultural Affairs Officer of the Brazilian embassy, stated that it is better under the official programs to send one man who enjoys the work and can benefit from the experience than twenty or thirty who return dissatisfied.[14]

Likewise, in a report prepared at the request of the United States Advisory Commission on Educational Exchanges, Dr. Walter H. C. Laves made his number one recommendation, "That the Government limit its programs to those for which it can assure high quality of content and of administration."[15]

The difficulties and dangers involved in large-scale exchange programs and the extent to which they quickly tend to become infiltrated with status seekers and empire builders are brought out in a series of studies made by faculty members of Michigan State University. They conclude: "Better a few professors obviously suited to the needs of the host institution than a situation where administrators search desperately to find men who are willing and able to accept foreign assignments simply because there are 'vacancies' to be filled," and further that the cause of international education "is not advanced by endorsing frauds."[16] A warning that the honorable position of the universities "might be degraded by the universities' reluctance to say no to dollars offered, even when their contribution might be dubious" was made by John W. Gardner, president of the Carnegie Corporation of New York, before the forty-second annual meeting of the American Council on Education. Mr. Gardner added that as long as the universities have no conception of themselves other than as supermarkets, "they will have to resign themselves to the fact that people will walk in off the street, buy a box of Wheaties, and walk out."[17] Similar comments have been made by a well-known anthropologist with wide experience and exceptional opportunities for observation of our Latin American programs. Referring, à la Veblen, to present-day "conspicuous giving," he warns against the "promotional excesses of conspicuous administration" in most of our programs. He also finds an apt illustration of Parkinson's Law in the fondness of our overseas administrators for the type of program which permits an almost unlimited expansion of subordinates. He points out that Americans operating in a foreign country tend to arouse envy on the part of nationals and that this envy frequently turns into hatred and anti-Americanism.[18]

Despite these words of caution, there were signs from the beginning of the Kennedy administration that a substantial expansion of our international cultural efforts was in the offing. At a combined meeting of the advisory boards of educational exchange and foreign scholarships on February 27, 1961, President Kennedy stated that "there is no better way" to help "the new nations . . . than by assisting them to develop their human resources through education." He also expressed the need for "centering responsibility" in this field, and on March 31 named an Assistant Secretary of State for Educational and Cultural Affairs (Philip H. Coombs), the first Assistant Secretary with this title, although in 1959 a Special Assistant to the Secretary of State had been appointed to assure greater recognition of the department's work in the internecine struggle with other agencies in this field, such as the United States Information Agency and the International Cooperation Administration (now the Agency for International Development).

A further step was taken with the enactment, on September 21, 1961, of the Mutual Educational and Cultural Exchange Act of 1961 (Public Law 87-256). Senator J. W. Fulbright, who with Representative Wayne L. Hays had sponsored this legislation, stated that its purposes were to consolidate in one piece of legislation the many provisions of law relating to the programs, to provide more flexibility in administration, and to increase the size and scope of the programs. Under the original Fulbright Act of 1946, assistance was limited to those countries where counterpart funds were available from sales of surplus property. Under the new legislation, the President is given broad authority, when he considers that it would strengthen international cooperative relations, to carry out educational and cultural exchanges and participation in international fairs and expositions. Among the other changes introduced in the new law is the provision that all foreign students in the United States are eligible to receive government-supported orientation and counseling services. Greater flexibility is permitted in making use of either dollars or foreign currencies to provide funds for the programs. United States tax and immigration provisions are also liberalized for the benefit of exchange visitors.

In order to meet these enlarged responsibilities, the appropriation for educational and cultural operations was increased for the fiscal year 1961-62, much of the increase being earmarked for improved reception and orientation facilities for foreign students in the United States—a program rendered acute by the influx of large numbers of poorly prepared African students.

There has also been some increase in the appropriation for the Latin American activities of the State Department's Bureau of Educational and Cultural Affairs, but the larger part of the United States government's aid to education has been handled by the Agency for International Development as a part of the Alliance for Progress.[19] After two decades of emphasis on ample provision of capital as the key factor in the process of economic development, educational and institutional factors have recently come in for increased attention. At a Policy Conference on Economic Growth and Investment in Education, held at Washington October 16-20, 1961, under the auspices of the Organization for Economic Cooperation and Development, Secretary Rusk, in the opening address, stated that "in our aid programs we shall devote increasing proportions to educational developments."

It is not within the purview of this discussion to attempt to assess the relative merits of the various aid, cultural, and information programs, nor judge the organizational machinery involved in their execution. There is, no doubt, room for considerable difference of opinion as to which programs need more funds and which might better be de-emphasized or suppressed, but in some cases it is hard to escape the conclusion that what is needed is not more money[20] but more wisdom and restraint.[21]

It is possible that our program for translation into Spanish and Portuguese of books published in the United States might illustrate this point. There has been no lack of such translations in the past, made either in a Latin American country or in Spain or Portugal. The fact that the people of the countries themselves undertook the translation and publication reflected a genuine interest in the work. Now that the United States government is undertaking the translations, and is mobilizing its agents to assure adequate circulation, the books tend to become propaganda tools rather than intellectual contributions, and are rated accordingly.

Culture vs. Propaganda

Since the war our cultural and informational programs have at times been bedeviled by organizational problems and by a divergence in philosophy between those who feel that all our programs should be tailored to have immediate propaganda impact and demonstrate the democratic way of life and the virtues of private enterprise, and those believing that our cultural exhibits and interchanges should be mutual and make their way on their merits without direct political motivation. At the end of the war, the public relations point of view was in the ascendant, with the result that cultural affairs were dominated by the much larger information programs, and became an instrument of the cold war. This approach was emphasized during the years 1945-47, when William Benton, a successful advertising executive, was Assistant Secretary of State for Public Affairs. Subsequently there developed some recognition of the need to treat educational and cultural matters separately from public relations, with the result that in 1953 the press, radio, and public affairs programs were assigned to the newly created United States Information Agency, while other relations remained in the Department of State. In 1959 a Special Assistant to the Secretary of State was appointed to supervise the educational and cultural work of the department, and in 1961 the position of Assistant Secretary for Educational and Cultural Affairs was created.

That the struggle is not yet over is indicated by a recent statement by former Senator Benton that "the U.S.I.A. should be reintegrated into the State Department and merged with the cultural affairs area, from which it should never have been separated."[22] Unfortunately this internecine warfare is exacerbated by the competition for position and power. For example, one of the major recommendations of a study prepared for the United States Advisory Commission on Educational Exchange early in 1961 was that "an *Under*-Secretary of State for Educational and Cultural Affairs be designated."[23] As noted above, they did not get an Under-Secretary but did get an Assistant Secretary. The United States Advisory Commission on Information, it may be noted, had already gone on record in its Sixteenth Report to Congress, as favoring the consolidation of foreign information, education, and cultural programs in an independent agency under a director general having Cabinet status.[24] Needless to say, these exalted officials, in order to justify their rank, would feel it necessary to have large staffs both at home and abroad and constantly expanding budgets.

The argument is frequently made, in support of massive cultural and information programs, that foreign distrust and suspicion of the United States arise out of ignorance of the United States, the high level of its culture, and the generosity of its motives. Congressmen returning from a trip southward have, on various occasions, lamented the lack of knowledge in Latin America of what we are doing for them, and conclude that we must do more to "tell our story." Actually, the real difficulty is just the opposite: the man in the street in Ecuador or Uruguay may not know all about our activities, but he knows enough to be startled and wonder what it is all about. Latin

Americans are not unappreciative of what has been done to make Latin American literature and art known in this country, nor do they object to our footing the bill for the salaries and travel expenses of some qualified American personnel to teach specialized subjects in their institutes and universities. But a high-pressure program at once arouses resistance and suspicions. In some fields responsible government officials realize that the United States can do more for them than any other country, but in other fields they would prefer to accept cultural assistance from the smaller and weaker countries, or from an international agency, although the latter has also become suspect in some quarters. They object to the attempts of the United States to monopolize the field, and it is partly in reaction against a too close embrace from the northern colossus that they become more sympathetic to Soviet contributions. In any case, they feel that they can enjoy Russian art, music, ballet, literature, and movies without becoming either czarist or communist. It is not without significance that the Bolshoi Ballet, virtually unchanged since czarist times, was a great success in Latin America. On the other hand, we work too hard at our propaganda and hence often miss the mark. *Porgy and Bess* is perhaps a case in point; it was fairly successful, but it offended some, and at times showed to half-empty houses.

Authoritative evidence on this point is contained in the testimony of George V. Allen, former Director of the United States Information Agency who has also served as Ambassador in various countries: "Let us be frank enough to face the fact that many people in foreign countries are concerned about American cultural imperialism. They are inclined to worry lest the culture of the United States be superimposed on them or that their own culture be swamped by the superior ability of the United States to send our people and our books and films and TV programs abroad."[25]

Those who are constantly urging bigger programs overlook the fact that the law of diminishing returns sets in fairly quickly on all types of foreign-based operations. Even if our programs were perfectly conceived and executed by saints, they would still be suspect if, taken in conjunction with all of our other activities in the country, they begin to appear disproportionately large in their particular setting. As early as 1945 a distinguished Peruvian scholar and educator asked why the United States was trying "so desperately and so methodically to win our friendship?"[26] The House Committee on Education and Labor, in the report mentioned above, stated: "The Latin Americans with whom we spoke were extraordinarily sensitive about receiving funds . . . directly from the United States Government."[27] The private foundations and some individuals and companies have done some fine work in the educational and cultural fields, but it is possible even for private operators to try to do too much.

The postwar position of leadership of the United States naturally makes it the center of interest and attraction throughout the world. Without any need for promotional activities on our part, young people want to learn English both because of its prestige value and because it opens the doors to new opportunities. It is right and proper that the United States government should provide some facilities to those wishing to learn more of our language, literature, economy, and customs, but it would be unwise to expect much cold-war mileage out of such things, and attempts to distort them for propaganda purposes are apt to be counterproductive.

Long before our present preoccupation with our image abroad, Latin Americans were familiar, either in the original or in translation, with our literary classics and our public documents. Manuel Belgrano, the Argentine patriot, carried a copy of Washington's Farewell Address with him during his military campaigns.[28] Even Dr. Francia of Paraguay, although a ruthless dictator, called Franklin "the first democrat of the world and our model for imitation."[29] During the 1920's and 1930's, there appeared in translation in Spanish (and frequently in Portuguese, too) a wide variety of books reflecting various phases of American life: success stories like the life of Henry Ford, anthologies of plays and poetry, textbooks, westerns, detective stories, and practically all of the best sellers, such as Sinclair Lewis, Ernest Hemingway, John Steinbeck, and John Dos Passos. Writers like Waldo Frank and Upton Sinclair had a wide circulation and were rated higher by Latin American than by American critics.

The uses and abuses of culture in international relations undoubtedly deserve careful study. Every country feels flattered when foreigners show a knowledge of and genuine liking for its distinctive cultural products. Many Latin American businessmen know our art museums better than most United States citizens and perhaps better than some of our official cultural representatives abroad. In Latin America it is almost *de rigueur* for a Minister of Foreign Affairs to be also a man of letters, and the diplomatic corps of the various countries include some of the outstanding national poets, novelists, essayists, philosophers, and historians. International recognition as a novelist led to the presidency in one country—for a brief period, at least. It does not necessarily follow that the United States should choose its Presidents or Secretaries of State from among our literary luminaries. Each nation should follow its own bent. But how many of our ambassadors in Latin America have a working knowledge of our poetry, to say nothing of Spanish, Portuguese, or Latin American poetry? A diplomat who can quote Rubén Darío might well do more to earn good will than cultural presentations costing hundreds of thousands of dollars. Unfortunately, until recently, at least, and perhaps still today, any United States representative who was caught reading Latin American novels or poetry would have been considered a suspicious character.

What is good and valuable in our culture will surely be appreciated, perhaps the more if we do not strive too hard to sell it. But we should not assume that our cultural concepts will necessarily be the same as those of other countries. Latin Americans place a high value on literary and artistic culture, but their point of view is essentially an elite concept, as is clearly brought out in Rodó's *Ariel*. Likewise, the Mexican historian, Daniel Cosío Villegas has pointed out the weaknesses of the United States' cultural programs; namely, that the very size of the programs prevents any refinement or high standards.[30] In Latin America, poetry occupies a vital place in the life of many people that has no parallel in the United States. Every Latin American young man carries some verses in his pocket. In the opening paragraphs of Machado de Assís' great novel, *Dom Casmurro*, the narrator was going home on a commuter train out of Rio de Janeiro, and happened to sit next to a young man from his neighborhood. The young man "talked of the moon and the government," and ended by taking some verses of his own composition from his pocket and reading them. The young man was offended because Dom Casmurro was

213

tired and preoccupied and did not show sufficient enthusiasm for the verses.

Authorship of a few essays or of a thin sheaf of poems is the best assurance of political preferment in Latin America (following family connections, of course). In fact, not a few public men have been concerned about their countrymen's preference for poets over production managers. Juan Bautista Alberdi, who drafted the Argentine constitution of 1853, stated that "next to the liberators, the poets are the most dangerous enemies of liberty in South America."[31] The Argentine editor, Julio R. Barcos, in concurring with Alberdi's views, stated: "Everything remains to be done among us. . . . It is high time for us to come forth from the contemplative ecstasy of our soft and ideal life, in order to pass over to the dynamic life."[32] There are a large and increasing number of dynamos in Latin America. Is there an irreconcilable conflict between the dynamo and the Virgin, as Henry Adams came to believe? Most Latin Americans believe they can effect a working compromise between poetry and productivity.

Notes to Chapter VIII

1. *Cooperation in the Americas,* Report of the Interdepartmental Committee on Scientific and Cultural Cooperation, July 1946-June 1947, U.S. Department of State Publication 2971 (Washington D.C.: Government Printing Office, 1948), p. 100.

2. *Ibid.,* p. 101.

3. *Ibid.,* p. 97.

4. *Books in the Americas,* (Washington, D.C.: Pan American Union, 1960), pp. 25, 82.

5. Concha Romero James, "Spanish American Literature and Art," in Charles Carroll Griffin (ed.), *Concerning Latin American Culture* (New York: Columbia University Press, 1940), p. 207.

6. The University of Arizona introduced courses in Spanish American literature as early as 1908—Sturgis E. Leavitt, *Some Phases of the Cultural Relationships Between the United States and Latin America During the Nineteenth and Twentieth Centuries* (Washington, D.C.: Pan American Union, 1938). Also see Leavitt, *The Teaching of Spanish in the United States,* Reports of Surveys and Studies in the Teaching of Modern Foreign Languages, published by the Modern Language Association, November, 1961.

7. Luis Alberto Sánchez, *América: Novela sin novelistas* (segunda edición corregida, Santiago de Chile: Ediciones Ercilla, 1940), p. 38. The first edition was issued at Lima in 1933.

8. John A. Crow, "A Critical Appraisal of the Contemporary Spanish-American Novel," *Hispania,* XXXIV (May, 1951), 162. The critic John Peale Bishop found Latin American novels and short stories "invincibly second-rate," and Dudley Fitts, who cites this comment, is in general agreement with it, but feels that two Argentines—Jorge Luis Borges and Eduardo Mallea—should be ex-

cepted from the sweeping condemnation. Dudley Fitts, "Is There a Spanish Temper?" in *The Hudson Review,* VII (Autumn, 1954), 454-59. During the decade since Fitts made this comment Borges has received critical recognition in Europe and the United States, as well as in Latin America.

9. Max Daireaux, *Panorama de la littérature hispano-américaine* (Paris, 1930), p. 190. Also: "moins imaginatif qu'observateur, plus violent que sensible . . . l'écrivain d'Amerique latine excelle dans le recit rapide où la brusquerie l'emport sur l'analyse," p. 223.

10. Gresham's Law that the bad issues drive out the good operates with particular intensity in cultural matters.

11. U.S. National Commission for UNESCO, Final Report, Seventh National Conference, Denver, Colorado, September 29-October 2, 1959, *The Culture of the Americas,* p. 21.

12. *New York Times,* December 2, 1961.

13. House Committee on Education and Labor, 87th Congress, 1st session. *The University in Latin America: Argentina and the Alliance for Progress* (Washington, D.C.: Government Printing Office, 1961), p. 12.

14. Manuel Cardozo (ed.), *Higher Education in Latin America* (Washington, D.C.: The Catholic University of America Press, 1961), p. 48.

15. *Toward a National Effort in International Educational and Cultural Affairs,* Department of State Publication 7238, International Information and Cultural Series 78 (Washington, D.C.: Government Printing Office, 1961), p. 9. A little further on Dr. Laves forgets his caution and urges "That virtually all programs be increased in magnitude and be more adequately financed." Some idea of the magnitude of the proposed effort may be gathered from his further recommendations that "much greater emphasis to placed upon (a) Programs designed to improve the education of the American people for their role in world affairs, and (b) Programs designed to strengthen democratic institutions abroad."

16. John A. Garraty and Walter Adams, *From Main Street to the Left Bank: Students and Scholars Abroad,* pp. 172, 194. Also see Walter Adams and John A. Garraty, *Is the World Our Campus?* and Richard N. Adams and Charles C. Cumberland, *United States University Cooperation in Latin America: A Study Based on Selected Programs in Bolivia, Chile, Peru, and Mexico.* Institute of Research on Overseas Programs (East Lansing: Michigan State University Press, 1960).

17. *New York Times,* October 9, 1961.

18. Erasmus, *op. cit.,* pp. 163, 167, and 179.

19. See chapters VII and IX. Many Peace Corps volunteers are also engaged in teaching.

20. The extent to which we have become committed to a monetary solution of our foreign problems is pithily summarized in the conclusion of Senator Wayne Morse that "There is nothing wrong with U.S. policies in Latin America that could not be cured by more . . . money." *South America: Argentina, Bolivia, Brazil, Chile, Colombia, and Venezuela.* Committee Print. 86th Congress, 2nd session (Washington, D.C.: Government Printing Office, 1960), p. 1. This is the report of Senator Morse's trip as Chairman of the Subcommittee on American Republics Affairs of the Senate Foreign Relations Committee. In fairness to Senator Morse, it should be pointed out that he was primarily concerned with more loan money and furthermore that he favored "a drastic reduction in military aid to Latin America." But it is symptomatic that more money as the cure for our problems should be emphasized in the opening sentence.

21. Needless to state, these observations on the effect of our programs in Latin America, viewed in the aggregate, should not be taken as reflecting on the indi-

viduals engaged in the programs. The officials known personally to the author are, in most cases, competent and dedicated men and women.

22. *The Voice of Latin America* (New York: Harper and Brothers, 1961), p. 174. For a statement of a different point of view, see John McCormick, "The United Snopes Information Service," *The Kenyon Review,* XXIV (Spring 1962), 330-50.

23. *Toward a National Effort in International Educational and Cultural Affairs,* a report prepared by Walter H. C. Laves. Issued as Department of State Publication 7238, International Information and Cultural Series 78 (Washington, D.C.: Government Printing Office, 1961), p. 8.

24. Press release, United States Advisory Commission on Information, Washington, D. C., February 13, 1961.

25. *Mutual Educational and Cultural Exchange Act.* Hearings before the Committee on Foreign Relations, United States Senate, 87th Congress, 1st session, on S. 1154, March 29, 1961 (Washington, D.C.: Government Printing Office, 1961). p. 25.

26. Luis Alberto Sánchez, "What's Left of Inter-Americanism?" *The Inter-American* (January, 1945), 14.

27. *The University in Latin America.*

28. José de Onís, *The United States as Seen by Spanish American Writers (1776-1890)* (New York: Hispanic Institute in the United States, 1952), p. 36.

29. *Ibid.,* p. 37, p. 90, note 2.

30. In Franz M. Joseph (ed.), *As Others See Us: The United States Through Foreign Eyes* (Princeton, N. J.: Princeton University Press, 1959), p. 295.

31. Quoted by Samuel Guy Inman, in *Modern Hispanic America,* A. Curtis Wilgus (ed.) (Washington, D.C.: George Washington University Press, 1933), p. 197.

32. *Ibid.,* pp. 197-98. Even today some Argentines are doubtful of too much emphasis on literary matters. Jorge Luis Borges and Adolfo Bioy Casares, two distinguished Argentine scholars, writers and critics, opposed the spending of five million pesos on a meeting of the International Pen Club at Buenos Aires in 1962 at a time when the government owed back salaries to its employees. *Vea y Lea,* año XVI (Buenos Aires, 25 octubre de 1962).

Unfinished Business

Writing on Latin America presents some special hazards. The area has never been a favorite with the reading public; among publishers it is a truism that anything about South America bears the kiss of death. A former editor of *Newsweek* has been quoted as saying that the circulation of his magazine was visibly depressed whenever a Latin American personality was positioned on the cover.[1]* Part of this unpopularity is accounted for by the inevitable reaction against wartime propaganda and the inflated claims of business, religious, and political groups having special interests in the area. There was also a decline in the enrollment of students in Latin American subjects in American universities during the 1950's, as more interesting or greener fields (judged by anticipated job opportunities) appeared, following shifts in public and official interest. In this battle of the continents, the official spotlight has recently been shifted to Africa.

With the exception of Mexico, which has always had a special hold on the American imagination, most of the Middle and South American countries have the disadvantage of being too much like the United States to make an exotic appeal, being at the same time sufficiently different in language, customs, and institutions to give rise to misunderstandings. No doubt much of the sourness on the part of large groups in the United States is due to the disparity between the political and social reality in some countries and the unrealistic claims of the public relations representatives of the governments. The average reader in the United States or visitor from these shores hardly expects to find much democracy in Iran or Abyssinia, and would doubtless be rather disappointed if he did, but the Latin American republics have so often been held up as democratic countries and part of the free world that we tend to be rather shocked when we

*Notes to chapter IX begin on page 234.

learn that some countries not only do not follow the Anglo-American norms but have no intention of doing so. The overemphasis on the neighbors theme has led to numerous misunderstandings.[2]

THE AMERICAN NEIGHBORHOOD

The concept of the American neighborhood has considerable validity historically and actually, but it has at times been stretched to cover too much ground. As sometimes used, the term presumes a much greater similarity in customs, tastes, interests, and political and social organization than actually exists. Not a few Latin American intellectuals also have objected to our insistent attempts to force them into the mold of United States institutions. For example, Daniel Cosío Villegas has on various occasions pointed out that Mexicans and Americans "are two radically different beings, in their scales of values and in their overall attitudes toward life and the world."[3] In this same article Cosío Villegas pays a tribute to the United States as the "only country in the world that has tried to create a democratic society, and the only one that has attained this on a large scale," but it is precisely this mass culture that makes the United States an unacceptable model for most other countries.[4] A sophisticated diplomat like Sumner Welles could appreciate the value of personal and political friendships with other citizens of the Americas without attempting "to pass judgment upon what . . . [they] . . . are doing within the realm of their strictly domestic affairs,"[5] but among large sections of the American public there has been an increasing tendency to assume that our criteria of democracy and the good life have universal validity and hence must be accepted south of the border.

Another possible objection to the good neighbor theory of international relations, which has now been extended to all countries, is the belief that if we can only drop in for a visit often enough, all of our problems and differences will be resolved. This is, no doubt, in part a rationalization of the sudden upsurge of interest in foreign travel on the part of all classes of our people. Superficially it seems like a pleasant method of creating international good will and understanding, but there is very little evidence either in history or in current experience to demonstrate that it works out that way. Aside from the historic feuds among neighbors in Europe and Asia, in this hemisphere Mexico and the United States have long had a vast exchange of peoples, goods, and ideas, but this has not assured an identity of views on either national or international affairs. Neither Cuba nor Mexico provide much support for the thesis of our public relations buffs that wider circulation of American publications and news and more exchanges will create sentiment favorable to United States policy objectives. Both Cuba and Mexico have for several generations received most of their news through American channels, and in both countries American newspapers, magazines, and books, in English as well as in Spanish translation, have circulated freely. Both countries have received not only vast numbers of tourists, but also many teachers, writers, artists and scholars. In both, there have been large colonies of resident United States citizens, and both countries have for many years sent many visitors, students, workers, and businessmen to this country. What has been the result of this saturation? Mexico has been the one country least disposed to accept United States economic and cultural aid, and has made difficulties on those projects it has been pressured into accepting. Mexico has been the chief holdout, both in the OAS and in the United Nations, on projects dear to the heart of our policy makers.

In Cuba the result is well known: the inevitable reaction brought Castro into power. The course of events in Cuba also casts doubts on one of the basic assumptions of our foreign aid program, namely, that rapid economic growth is the best antidote against communism. As has been pointed out earlier, Cuba was in the top brackets of the Latin American countries as regards per capita income. Its prosperity during the postwar years had enabled Cuba to buy out many foreign holdings, such as sugar mills and the railways. Not only was labor better off than ever before in history, but there was a comparatively large and growing middle-income group. As late as 1957, members of the American colony in Havana were assuring visitors that Cuba was democracy's best hope in Latin America.

Principal Areas of Conflict

It appears likely that the United States' relations with the other American republics will pass through a period of considerable strain

219

and stress during the 1960's. Nor is it to be expected that any grandiose programs in the economic, cultural or public relations field can exorcise the difficulties—indeed, they might well exacerbate the problem.

The two major areas of conflict yet to be resolved are the nationalistic pressures on large American enterprises established in Middle and South America, and the problem of communism. It is also possible that some friction will arise in connection with trade problems (United States import restrictions and export subsidies, preferential tariffs under the Latin American Free Trade Association, policies of the European Common Market), but these are not expected to generate the same heat as the other two problems.

The size of our investment in most of the countries leaves us very little room for maneuver, since the first consideration has to be the possible effect of any measure on our holdings. One of the reasons why many Latin Americans have kept their fingers crossed concerning the Alliance for Progress is the feeling that it was designed primarily to salvage the position of the United States' interests.

As regards communism, there are so many crosscurrents in Latin America that it is difficult to generalize, but on balance it may be said that the Latin American attitude is somewhat similar to that of the Latin countries in Europe, especially Italy, where substantial proportions of the population regularly vote the communist ticket. In Latin America it is not unusual for a conservative candidate for office to make a deal with the extreme left, since both are opposed to genuine reform. Likewise, some of the dictators have played footsie with the communists. It is reported that the late Anastasio Somoza "supplied the campaign money with which communist labor leaders won the top offices in Nicaragua's labor federation."[6] Likewise, Batista in Cuba[7] and Trujillo in the Dominican Republic,[8] had working arrangements with the communists. In Brazil a leading industrialist subsidized a communist campaign—including student demonstrations—against an American company when the latter proposed to establish a plant competing with his established operations.[9] The military junta in Peru in 1962 let the communists build up their forces in the trade unions in order to oust the Aprista members as leaders.[10]

The fact is that Latin American ideological and institutional conditioning tends to make all classes sympathetic to an authoritarian solution. It should not be forgotten that Perón in Argentina and Vargas in Brazil received heavy majorities at the polls, either in spite of their dictatorial tendencies, or perhaps primarily because the voters expected them to use dictatorial methods to achieve results.

Very few Latin Americans look at the communist question in global terms. They do not want the communists to take over their own country, but they are not unwilling to see local Reds run interference for them, such as support for nationalistic legislation in the economic field. Some of the operations of the Central Intelligence Agency in Latin America, such as the buying off of presidential candidates,[11] have in the view of many Latin Americans blunted the edge of our criticisms of Soviet machinations.

Although Latin America's experience with governmental planning and state intervention is far from encouraging, our strictures on "creeping socialism" have not succeeded in changing the course of Hispanic tradition in these matters, but may have become counter-productive by making many Latin Americans look with more sympathy upon centrally planned economies. The Latin American countries, like Russia, have not been happy with the international status quo, and hence they are willing to take some lessons from Russia, especially in matters of economic development, even though they do not like communism. There is room for differences of opinion and taste as to whether highly socialized countries like Scandinavia and Finland in Europe and Uruguay and Costa Rica in Latin America represent the *summum bonum,* but there can be no doubt that they have been among the staunchest in resisting the blandishments of communism. No doubt we could afford to be more tolerant of Latin American *étatisme* if it were not for the fact that many state enterprises in Latin America are created for the specific purpose of nationalizing or domesticating foreign-owned activities in fields local private investors are unwilling or unable to undertake.

As the currents of nationalism are running deep in the Americas, some of these problems will not be easy to resolve.

221

THE ALLIANCE FOR PROGRESS SUCCEEDS THE ACT OF BOGOTÁ

By the closing years of the Eisenhower administration it had become clear that new measures were needed to cope with the rising tide of dissatisfaction in the other American republics. The solution proposed, which was embodied in the Act of Bogotá concluded in September, 1960, envisaged an attack on the social problems of the area, backed by a substantial contribution from the United States to be administered chiefly through the new regional institution, the Inter-American Development Bank. Previously the existing public financial institutions, such as the Export-Import Bank of Washington, had in general declined to finance social undertakings, such as housing and education, which either involved local materials and labor chiefly or were not considered bankable. Now it is popular to talk about investment in the human factor, although many economists demur at this usage of economic terminology.

At the outset of his administration, President Kennedy endorsed the objectives of the Act of Bogotá by requesting and obtaining from Congress the appropriation of $600 million, including $100 million for Chilean reconstruction, authorized the previous August, and went a step further in proposing a new name (Alliance for Progress) and a broader coverage for the joint attack on Latin American economic underdevelopment. The Alliance was established by the Charter of Punta del Este in August, 1961, approved by all of the American republics except Cuba.

The Alliance was patterned after the Marshall Plan for Europe, but there are important differences. The European Recovery Program involved large grant aid, but under the Alliance most of the financial resources are to be in the form of credits and private investment, although part of the credit is expected to be for long terms and without interest. The Alliance provides that each government is to submit a national development program to the governments and institutions prepared to extend financial and technical assistance under the program. The United States pledged itself to "provide a major part of the minimum of $20 billion, principally in public funds, which Latin America will require over the next ten years from all external sources in order to supplement its own efforts." According

222

to subsequent statements by United States officials, one-fourth of this amount is expected to come from European and Japanese sources.

Although the larger part of the promised financial resources will presumably go to economic development projects, allocations will depend upon approval by participating countries of programs establishing "self-help measures, economic policies and programs consistent with the goals and principles" of the Charter. These goals include "a more equitable distribution of national income," "comprehensive agrarian reform," the reform of tax laws, price stability, and far-reaching measures in connection with health, education, and housing. Emphasis on social measures also has prevailed in the distribution of the $500 million appropriated by Congress for American Republics projects. Of this total, $394 million was designated as a Social Progress Trust Fund to be administered by the Inter-American Development Bank for projects involving housing for low income groups, land settlement, and improved land use, rural credit, and community water supply and sanitation facilities. Six million dollars were allocated to the Pan American Union to strengthen the economic and technical studies involved in the Alliance programs, and $100 million was reserved for the United States' bilateral aid programs in the fields of education and health.

One difference of opinion that developed at Punta del Este in 1961—not unlike the divergence appearing at the Foreign Ministers Meeting at the same place in 1962—was between the larger and smaller countries, the latter favoring the granting of fairly extensive powers to a central review board to pass on projects and recommend granting of credit. The larger countries wanted to retain independence both as regards decisions on national planning and as regards contact with lending agencies. The viewpoint of the larger countries prevailed, in substance, although under the Charter as approved, a panel of nine experts ("the nine wise men") was created, so that "each government, if it so wishes, may present its program for economic and social development for consideration by an ad hoc committee, composed of no more than three members drawn from the panel of experts . . . together with an equal number of experts not on the panel." This split involved something more than the right of the countries to maintain bilateral relations with the United States and the public lending agencies; it also reflected the resistance of some countries to the "interventionist trend of Pan Americanism."[12]

It is difficult to judge the Alliance on the basis of its first year's performance, but one thing is clear: it did not set the woods on fire. In fact, its reception south of the border was not unlike that which Secretary of State Marshall encountered at Bogotá in 1948. On the eve of the ministerial meeting at Mexico City of the Inter-American Economic and Social Council, at which the Alliance was subjected to a searching review, the *New York Times* correspondent observed that "the concepts of the Alliance . . . have not gained significant acceptance in Latin America."[13] In the Report of the Panel of Experts to the Inter-American Economic and Social Council, the wry comment is made that "if one notes the few expressions of favorable public opinion in the hemisphere . . . he may reach the conclusion that the Alliance for Progress is in fact encountering serious difficulties."[14] In an address at the Pan American Union accepting his appointment to prepare a report (in conjunction with Dr. Juscelino Kubitschek, former President of Brazil) on the organization and functioning of the inter-American system, Dr. Alberto Lleras Camargo remarked on the apathy with which the Alliance had been received: "The program is fascinating, and the surprising thing is that it fails to fascinate. It is attractive, and it is astounding that it does not attract as it should those who are going to be its immediate beneficiaries."[15]

Despite the blare of trumpets that greeted the signing of the Charter of Punta del Este, the Alliance for Progress has not resulted in an alliance in any real sense. To most people it has remained a Washington bureaucratic operation, not a community endeavor. In their form and language the Alliance documents attempt to recapture something of the spirit of the Marshall Plan, but that was long ago and far away. In a commendable burst of frankness, Teodoro Moscoso, the able American coordinator of the Alliance, admitted that "the very fact that the Alliance program was proclaimed by a United States President, and that the United States fulfilled its pledge to commit one billion dollars to the program during the first year, all this has contributed to the prevailing psychology that the Alliance is just another U.S. aid program." Mr. Moscoso referred to the "ambivalence of Latin America's relationship with the United States," an

224

ambivalence "born out of a complex mixture of feelings: reliance on us, resentment of that very reliance, and the tendency to exaggerate the faults and minimize the achievements of the strong and powerful brother."[16]

Theoretically, the Alliance has much to recommend it, since it represents the first serious attempt since the 1930's on the part of Washington officialdom to get at a better understanding of Latin American problems and misgivings. Likewise, a good theoretical case can be made for the attempt to point up the social and institutional factors which are obstacles to economic development. Not a few Latin Americans are conscious of the need for social and economic reform and welcome any support they can get from external pressure. But the problems involved in translating these pressures into effective programs of national action are formidable. In the United States nationalization of an industry not only affects specific vested interests but also challenges the prevailing climate of opinion regarding private enterprise. On the other hand, tax and land reforms are more acceptable in the United States, in theory at least, even though each group or class tries to shift the burden of incidence to others so far as possible. In Latin America the situation is just the reverse: there is no popular objection to state-owned steel or power industries, but attempts to break up large estates, which are important status symbols as well as the source of political and economic power, or to shift some of the burden of taxation to the shoulders of the wealthy, at once encounter sharp resistance.

Under our prodding, most of the governments have taken some steps to implement the type of reforms envisaged by the Charter of Punta del Este, and some of these measures may have enduring effects. The Alliance, backed by official and private funds from the United States, as well as increased national appropriations, is making some dent in the field of education. But the majority of the governments have made it clear that their chief interest is to obtain more liberal financial assistance from the United States with as few strings as possible attached to the dollars. The one common denominator has been the desire to get as much cash as possible, and that quickly. Not all of the governments have been as frank as that of Haiti, which made its support of the United States' position at the Meeting of

Foreign Ministers in January, 1962, conditional on the receipt of additional aid, but the difference has been one of tactics rather than of objectives. Historians who have studied the results of our foreign aid and technical missions over the years have observed that "foreign receptivity to American ideas" tends to fade rapidly once the chief objective, a loan or grant, has been achieved.[17]

The Latin Americans have tended to justify their cynicism on the grounds that the United States refused to take their complaints seriously until we needed their support against Castro. In fact, the Alliance for Progress has frequently been referred to as the "Castro Plan," and well-informed journalists reported from the Foreign Ministers Meeting at Punta del Este that the reason why some countries held back on our proposals to eliminate Castro was their desire to keep him as a sort of hostage for United States economic performance.[18]

Some observers foresee the possibility of new inter-American antagonisms growing out of our entry into the "uncharted territory" of promoting social change in the other Americas.[19] There are, theoretically at least, two alternative approaches to the attainment of the social objectives. One would call for technical studies, such as have already been initiated in connection with the various topics, in the hope that these will stimulate action along sound lines, but leaving final judgment to the national authorities as regards timing and specifics. As regards land reform, for example, who is to judge what is politically, economically and institutionally desirable and feasible in a given country?[20] But expectations of more radical action have been aroused both in the United States and in Latin America. Some members of Congress, who have been waiting for years for the miracles promised by Point Four, are getting impatient over the reluctance of Latin American governments to act quickly. In Latin America there are groups who were impressed by President Kennedy's promise, in his address to Latin American Ambassadors at the White House on March 13, 1961, "to complete the revolution of the Americas," and want to get going. They are not convinced, however, that the transition from the old order can be made smoothly and peaceably. On the other hand, the established conservative elements, who have defeated attempts at tax and land reform in the past, are not disposed to get on the Alliance bandwagon. Some of the more progressive emphasize mechanization and technical and economic progress in the hope that social improvement will follow. Although British Guiana is not one of the American republics and was not a signer of the Charter of Punta del Este, the violence which broke out in Georgetown in February, 1962, following the enactment of new tax measures recommended by a British economist may give a foretaste of what is in store elsewhere.

A substantial segment of the American business community also has been critical "of the apparent tendency on the part of some officials of the United States Government to stress social reform as the prime target and sometimes to the detriment of economic growth,"[21] and the Luce publications have protested against allowing the Alliance for Progress "to become identified with the ECLA movement," meaning by "the ECLA movement" a certain sympathy for vigorous government action to spark economic development.[22] In an article entitled "Latin America: Bureaucracy or the Market," a *Fortune* writer stated that "the long-range goals of hemisphere policy will be frustrated if U.S. dollars are used to nourish an oppressive Latin-American statism."[23]

Although one of the objectives of the Alliance is the achievement in each country of a rate of economic growth of not less than 2.5 per cent per capita per year, it can hardly be called a plan of economic development. It would be considerable exaggeration to blame the Alliance for the political and economic upsets that have occurred since the signing of the Charter of Punta del Este, but it is true that the Alliance so far has not been able to create the conditions of confidence necessary to attract foreign and domestic investment on an important scale. According to some estimates, the outflow of foreign capital in 1962 exceeded the inflow, and furthermore the flight of native capital has been at an alarming rate. There has also been an exodus of peoples from some of the countries, particularly from Argentina and Venezuela.

Perhaps the chief danger of the Alliance lies in its tutelary character. Granted that the United States, by virtue of its world position and its control of capital resources, is bound to have an impact upon other countries, and that it can properly provide assistance and advice, it

227

is not certain that we are wise to take upon ourselves so much moral as well as political and financial responsibility for the course of events we can only dimly perceive and cannot control. There is danger that the Alliance will weaken, rather than strengthen, inter-American cooperation and friendship by insisting on too close an embrace. As has been pointed out in preceding chapters, Latin America yearns for a soul and voice of its own and a chance to follow the line of its own internal evolution. It is obvious to us that the Latin Americans will have more choice under our tutelage than under communist domination, but to most Latin Americans this is not the alternative: they do not want to be excluded from world contacts, and they hope to avoid the role of satellite in any camp. If we put them on the spot, they may be pressured into making choices that might otherwise have been avoided. Recently *Visão* magazine (Rio de Janeiro) published a cartoon showing Janio Quadros, the peripatetic philosopher and ex-President of Brazil, kneeling on the bunk in his ship's cabin and engaged in removing a portrait of Lincoln and putting up one of General de Gaulle.[24]

Our commendable desire to use our wealth and strength for broad international objectives is generally appreciated, but unfortunately our zeal has frequently outstripped our discretion. In the last analysis we will be judged not by the number of Americans abroad, the amount of tourist expenditures, the mileage of our officials, or the number of inches of newspaper coverage, but by what we are ourselves, in our homes, in our offices, in public places. A wise teacher has observed, "There is danger of making a ritual of exchange and movement."[25]

THE NONINTERVENTION RULE

In concluding this review of unresolved issues of the inter-American system, mention must be made of the doubts widely entertained both in the United States and in Latin America regarding the current rigidity of interpretation of the doctrine of nonintervention as written into the Charter and other basic documents of the OAS.

In the United States there has been a vigorous revival of interest in the right of intervention, both unilateral and collective. This new faith is shared by both liberals and conservatives, and is justified as a means of promoting democracy, protecting human rights, combating communism and fascism, protecting the foreign investor, and enforcing good behavior on unruly neighbors. During his tenure in office Assistant Secretary of State Spruille Braden argued that nonintervention was a practical impossibility and that the United States should abandon the fiction and use its power and influence to promote democratic and cooperative regimes in Latin America.[26] Likewise, former Assistant Secretary of State Adolf A. Berle has expressed the view that the right of unilateral or collective self-defense granted under the Rio Treaty can be interpreted to cover any situation involving national interest. Dr. Berle would use this right only to prevent encroachments by foreign ideologies and in the assumed interest of the Latin Americans themselves, but apparently he does not question the right of the United States to judge each case.[27] One writer goes all the way back to the pre-World War I imperialistic doctrines to insist that the United States as a great power has the obligation to see to it that its smaller neighbors maintain stable governments, honor their commitments, and recognize the human decencies.[28]

Other observers have been concerned that as the result of our acceptance of the principle of nonintervention we have lost all leverage in diplomatic or other action designed to protect United States investment in Latin America. In practice, the argument runs, the freedom of Latin America from intervention has meant freedom to treat foreign corporations as the Latin American countries think best. As reciprocity for its removal of the threat of intervention or interposition, the United States has expected to receive appropriate treatment of United States business enterprises, but has sometimes been disappointed. New policy techniques such as withholding financial aid or manipulation of the sugar quota have not always been effective.[29]

Part of the difficulty with the doctrine of nonintervention arises from the fact that the coverage of the word "intervention" has been so overextended that it is practically impossible for any country, in the normal course of its official and unofficial relations with other countries, to avoid some acts which might be brought within the definition of "intervention". Article 15 of the OAS Charter not only prohibits direct intervention but also indirect (without defining the term). It prohibits not only the use of armed force "but also any other form of interference or attempted threat against the personality of the State or against its political, economic, and cultural elements."

It is generally agreed that each state retains the right of self-defense within the terms of article 51 of the United Nations, that is, "if an armed attack occurs."

It is reasonable to anticipate that the doctrine of nonintervention, like all human concepts, will undergo some evolution and reinterpretation over the years. It is likely that occasions justifying joint intervention will arise, either for security reasons, to preserve the peace of the Americas, or for humanitarian reasons. Furthermore, it is likely that inter-American cooperation will be obtainable in such cases, provided the ostensible reason is the real one. Since the OAS was established in its present form in 1948, the American republics have, acting through the Council of the OAS, through Meetings of Consultation of Ministers of Foreign Affairs, through the Inter-American Peace Committee, or through *ad hoc* machinery, taken a number of important steps to deal with situations disturbing, or threatening to disturb, the peace of the hemisphere. Likewise, important precedents have been established in the case of sanctions against the Dominican Republic and quarantine against Castro's Cuba.

At the same time, it is far from certain that the majority of Latin Americans will accept the view that nonintervention is a fiction. In any case, it may be doubted whether the so-called rigidity of the nonintervention doctrine presents quite as much of a problem as may appear at first sight. During the 1940's Roosevelt obtained Latin American cooperation against Nazi aggression, and in 1962 Kennedy secured OAS support as soon as a case of Soviet intervention became reasonably clear. Latin Americans have been conservative about raising the bar to intervention because they have known that if they voted for intervention every time some important individuals, groups, or countries raised the cry of communism or fascism, no Latin American country would have escaped intervention. Furthermore, it is useful to keep in mind the tolerance Latin Americans have shown to infractions of the strict letter of the doctrine when they were convinced that such deviations were prompted by generous motives. Most

Latin Americans respect the memory of Woodrow Wilson despite the fact that he intervened in Latin America more than any other American president. Franklin D. Roosevelt boasted of writing the constitution of Haiti at the time the country was under United States military occupation, and he was serving as Assistant Secretary of the Navy when our warships bombarded Veracruz, Mexico. At a press conference in 1938, Roosevelt, as President, put the hypothetical question: If certain European governments attempted to organize a Fascist takeover in Mexico, "Do you think that the United States could stand idly by and have this European menace right on our own border? You could not stand for it."[30] As Ambassador to Cuba, Sumner Welles pulled the rug out from under President Gerardo Machado and was prepared to use military intervention to influence the succession.[31] The stationing of United States naval units within sight of Santo Domingo during the political crisis of November, 1961, brought outcries from Cuba but does not appear to have caused much concern elsewhere.

In these and other instances most Latin Americans judged events in the broad context of our overall policy, and were prepared to forgive mistakes provided they were convinced that our objectives were in accordance with justice and democratic aspirations. On the other hand, Latin American public opinion has condemned interventions designed to protect large foreign interests or promote purely American objectives that encroached on the rights of other peoples. Many recent commentators have pointed out that the United States is suspected "of exaggerating the threat of communism to hide a fundamental opposition to any movement in the direction of social justice."[32]

The shocking brutalities of some of the worst Latin American dictators in recent decades have stimulated interest in proposals to use the inter-American mechanism to protect human rights. The Fifth Meeting of Consultation, as stated in chapter II, focussed attention on this problem and created an Inter-American Commission on Human Rights, composed of seven members elected as individuals by the Council of the OAS from panels submitted by the member governments. The powers of the Inter-American Peace Committee were expanded to include examination of "the relationship between viola-

231

tions of human rights or the non-exercise of representative democracy, on the one hand, and the political tensions that affect the peace of the Hemisphere, on the other."

The Inter-American Commission on Human Rights was organized in June, 1960, and has held periodic sessions since that time. At its fifth session, in September-October, 1962, the Commission applied to the Cuban, Haitian, and Nicaraguan governments for permission to meet in those countries and consider complaints lodged with the Commission. The Cuban government ignored the request, and the Haitian government refused it. The Commission also solicited information from Paraguay concerning alleged violations of human rights. The government of Paraguay agreed, in principle, to supply the information but was dilatory in taking action.[33] In 1963 Nicaragua invited three observers from the OAS to be present at the February 5 elections.

There has been some tendency to criticize the Commission because of its lack of enforcement authority, but there is also an important school of thought which feels that more enduring results can be achieved through vigilance and publicity than through the use of force. The latter view has received strong support from Dr. Alberto Lleras, who said, "A group of democratic nations may destroy an anti-democratic government by coercion and intervention, but who is going to guarantee that a coalition of anti-democratic governments will not proceed in this identical form against a pure and democratic government?"[34]

Much of the animus against the nonintervention doctrine derived from the feeling of frustration over the problem presented by the existence of a communist state within ninety miles of the United States shore line. Although most of the Caribbean countries would doubtless have supported armed intervention in Cuba, President Kennedy's choice in October, 1962, of a quarantine instead of an invasion reflected the judgment that an irreversible military action might well have had some serious repercussions both within the Americas and in other areas of the world. The United States clearly had the resources to dispose of Castro in short order, but such action might well have created a new wave of communist sympathy, especially in critical countries like Brazil, and furthermore might have wrecked the inter-American system. Although President Kennedy gave public assurance on various occasions that "there will not, under any circumstances, be an intervention in Cuba by U.S. armed forces,"[35] he nevertheless made it clear that all means short of a military invasion will be used to end communist rule in the hemisphere. President Kennedy did not present a blueprint of his anti-Castro strategy, but he talked of economic measures, quarantine or blockade, stimulus to internal revolt, and harassment through observation and photographic flights over Cuban territory. In an interview in December, 1962, the President said, "Mr. Castro could not permit us to continue indefinitely flights over his island at 200 feet every day, and yet he knew if he shot down one of our planes, that then it would bring a much more serious reprisal on him."[36] Ten days later the President interrupted his holiday in Florida to appear at Miami before the veterans of the Bay of Pigs invasion, and to take occasion in the course of his remarks to express his confidence that many Cubans, including men in the government and the army, "hold to this freedom faith."

Several well-informed newsmen have referred to the possibility that Castro might start shooting down the United States' reconnaissance planes, "precipitating a conflict that might destroy him."[37] So far Castro has shown remarkable restraint in avoiding a brush with United States military forces. At the end of 1962 Castro had completed four years in power. With the opening of 1963 the United States made further efforts to isolate Cuba by tightening restrictions on trade, travel, transport, and movement of funds, and by providing inducements to the Latin American countries to act along the same lines. At the same time, as the harassing tactics of the Cuban refugees were made difficult, and further political or military confrontation with Russia was avoided, some observers believed that we were entering a period of coexistence. Certainly the prospects of invasion or direct intervention appeared to have receded, although there remained the possibility of dramatic and unexpected events. Meanwhile there was growing conviction that Castro's future was tied up with the outlook for successful Castroite takeovers elsewhere in the hemisphere.

No doubt there will be many occasions in the future, as in the past, when some important groups in the United States and Latin America will insist that the United States use its superior strength to eliminate some troublesome issue in the southern latitudes. There can be no question that the United States possesses the resources to carry through such measures as it feels are essential for its safety or required by paramount national interest. The real question is, whether our objectives will be achieved through the use of military and economic power in a manner that will leave a running sore, or on the basis of understanding and cooperative policies that will inspire respect and continuing cooperation. Used with discretion and restraint, the power of the United States can serve as a valuable positive element in the vitality of the inter-American system, but abuse or frittering away of its strength can quickly arouse hostility and put sand in the machinery of mutual endeavor.

There are ample grounds for optimism that, if we proceed with serenity,[38] sobriety,[39] and good faith, we will encounter reciprocity on the part of the other peoples of the hemisphere. Once we relax our efforts to force other countries into our economic, social, and ideological mold, we will find the Latin Americans less attracted by other alien molds. Since a large segment of American internationalists have come to think of international relations in terms of group integration or community, the power disparity and the institutional differences between the United States and Latin America have come in for added emphasis. As a consequence, not all of the Latin American countries are now willing to accept the United States as their spokesman in world affairs, but most of them would doubtless gladly accept the United States as leader of a Western, democratic bloc, once we have learned the hard lessons of leadership.

NOTES TO CHAPTER IX

1. Quoted by William C. Baggs, "The Gringo and the Revolution in Latin America," *The American Scholar*, XXX (Autumn, 1961), 567.

2. It is worthy of note that the word "neighbors" has been used in connection with the Far East almost as long as with reference to Hispanic America. Secretary of the Treasury Robert J. Walker in his *Annual Report* for 1848 announced that "Asia has suddenly become our neighbor." Even Colonel Henry L. Stimson, who shared some of the popular myths about the Far East, spoke of China as geographically adjacent to the United States and as a neighbor. William L. Neu-

mann, in George L. Anderson, *Issues and Conflicts: Studies in Twentieth Century American Diplomacy* (Lawrence: University of Kansas Press, 1959) pp. 4, 6.

3. Section on Mexico in Joseph, *op. cit.,* p. 302.

4. *Ibid.,* p. 298.

5. "On the Need for a Spirit of Tolerance in Inter-American Relationships," *Pan Americanism: Its Justification and Its Future* (Washington, D.C.: George Washington University Press, 1938), p. 13.

6. Lester Velio, "New Time Bomb in the Caribbean," *Reader's Digest,* LXXX (January, 1962), 213.

7. Robert F. Smith, *The United States and Cuba: Business and Diplomacy, 1917-1960* (New York: Bookman Associates, 1960), p. 181, and Ruby Hart Phillips, *Cuba: Island of Paradox* (New York: McDowell, Obelensky, 1959), pp. 207, 350-57.

8. Victor Alba, "República Dominicana, La Herencia del 'Benefactor,' " *Cuadernos,* No. 63 (August, 1962), p. 71.

9. *Business Week,* CLXXXIV (September 22, 1962), 164. For background on Vargas' flirting with the communists, see Robert J. Alexander, *Prophets of the Revolution* (New York: The Macmillan Co., 1962), the chapter on Vargas.

10. *Washington Daily News,* March 6, 1963; *The Vision Letter,* February 12, 1963; *The New Republic,* CXLVIII (January 19, 1963), 5.

11. See C. L. Sulzberger, "Foreign Affairs: Problems of Progress-IV. Mistaken Gifts," *New York Times,* December 25, 1961, p. 22.

12. Jorge Castañeda, *Mexico and the United Nations* (New York: Manhattan Publishing Co., 1958), p. 194.

13. October 21, 1962.

14. OAS, Inter-American Economic and Social Council, First Annual Meetings, *Report of the Panel of Experts to the Inter-American Economic and Social Council,* Doc. 17, provisional English translation, September 30, 1962, p. 39.

15. OAS, Press Release, E-512/62, *Address delivered by Dr. Alberto Lleras Camargo, at the Protocolary Session in his honor . . . held by the Council of the OAS . . . on December 14, 1962.*

16. Address before the World Affairs Conference, Marquette University, September 29, 1962, Press Release.

17. Merle Curti and Kendall Birr, *Prelude to Point Four: American Technical Missions Overseas 1838-1938* (Madison: University of Wisconsin Press, 1954), pp. 206-7.

18. Philip Geyelin, *Wall Street Journal,* January 17, 1962.

19. Hirschman, "Second Thoughts on the 'Alliance for Progress,' " *The Reporter,* XXIV (May 25, 1961), 20-23, and Ambassador John C. Dreier (U.S. representative to the Organization of American States for nine years), in an address at the Conference on Latin American History, 76th Annual Meeting of the American Historical Association, reported in the *Washington Post,* December 29, 1961.

20. According to press reports, the United Fruit Company has cut back on new investments in Honduras as the result of the new agrarian law in that country. While the President of Honduras was in Washington it was "suggested diplomatically that his agrarian program was too 'punitive' against large landowners." *Washington Post,* March 12, 1963.

21. David Rockefeller, "Responsibilities of Business in a Troubled World," address before the Wharton School Alumni Society, November 16, 1961, published in brochure form by the Chase Manhattan Bank, New York p. 13.

22. Editorial, *Fortune,* LXV (February, 1962), 80.

23. *Ibid.,* p. 85. This issue quotes Dr. Raúl Prebisch, Director General of

ECLA, as follows: "One of the things that have most fired the imagination and enthusiasm of our people, particularly the younger generation, has been the very significant lesson to be learned from the Soviet method of economic development: No matter how rudimentary their technology in underdeveloped countries, no matter how high the rate of illiteracy, there is nothing which in time these countries cannot learn and practice—from the exploitation of their natural resources to the more advanced industrial technology" (p. 86).

24. XX (February 2, 1962), 12.

25. Henry Roberts (Director of Columbia University Russian Institute), "The Exchange of Scholars with the Soviet Union," *Columbia University Forum I* (1958), pp. 28-29.

26. "Not to use our power in the interest of peace and freedom may be misusing that power just as much as if we brought our influence to bear on the wrong side of the issue." Department of State, Inter-American Series No. 28, January 4, 1946.

27. *Latin America: Diplomacy and Reality* (New York: Harper & Row for the Council on Foreign Relations, 1962), chapter V.

28. Irving Kristol, "The Case for Intervention in Cuba," *New Leader,* October 15, 1962, p. 10.

29. Wood, *The Making of the Good Neighbor Policy,* p. 330.

30. *Ibid.,* p. 154.   31. *Ibid.,* chapter II.

32. M. Margaret Ball, "Issue for the Americas: Non-Intervention v. Human Rights and the Preservation of Democratic Institutions," *International Organization,* XV (Winter, 1961), 27.

33. OAS press release, "Inter-American Commission of Human Rights Reports on Its Fifth Session," October 17, 1962.

34. *New York Times,* August 24, 1959. Quoted in Mecham, *The United States and Inter-American Security,* p. 417.

35. Report on news conference, *New York Times,* April 13, 1962.

36. *Washington Post,* December 18, 1962.

37. Tad Szulc, *New York Times Magazine,* December 9, 1962. Also see Chalmers M. Roberts in the *Washington Post,* December 27, 1962.

38. The author is indebted for this word to John Paton Davies, Jr., "A New Look at a Global Puzzle," *New York Times Magazine,* February 11, 1962. Reference may also be made to Operation Serenity (supplementing Operation Bootstrap and Operation Commonwealth) of Governor Luis Muñoz Marín of Puerto Rico, meaning "the pursuit of happiness with some hope of really catching up with her."

39. Freyre has pointed out that many Latin Americans have come to have a nostalgia for the "sobriety and elegance" of the earlier eras before the United States became the world arbiter. *New World in the Tropics,* p. 262.

Suggested Readings

This reading list has been compiled for the convenience both of the general reader and of the student who might wish to pursue his investigation of inter-American affairs. Inevitably the list is highly selective but some of the titles listed include extensive bibliographies. Additional references can be found in the notes to the chapters of this volume. The serious student would do well to consult the *Handbook of Latin American Studies,* published annually since 1935. It is currently prepared by the Hispanic Foundation of the Library of Congress and published by the University of Florida Press at Gainesville.

GENERAL

A Mexican Ulysses: The Autobiography of José Vasconcelos. Translated and abridged by W. Rex Crawford. Bloomington: Indiana University Press, 1963.

Bryce, James. *South America; Observations and Impressions.* New ed., cor. and rev. New York: The Macmillan Co., 1920.

Cosío Villegas, Daniel. *Extremos de América.* México, D.F.: Tozontle, 1948.

——. *Change in Latin America: The Mexican and Cuban Revolutions.* Lincoln: University of Nebraska Press, 1961.

Dozer, Donald M. *Are We Good Neighbors?* Gainesville: University of Florida Press, 1959.

García Calderón, Francisco. *Latin America, Its Rise and Progress.* Pref. by Raymond Poincaré; translated by Bernard Miall. New York: Charles Scribner's Sons, 1913.

Griffin, Charles C. *Latin America: An Interpretation of Main Trends in Its History.* Ithaca: Cornell University Press, 1944.

Haya de la Torre, Víctor Raúl. *¿A donde va Indoamérica?* Santiago de Chile: Editorial Ercilla, 1935.

Hirschman, Albert O. (ed.). *Journeys Toward Progress: Studies of Economic Policy-Making in Latin America.* New York: Twentieth Century Fund, 1963.

Inman, Samuel G. *Latin America: Its Place in World Life.* Rev. ed. New York: Harcourt, Brace & Co., 1942.

——. *Social and International Conflicts in Latin America.* New York: The Church Union, 1933.

——. *Problems in Pan Americanism.* New York: Doran, 1921 and 1925.

James, Preston E. *Latin America.* 3d ed. New York: The Odyssey Press, 1959.

Masur, Gerhard. *Simón Bolívar.* Albuquerque: University of New Mexico Press, 1948.

Matthews, Herbert L. (ed.). *The United States and Latin America.* New York: The American Assembly, Columbia University, 1959.

Rowe, L. S., Haring, Clarence H., Duggan, Stephen, and Munro, Dana G. *Latin America in World Affairs, 1914-1940.* University of Pennsylvania, Bicentennial Conference. Philadelphia: University of Pennsylvania Press, 1941.

Tannenbaum, Frank. *Ten Keys to Latin America.* New York: Alfred A. Knopf, 1962.

United States Senate. 86th Congress, 2d session. Doc. No. 125. *United States-Latin American Relations.* Compilation of studies prepared under the direction of the Subcommittee on American Republics Affairs of the Committee on Foreign Relations, pursuant to S. Res. 330, 85th Congress, S. Res. 31 and S. Res. 250, 86th Congress. Washington, D.C.: Government Printing Office, 1960.

Wilgus, A. Curtis. *Latin America in Maps: Historic, Economic, Geographic.* New York: Barnes & Noble, 1943.

———— (ed.). *The Caribbean at Mid-Century.* Gainesville: University of Florida Press, 1951. (Also see annual volumes in this series since 1951.)

———— (ed.). *Readings in Latin American Civilization.* New York: Barnes & Noble, 1946.

INTER-AMERICAN AND INTERNATIONAL

Aguirre, Aureliano (ed.). *Uruguay and the United Nations.* New York: Carnegie Endowment for International Peace, 1958.

Anglin, Douglas G. "United States Opposition to Canadian Membership in the Pan American Union: A Canadian View," *International Organization,* XV (Winter, 1961), 1-20.

Ball, M. Margaret. *The Problem of Inter-American Organization.* Stanford: Stanford University Press, 1944.

Bemis, Samuel Flagg. *The Latin American Policy of the United States.* New York: Harcourt, Brace & Co., 1943.

Burr, Robert N., and Hussey, Roland D. (eds.). *Documents on Inter-American Cooperation.* 2 vols. Philadelphia: University of Pennsylvania Press, 1955.

Canyes, Manuel. *The Organization of American States and the United Nations.* 5th ed. Washington, D.C.: Pan American Union, 1960.

————. *The Meetings of Consultation: Their Origin, Significance and Role in Inter-American Relations.* 3d ed. rev. Washington, D.C.: Pan American Union, 1962.

Castañeda, Jorge. *Mexico and the United Nations.* New York: Manhattan, 1958.

Cosío Villegas, Daniel. "Los problemas de América," *Cuadernos Americanos,* año VIII (March-April, 1949), 7-23.

————. "Las relaciones de Estados Unidos e Iberoamerica," *Jornadas,* No. 10. México, D.F.: Colegio de México, Centro de Estudios Sociales, 1944.

Dreier, John C. (ed.). *The Alliance for Progress: Problems and Perspectives.* Baltimore: The Johns Hopkins Press, 1962.

————. *The Organization of American States and the Hemisphere Crisis.* Published for the Council on Foreign Relations. New York: Harper & Row, 1962.

Duggan, Lawrence. *The Americas: The Search for Hemisphere Security.* New York: Henry Holt & Co., 1949.

Fenwick, Charles G. *The Inter-American Regional System.* A Holy Cross College Press Publication. New York: Declan X. McMullen Co., 1949.

Finch, George A. "Elihu Root's Contribution to Pan Americanism," *Bulletin of the Pan American Union,* LXXIX (February, 1945), 63-73.

Gómez Robledo, Antonio. *Idea y experiencia de América.* México, D.F.: Fondo de Cultura Económica, 1958.

Humphrey, John T. P. *The Inter-American System. A Canadian View.* Toronto: The Macmillan Co., 1942.

Hughes, Charles Evans. *Our Relations to the Nations of the Western Hemisphere.* Princeton: Princeton University Press, 1928.

Jessup, Philip C. *Elihu Root.* New York: Dodd, Mead & Co., 1938.

Manger, William (ed.). *The Alliance for Progress: A Critical Appraisal.* A Georgetown University Symposium. Washington, D.C.: Public Affairs Press, 1963.

McGann, Thomas F. *Argentina, the United States, and the Inter-American System, 1880-1914*. Cambridge: Harvard University Press, 1957.
Pan American Union. *The Basic Principles of the Inter-American System*. Prepared under the direction of the Executive Committee on Post-War Problems of the Governing Board of the Pan American Union. Washington, D.C.: Pan American Union, 1943.
Perkins, Dexter. *A History of the Monroe Doctrine*. Rev. ed. Boston: Little, Brown & Co., 1955.
————. *The United States and Latin America*. Baton Rouge: Louisiana State University Press, 1961.
————. *Foreign Policy and the American Spirit*. Essays by Dexter Perkins. Edited by Glyndon G. van Deusen and Richard C. Wede. Ithaca: Cornell University Press, 1957.
Rippy, J. Fred. *Latin America in World Politics*. 3d ed. rev. New York: Crofts, 1938.
————. *Globe and Hemisphere: Latin America's Place in the Postwar Foreign Relations of the United States*. Chicago: Henry Regnery Co., 1958.
Spykman, Nicholas John. *America's Strategy in World Politics*. New York: Harcourt, Brace & Co., 1942.
Whitaker, Arthur P. "Development of American Regionalism: The Organization of American States," *International Conciliation*, No. 469 (March, 1951), pp. 121-64
Yepes, Jesús María. *La panaméricanisme au point de vue historique, juridique et politique*. Preface de J. G. Guerrero. Paris: Les Éditions Internationales, 1936.

GOVERNMENT AND NATIONALISM

Belaunde, Victor A. *Bolivar and the Political Thought of the Spanish American Revolution*. Baltimore: The Johns Hopkins Press, 1938.
Brasileiros contra o Brasil; antologia nacionalista. Presented by the Movimento Nationalista Brasileira. Sao Paulo: Editôra Fulgor, 1958. Preface by Gabriel Passos. Other contributors: Adelgisa Nery, Caio Prado Junior, Elias Chaves Nato, Gondin da Fonseca, Oswaldo Costa, Osny Duarte Pereira, Paulo F. Alves Pinto, and Pompeu Accioly Borges.
Christensen, Asher N. (ed.). *The Evolution of Latin American Government: a Book of Readings*. New York: Henry Holt & Co., 1951.
Correo, Gustavo. "El nacionalismo cultural en la literatura hispanoamericana," *Cuadernos Americanos*, ano XVII, v. XCVIII (marzo-abril de 1958), 225-36.
Davis, Harold E. (ed.). *Government and Politics in Latin America*. New York: The Ronald Press, 1958.
Donoso, Ricardo, *Desarrollo político y social de Chile desde la Constitución de 1833*. 2d ed. Santiago, Chile: Imprenta Universitaria, 1942.
Fitzgibbon, Russell H. (ed.). *The Constitutions of the Americas*. Chicago: University of Chicago Press, 1948.
Graña, César."Cultural Nationalism: the Idea of Historical Destiny in Spanish America," *Social Research*. I, in 29:4 (Winter, 1962), 395-418; II, in 30:1 (Spring, 1963), 37-52.
Jane, Cecil. *Liberty and Despotism in Spanish America*. Oxford: Clarendon Press, 1929.
Jorrín, Miguel. *Governments of Latin America*. New York: D. Van Nostrand Co., 1953.

Kennedy, John J. *Catholicism, Nationalism, and Democracy in Argentina.* Notre Dame: University of Notre Dame Press, 1958.

Latin American Nationalistic Revolutions. Foreword by Robert N. Burr. (Annals of the American Academy of Political and Social Sciences, CCCXXXIV, March, 1961.)

MacDonald, Austin F. *Latin American Politics and Government.* 2d ed. New York: Thomas Y. Crowell Co., 1954.

Martí, José. *The America of José Martí; Selected Writings.* Translated by Juan de Onís. New York: The Noonday Press, 1953.

Pierson, William W., and Gil, Federico G. *Governments of Latin America.* New York: McGraw-Hill Book Co., 1957.

Reyes, Alfonso. *The Position of America and Other Essays.* Selected and translated by Harriet de Onís. New York: Alfred A. Knopf, 1950.

Stokes, William S. *Latin American Politics.* New York: Thomas Y. Crowell Co., 1959.

Whitaker, Arthur P. *Nationalism in Latin America.* Gainesville: University of Florida Press, 1962.

Zavala, Silvio A. *New Viewpoints on the Spanish Colonization of America.* Philadelphia: University of Pennsylvania Press, 1943.

――――. *The Political Philosophy of the Conquest of America.* Translated by Teener Hall. Mexico City: Editorial Cultura, 1953.

Agrarian Problems

Beckett, James, "Land Reform in Chile," *Journal of Inter-American Studies,* V (April, 1963), 177-211.

Beyer, Robert Carlyle, "Land Distribution and Tenure in Colombia," *Journal of Inter-American Studies,* III (April, 1961), 281-90.

Carroll, Thomas F. "The Land Reform Issue in Latin America," in *Latin American Issues,* Albert O. Hirschman (ed.). New York: Twentieth Century Fund, 1961, pp. 161-201.

Fernández y Fernández, Ramón, and Acosta, Ricardo. *Política agrícola; ensayo sobre normas para México.* México, D.F.: Fondo de Cultura Económica, 1961.

Hirschman, Albert O. *Journeys Toward Progress: Studies of Economic Policy-Making in Latin America.* New York: Twentieth Century Fund, 1963. Chapter 1, "Brazil's Northeast," and chapter 2, "Land Use and Land Reform in Colombia," are of special interest.

McBride, George McCutcheon, "Land Tenure," Latin American Section, *Encyclopedia of the Social Sciences,* IX (1933), 118-22, 127.

Peake, Harold E. J. "Village Community," *Encyclopaedia of the Social Sciences,* XV (1935), 253-59.

Phipps, Helen. *Some Aspects of the Agrarian Question in Mexico: A Historical Survey.* Austin: University of Texas Bulletin No. 2515, April 15, 1925.

Senior, Clarence Ollson. *Land Reform and Democracy.* Gainesville: University of Florida Press, 1958.

Economics

Baldwin, Robert E. "Secular Movements in the Terms of Trade," *American Economic Review,* XLV (May, 1955), 259-69.

de Vries, Egbert, and Medina Echavarría, José, *Social Aspects of Economic Development in Latin America.* Paris: UNESCO, 1963.

Fetter, Frank W. "History of the Public Debt in Latin America," *American Economic Review*, XXXVII (May, 1947), 147-48.

Hanson, Simon G. *Economic Development in Latin America*. Washington, D.C.: The Inter-American Affairs Press, 1951.

Jenks, Leland Hamilton. *Our Cuban Colony: A Study in Sugar*. New York: Vanguard Press, 1928.

Jones, Chester Lloyd. *Caribbean Background and Prospects*. New York: Appleton, 1931.

Jones, Clarence F. *Commerce of South America*. New York: Ginn & Co., 1928.

Knight, Melvin M. *The Americans in Santo Domingo*. New York: Vanguard Press, 1928.

League of Nations. *Industrialization and Foreign Trade*. Geneva, 1945.

Levin, Jonathan V. *The Export Economies. Their Pattern of Development in Historical Perspective*. Cambridge: Harvard University Press, 1960.

Marsh, Margaret Alexander. *The Bankers in Bolivia*. New York: Vanguard Press, 1928.

Mikesell, Raymond F. *Foreign Investment in Latin America*. Washington: Pan American Union, 1955.

Nash, Manning. *Machine Age Maya: the Industrialization of a Guatemalan Community*. Glencoe, Ill.: Free Press, 1958.

Pizer, Samuel, and Cutler, Frederick. *U. S. Investment in the Latin American Economy*. Washington, D.C.: Government Printing Office, 1957

Rippy, J. Fred. *The Capitalists and Colombia*. New York: Vanguard Press, 1931.

Tax, Sol. *Penny Capitalism: a Guatemalan Indian Economy*. Washington, D.C.: Government Printing Office, 1953.

United Nations, Department of Economic and Social Affairs. *Foreign Capital in Latin America*. New York, 1955.

———, Economic Commission for Latin America. *Economic Development, Planning and International Co-operation*. Santiago, Chile: United Nations, 1961.

———, ———. *The Latin American Common Market*. New York, 1959.

United States Department of Commerce, Office of International Trade. *Factors Limiting U.S. Investment Abroad: Part 1. Survey of Factors in Foreign Countries*. Washington, D.C.: Government Printing Office, 1953.

Viallate, Achille. *Economic Imperialism and International Relations During the Last Fifty Years*. New York: The Macmillan Co., 1923.

Wythe, George. *An Outline of Latin American Economic Development*. New York: Barnes & Noble, 1949.

———. *Industry in Latin America*. 2d ed. New York: Columbia University Press, 1949.

———, et al. *Brazil: An Expanding Economy*. New York: Twentieth Century Fund, 1949.

———. "Farms or Factories: Three Views of Mexico's Industrial Revolution," *Inter-American Economic Affairs*, IV (Summer, 1950), 35-44.

———. "Brazil: Trends in Industrial Development," in Kuznets, Simon, et al. (eds.). *Economic Growth: Brazil, India, Japan*. Durham: Duke University Press, 1955, pp. 29-77.

EDUCATION, LITERATURE, PHILOSOPHY

Cohen, J. M. "Borges," *Encounter*, XVIII (June, 1962), 48-49.

Dimmick, Ralph Edward. "The Brazilian Literary Generation of 1930's," *Hispania*, XXXIV (May, 1951), 181-87.

Ellison, Fred P. *Brazil's New Novel: Four Northeastern Masters: José Lins do Rêgo, Jorge Amado, Graciliano Ramos, Rachel de Queiros.* Berkeley: University of California Press, 1954.

Flores, Angel. "Magical Realism in Spanish American Fiction," *Hispania,* XXXVIII (May, 1955), 187-92.

Frondizi, Risieri. "Tendencies in Contemporary Latin American Philosophy," *Inter-American Intellectual Interchange.* Austin, Texas: Institute of Latin American Studies, 1943.

Griffin, William J. "Brazilian Literature in English Translation," *Revista Interamericana de Bibliography* (January-June, 1955), pp. 21-37.

Henriquez Ureña, Max. "The Novel in Spanish America," in Río, Angel del (ed.). *Responsible Freedom in the Americas.* New York: Doubleday & Co., 1955.

Henriquez Ureña, Pedro. *Literary Currents in Hispanic America.* Cambridge: Harvard University Press, 1945.

Hespelt, E. Herman, and Associates. *An Outline History of Spanish American Literature.* Prepared under the auspices of the Instituto Internacional de Literatura Iberoamericana. New York: Crofts, 1941.

Johnson, Harvey L. "A Backward Glance at Portuguese and Brazilian Studies in the United States," *Journal of Inter-American Studies,* I (October, 1959), 477-87.

Lanning, John Tate. *Academic Culture in the Spanish Colonies.* New York: Oxford University Press, 1940.

———. *The Eighteenth-Century Enlightenment in the University of San Carlos de Guatemala.* Ithaca: Cornell University Press, 1956.

———. *The University in the Kingdom of Guatemala.* Ithaca: Cornell University Press, 1955.

Monguió, Luis. "Nationalism and Social Discontent as Reflected in Spanish-American Literature," *Latin American Nationalistic Revolutions.* (Annals of the American Academy of Political and Social Science, CCCXXXIV, March, 1961), 53-73.

Moser, Gerald M. "Histories of Brazilian Literature: A Critical Survey," *Revista Interamericana de Bibliografía* (abril-junio de 1960), pp. 117-46.

Picón-Salas, Mariano. *A Cultural History of Spanish America. From Conquest to Independence.* Translated by Irving A. Leonard. Berkeley: University of California Press, 1962.

Putnam, Samuel. *Marvelous Journey: A Survey of Four Centuries of Brazilian Writing.* New York: Alfred A. Knopf, 1948.

Ramos, Samuel. *Profile of Man and Culture in Mexico.* Translated by Peter G. Earle. Austin: University of Texas Press, 1962.

Rodríguez Alcalá, Hugo. "Sobre el americanismo filosófico: La teoría de J. B. Alberdi renovada por Alejandro Korn." *Hispanic Review,* XXXI (January, 1963), 40-60.

Romanell, Patrick. *Making of the Mexican Mind: A Study in Recent Mexican Thought.* Lincoln: University of Nebraska Press, 1952.

———. "Ortega in Mexico: A Tribute to Samuel Ramos," *Journal of the History of Ideas,* XXI (October-December, 1960), 600-8.

Sánchez Reulet, Aníbal (ed.). *Contemporary Latin American Philosophy.* Translated by W. R. Trask. Albuquerque: University of New Mexico Press, 1954.

Spell, Jefferson Rea. *Contemporary Spanish-American Fiction.* Chapel Hill: University of North Carolina Press, 1944.

Torres-Rioseco, Arturo. *The Epic of Latin American Literature.* Berkeley: University of California Press, 1959.

————. *New World Literature: Tradition and Revolt in Latin America.* Berkeley: University of California Press, 1949.

Zea, Leopoldo. *Dos etapas del pensamiento en Hispanoamérica: Del romanticismo al positivismo.* México, D.F.: El Colegio de México, 1949.

————. "Dialéctica de la conciencia en Mexico," *Cuadernos Americanos,* LVII (mayo-junio de 1951), 87-103. (This same issue of *Cuadernos Americanos,* under the general heading of "El Mexicano en busco del Mexicano," contains articles by Samuel Ramos, Emilio Uranga, and José Gaos.)

————. *América como conciencia.* México, D.F.: Ediciones Cuadernos Americanos 30, 1953.

Zum Felde, Alberto. *Indice crítico de la literatura hispano-americana.* 2 vols. Mexico: Editorial Guarania. I, *Los ensayistas,* 1954; II, *La narrativa,* 1959.

Also see the Annual Reports of the Carnegie Corporation of New York, the Ford Foundation, the Rockefeller Foundation, and the John Carter Brown Library.

SOCIAL THOUGHT AND INSTITUTIONS

Alba, Víctor. *Las ideas sociales contemporánea en México.* México, D.F.: Fondo de Cultura Económica, 1960.

Azevedo, Fernando de. *Brazilian Culture; an Introduction to the Study of Culture in Brazil.* Translated by William R. Crawford, ill. New York: The Macmillan Co., 1950.

Bastide, Roger. "Sociology in Latin America," in G. D. Gurvitch and W. E. Moore, *Twentieth Century Sociology.* New York: Philosophical Library, 1945.

Bernard, L. L. "The Development of Social Thought and Institutions: IX. Latin America," *Encyclopaedia of the Social Sciences,* I (1930), 301-20.

Crawford, W. Rex. *A Century of Latin American Thought.* Cambridge: Harvard University Press, 1944.

Davis, Harold Eugene. *Latin American Social Thought. The History of Its Development Since Independence.* With selected readings. Washington, D.C.: American University Press, 1961.

Leonard, Olen E., and Loomis, Charles P. (eds.). *Readings in Latin American Social Organization and Institutions.* East Lansing: Michigan State University Press, 1953.

Social Change in Latin America: Its Implications for United States Policy. By Richard N. Adams, John P. Gillin, Allan R. Holberg, Oscar Lewis, Richard W. Patch, and Charles Wagley. Introduction by Lyman Bryson. Published for the Council on Foreign Relations. New York: Harper & Brothers, 1960.

SELECTED WORKS ON INDIVIDUAL COUNTRIES AND REGIONS

Arnade, Charles W. The Emergence of the Republic of Bolivia. Gainesville: University of Florida Press, 1957.

Biesanz, John and Mavis. *The People of Panama.* New York: Columbia University Press, 1955.

Callcott, Wilfrid Hardy. *Liberalism in Mexico, 1857-1929.* Stanford: Stanford University Press, 1931.

Cline, Howard F. *The United States and Mexico.* Cambridge: Harvard University Press, 1953.

————. *Mexico: Revolution to Evolution, 1940-1960.* New York: Oxford University Press, 1962. (One of the series sponsored by the Royal Institute of

International Affairs; country volumes have been published on Argentina, Bolivia, Brazil, Chile, Colombia, Ecuador, Paraguay, Uruguay, and Venezuela.)

Dunn, Frederick Sherwood. *The Diplomatic Protection of Americans in Mexico* (*Mexico in International Finance and Diplomacy,* vol. II.) 2 vols. New York: Columbia University Press, 1933.

Freyre, Gilberto. *The Masters and the Slaves: A Study in the Development of Brazilian Civilization.* Translated by Samuel Putnam. 2d English-language ed., rev. New York: Alfred A. Knopf, 1956.

————. *The Mansions and the Shanties: The Making of Modern Brazil.* Translated by Harriet de Onís. Introduction by Frank Tannenbaum. New York: Alfred A. Knopf, 1963.

Hanson, Simon G. *Utopia in Uruguay.* New York: Oxford University Press, 1938.

Humboldt, Alexander von. *Personal Narrative of Travels to the Equinoctial Regions of South America During the Years 1799-1804.* Translated and edited by Thomasina Ross. 7 vols. London: 1818-29 (3 vols. London: Bell, 1907).

————. *Political Essay on the Kingdom of New Spain.* Book I translated and edited by Hensley C. Woodbridge. Lexington: University of Kentucky, 1957. (Also, complete, *Essai Politique sur le Royaume de la Nouvelle Espagne,* 5 vols. Paris, 1811.)

Jones, Chester Lloyd. *Costa Rica and Civilization in the Caribbean.* Madison: University of Wisconsin Press, 1935.

————. *Guatemala: Past and Present.* Minneapolis: University of Minnesota Press, 1940.

————. *The Caribbean Since 1900.* New York: Prentice-Hall, 1936.

Lewis, Oscar. *Life in a Mexican Village: Tepoztlán Restudied.* Urbana: University of Illinois Press, 1951.

————. *Five Families: Mexican Case Studies in the Culture of Poverty.* New York: Basic Books, 1959.

Molina Enríquez, Andrés. *Los grandes problemas nacionales.* México, D.F.: Imprenta de A. Carranza e Hijos, 1909.

Munro, Dana G., and Associates. *Refugee Settlement in the Dominican Republic.* Washington, D.C.: Brookings Institution, 1942.

Ostria Gutiérrez, Alberto. *The Tragedy of Bolivia: A People Crucified.* Translated by Eithue Golden, New York: Devin-Adair Co., 1958.

Pierson, Donald. *Negroes in Brazil: a Study of Race Contact at Bahia.* Chicago: University of Chicago Press, 1942.

Rennie, Ysabel F. *The Argentine Republic.* New York: The Macmillan Co., 1945.

Schneider, Ronald M. *Communism in Guatemala, 1944-1954.* New York: Frederick A. Praeger, 1958.

Sierra, Justo (ed.). *Mexico, Its Social Evolution.* Translated by G. Santiñón. 2 vols. in 3. México, D.F.: J. Ballesca y Cía., 1900-04.

Simpson, Lesley B. *Many Mexicos.* 4th ed. rev. Berkeley: University of California Press, 1957.

Smith, T. Lynn, and Marchant, Alexander (eds.). *Brazil, Portrait of Half a Continent.* New York: Dryden Press, 1951.

United States Department of Commerce, Bureau of Foreign Commerce. Series of country studies published under the title, "Investment in_____."

Whitaker, Arthur P. *The United States and Argentina.* Cambridge: Harvard University Press, 1954.

————. *Argentine Upheaval: Peron's Fall and the New Regime.* New York: Frederick A. Praeger, 1956.

244

Periodicals

It is still fashionable in some quarters to lament the lack of serious coverage of Latin American developments by the United States press, but the situation is actually more favorable than such complaints make it appear. There are several daily newspapers of national standing that give extensive and objective coverage (particularly the *New York Times*), and likewise several weekly news magazines that devote substantial space to the hemisphere. Furthermore, comments and analytical articles appear frequently in a large number of weekly, fortnightly, monthly, and quarterly magazines and journals of opinion, as well as in a wide variety of official and professional publications. For those who read Spanish, there are also several Spanish-language dailies.

Of the journals devoted primarily to inter-American topics, mention may be made of *Américas* (monthly, published by the Pan American Union in English, Spanish, and Portuguese), *Hispania* (monthly, published by the American Association of Teachers of Spanish and Portuguese), *Hispanic American Historical Review* (quarterly, published by the Conference on Latin American History of the American Historical Association), *Hispanic American Report* (monthly, published by the Hispanic American Society), *Inter-American Economic Affairs* (quarterly, published in Washington, D.C.), *Inter-American Review of Bibliography* (quarterly, organ of the Inter-American Committee on Bibliography), *Journal of Inter-American Studies* (published quarterly for the School of Inter-American Studies, University of Florida, by the Pan-American Foundation, Inc.), and the *Revista Iberoamericana* (published twice a year, under the auspices of the University of Iowa, organ of the Instituto Internacional de Literatura Iberoamericana). This list could be extended very considerably by including technical or professional journals that include considerable matter relating to the Americas along with other material, such as the *Hispanic Review,* the *Romantic Review, Modern Language Notes, Revista Hispánica Moderna,* and *PMLA.*

Three high-grade quarterlies published at San Juan de Puerto Rico (*La Torre, Asomante,* and *Revista del Instituto de Cultura Puertorriqueña*) follow the European humanistic traditions, with articles and comments on life, letters, and international affairs.

Many important journals are published in the Middle and South American countries. A useful reference list is given in Irene Zimmerman, *A Guide to Current Latin American Periodicals: Humanities and Social Sciences,* Gainesville: Kallman Publishing Co., 1961. The more important of these will normally be mentioned in the "Title List of Periodicals Cited" in the *Handbook of Latin American Studies.* Attention may be called here to several Mexican journals, not only because of their quality and significance in the inter-American field, but also because they are usually more readily available and have been going long enough to have acquired status and stability: *Cuadernos Americanos* (bimonthly, established in 1942 with the active participation of Spanish Republican refugees), *El Trimestre Económico* (published quarterly by the Fondo de Cultura Económica), and *Investigación Económica* (published quarterly by the Escuela Nacional de Economía, Universidad Nacional Autónoma de México).

Mention should also be made of *Anales de la Universidad de Chile,* published quarterly by the University of Chile, Santiago de Chile (Editorial Nascimento), which was founded in 1843 and claims to be the oldest scientific and literary review published in the Spanish language. Outstanding contributions frequently appear in such Venezuelan reviews as *Revista Nacional de Cultura,* published bimonthly at Caracas by the Ministerio de Educación, Dirección de Cultura y

245

Bellas Artes, and in *Cultura Universitaria,* quarterly review of the Dirección de Cultura de la Universidad Central de Venezuela, Caracas.

In Latin America, some of the best contributions in the fields of literature, history, sociology, economics, and international affairs first appear in the daily press. In contrast to the brief life expectancy of most serious journals in Latin America, there are not a few daily newspapers which can boast not only of considerable antiquity, but also of international reputations for their extensive news coverage, the high literary quality of their chief writers and editors, and the courage and independence of their directors.

Mention may also be made of the publications of the United Nations Economic Commission for Latin America. Of its periodical publications, the *Economic Bulletin for Latin America* appears twice a year. Most of the Commission's valuable output of economic, social, and demographic studies are issued in connection with its regular or special conferences.

Serious students should not neglect European commentators on the inter-American scene. *International Affairs* (quarterly) and the *World Today* (monthly), publications of the Royal Institute of International Affairs, London, are valuable, and some private journals, like *Encounter,* give considerable attention to Latin America. *Cuadernos,* a monthly published in Spanish at Paris, originally an organ of Spanish Republican exiles, is now edited by a Latin American. *Cuadernos Hispanoamericanos,* semi-official monthly published at Madrid, is devoted to the fostering of Hispanic ties between the old and the new world.

Index

AID (Agency for International Development). *See* Cultural interchanges: education

Aid programs, cooperative: assumptions based on, 152-59; neglect of in Latin America, 143-44; prewar, 144-48; types of, 148-52; under Kennedy administration, 160-64. *See also* Cultural interchanges

Alliance for Progress: and ECLA, 227; and Pan American Union, 223; establishment of, 222; judgment of, 224; loans and grants under, 160-61; objectives of, 191-92

Antarctic Treaty: territorial claims under, 82

Anti-Americanism: and U.S. investments, 129; genesis of, 16-23

Argentina *passim*

BETANCOURT, Rómulo, 47-48, 54

Bogotá. *See* Inter-American Conferences: Ninth; inter-American system: reorganization of; OAS: Charter of

Bogotá, Act of. *See* Latin America: future conflicts with

Bolívar, Simón, 8, 13, n13-62, 71, 80, n8-194

Bolivia *passim*

Brazil *passim*

Brazilian Institute of Afro-Asian Studies. *See* Nationalism: and national character

Buenos Aires. *See* Inter-American Conference for the Maintenance of Peace

CALLES, Plutarco Elías, 11, 97, 163

Calvo, Carlos, 37, 77

Calvo Doctrine, 37, n6-61, 130

Caracas. *See* Inter-American Conferences: Tenth

Caribbean, the, 6, 10, 47, 51, 60; dictatorial governments in, 41; police powers in, 2; tensions in, 44-45, 54, 58, 79

Castro, Fidel. *See* Cuba

Chaco War, 76

Chile *passim*

CIAA (Coordinator of Inter-American Affairs). *See* Cultural interchanges: cooperative programs of

Collective Measures Committee. *See* United Nations: Sixth Session

Colombia *passim*

Congress of Panama, n13-62

Convention on Rights and Duties of States, 35, 37

Córdoba reforms. *See* Cultural interchanges: education: interest in

Costa Rica *passim*

Couchiching Conference, 29th: Mexican statement at, 20

Cuba: case of, 49-60, 217-34; *passim*

Cultural interchanges, mutual: books: distribution of, 196-98—Latin American in U.S., 199-02—novels, 202-5—translation and publication of in Latin America, 198-99; cooperative programs of, 169-72; education: agencies of, 188-91—developments in, 191-93—interest in, 178-88—Latin American students in U.S., 174-76—U.S. assistance to Latin American schools, 176-78—U.S. schools in Latin America, 172-73—U.S. students in Latin America, 176; expansion of, 207-9; Hispanic studies in U.S., 165-69; propaganda in, 209-14; quality vs. numbers of, 205-7. *See also* Aid programs

DARÍO, Rubén, 10, 201-2

Dávila, Carlos, 120

Declaration of San José. *See* Meetings of Consultation of Ministers of Foreign Affairs: Sixth

Declaration of Santiago. *See* Meetings of Consultation of Ministers of Foreign Affairs: Fifth

Díaz, Porfirio, 9-11, 129

Dominican Republic *passim*

Drago Doctrine, n6-61, 130

249